54th Annual Meeting of the Association for Computational Linguistics (ACL 2016)

AA002206

Student Research Workshop

Berlin, Germany
7 – 12 August 2016

ISBN: 978-1-5108-2760-8

Printed from e-media with permission by:

Curran Associates, Inc.
57 Morehouse Lane
Red Hook, NY 12571

Some format issues inherent in the e-media version may also appear in this print version.

Copyright© (2016) by the Association for Computational Linguistics
All rights reserved.

Printed by Curran Associates, Inc. (2016)

For permission requests, please contact the Association for Computational Linguistics
at the address below.

Association for Computational Linguistics
209 N. Eighth Street
Stroudsburg, Pennsylvania 18360

Phone: 1-570-476-8006
Fax: 1-570-476-0860

acl@aclweb.org

Additional copies of this publication are available from:

Curran Associates, Inc.
57 Morehouse Lane
Red Hook, NY 12571 USA
Phone: 845-758-0400
Fax: 845-758-2633
Email: curran@proceedings.com
Web: www.proceedings.com

ACL 2016

The 54th Annual Meeting of the Association for Computational Linguistics

Proceedings of the Student Research Workshop

August 7-12, 2016
Berlin, Germany

Introduction

Welcome to the ACL 2016 Student Research Workshop!

Following the tradition of the previous years' workshops, we have two tracks: research papers and thesis proposals. The research papers track is as a venue for Ph.D. students, masters students, and advanced undergraduates to describe completed work or work-in-progress along with preliminary results. The thesis proposal track is offered for advanced Ph.D. students who have decided on a thesis topic and are interested in feedback about their proposal and ideas about future directions for their work.

We received in total 60 submissions: 14 thesis proposals and 46 research papers, more than twice as many as were submitted last year. Of these, we accepted 4 thesis proposals and 18 research papers, giving an acceptance rate of 36% overall. This year, all of the accepted papers will be presented as posters alongside the main conference short paper posters on the second day of the conference.

Mentoring programs are a central part of the SRW. This year, students had the opportunity to participate in a pre-submission mentoring program prior to the submission deadline. The mentoring offers students a chance to receive comments from an experienced researcher in the field, in order to improve the quality of the writing and presentation before making their final submission. Nineteen authors participated in the pre-submission mentoring. In addition, authors of accepted papers are matched with mentors who will meet with the students in person during the workshop. This year, each accepted paper is assigned one mentor. Each mentor will prepare in-depth comments and questions prior to the student's presentation, and will provide discussion and feedback during the workshop.

We are very grateful for the generous financial support from Google and the Don and Betty Walker Scholarship Fund. The support of our sponsors allows the SRW to cover the travel and lodging expenses of the authors, keeping the workshop accessible to all students.

We would also like to thank our program committee members for their constructive reviews for each paper and all of our mentors for donating their time to work one-on-one with our student authors. Thank you to our faculty advisers for their advice and guidance, and to the ACL 2016 organizing committee for their constant support. Finally, a huge thank you to all students for their submissions and their participation in this year's SRW. Looking forward to a wonderful workshop!

Organizers:

> He He, University of Maryland
> Tao Lei, Massachusetts Institute of Technology
> Will Roberts, Humboldt-Universität zu Berlin

Faculty Advisors:

> Chris Biemann, Technische Universität Darmstadt
> Gosse Bouma, Rijksuniversiteit Groningen
> Yang Liu, Tsinghua University

Program Committee:

> Gabor Angeli, Stanford University
> Tania Avgustinova, Saarland University
> António Branco, University of Lisbon
> Chris Brew, Ohio State University
> Wanxiang Che, Harbin Institute of Technology
> Danqi Chen, Stanford University
> Ann Copestake, University of Cambridge
> Michael Elhadad, Ben-Gurion University of the Negev
> George Foster, Google
> Kevin Gimpel, Toyota Technological Institute at Chicago
> Jiang Guo, Harbin Institute of Technology
> Nizar Habash, New York University Abu Dhabi
> Dilek Hakkani-Tur, Microsoft Research
> Keith Hall, Google
> Sanda Harabagiu, University of Texas at Dallas
> Xiaodong He, Microsoft Research
> Lars Hellan, Norwegian University of Science and Technology
> Eduard Hovy, Carnegie Mellon University
> Philipp Koehn, Johns Hopkins University
> Eric Laporte, Université Paris-Est Marne-la-Vallée
> Jiwei Li, Stanford University
> Junyi Jessy Li, University of Pennsylvania
> Wang Ling, Google Deepmind
> Wei Lu, Singapore University of Technology and Design
> Daniel Marcu, University of Southern California
> Taesun Moon, IBM Research
> Alessandro Moschitti, Qatar Computing Research Institute
> Karthik Narasimhan, Massachusetts Institute of Technology
> Graham Neubig, Nara Institute of Science and Technology
> Vincent Ng, University of Texas at Dallas
> Joakim Nivre, Uppsala University
> Kemal Oflazer, Carnegie Mellon University Qatar
> Miles Osborne, Bloomberg
> Yannick Parmentier, University of Orléans
> Nanyun Peng, Johns Hopkins University

Gerald Penn, University of Toronto
Emily Pitler, Google
James Pustejovsky, Brandeis University
Michael Riley, Google
Michael Roth, University of Edinburgh
David Schlangen, Bielefeld University
Satoshi Sekine, New York University
Richard Sproat, Google
Keh-Yih Su, Academia Sinica
Chenhao Tan, Cornell University
Christoph Teichmann, University of Potsdam
Simone Teufel, University of Cambridge
William Yang Wang, Carnegie Mellon University
Bonnie Webber, University of Edinburgh
Bishan Yang, Carnegie Mellon University
Dani Yogatama, Baidu USA
Alessandra Zarcone, Saarland University
Meishan Zhang, Singapore University of Technology and Design
Yuan Zhang, Massachusetts Institute of Technology
Yue Zhang, Singapore University of Technology and Design

Table of Contents

Controlled and Balanced Dataset for Japanese Lexical Simplification
Tomonori Kodaira, Tomoyuki Kajiwara and Mamoru Komachi 1

Dependency Forest based Word Alignment
Hitoshi Otsuki, Chenhui Chu, Toshiaki Nakazawa and Sadao Kurohashi 8

Identifying Potential Adverse Drug Events in Tweets Using Bootstrapped Lexicons
Eric Benzschawel 15

Generating Natural Language Descriptions for Semantic Representations of Human Brain Activity
Eri Matsuo, Ichiro Kobayashi, Shinji Nishimoto, Satoshi Nishida and Hideki Asoh 22

Improving Twitter Community Detection through Contextual Sentiment Analysis
Alron Jan Lam 30

Significance of an Accurate Sandhi-Splitter in Shallow Parsing of Dravidian Languages
Devadath V V and Dipti Misra Sharma 37

Improving Topic Model Clustering of Newspaper Comments for Summarisation
Clare Llewellyn, Claire Grover and Jon Oberlander 43

Arabizi Identification in Twitter Data
Taha Tobaili 51

Robust Co-occurrence Quantification for Lexical Distributional Semantics
Dmitrijs Milajevs, Mehrnoosh Sadrzadeh and Matthew Purver 58

Singleton Detection using Word Embeddings and Neural Networks
Hessel Haagsma 65

A Dataset for Joint Noun-Noun Compound Bracketing and Interpretation
Murhaf Fares 72

An Investigation on The Effectiveness of Employing Topic Modeling Techniques to Provide Topic Awareness For Conversational Agents
Omid Moradiannasab 80

Improving Dependency Parsing Using Sentence Clause Charts
Vincent Kríž and Barbora Hladka 86

Graph- and surface-level sentence chunking
Ewa Muszyńska 93

From Extractive to Abstractive Summarization: A Journey
Parth Mehta 100

Putting Sarcasm Detection into Context: The Effects of Class Imbalance and Manual Labelling on Supervised Machine Classification of Twitter Conversations
Gavin Abercrombie and Dirk Hovy 107

Unsupervised Authorial Clustering Based on Syntactic Structure
Alon Daks and Aidan Clark 114

Suggestion Mining from Opinionated Text
Sapna Negi 119

An Efficient Cross-lingual Model for Sentence Classification Using Convolutional Neural Network
Yandi Xia, Zhongyu Wei and Yang Liu 126

QA-It: Classifying Non-Referential It for Question Answer Pairs
Timothy Lee, Alex Lutz and Jinho D. Choi 132

Building a Corpus for Japanese Wikification with Fine-Grained Entity Classes
Davaajav Jargalsaikhan, Naoaki Okazaki, Koji Matsuda and Kentaro Inui 138

A Personalized Markov Clustering and Deep Learning Approach for Arabic Text Categorization
Vasu Jindal 145

Conference Program

Controlled and Balanced Dataset for Japanese Lexical Simplification
Tomonori Kodaira, Tomoyuki Kajiwara and Mamoru Komachi

Dependency Forest based Word Alignment
Hitoshi Otsuki, Chenhui Chu, Toshiaki Nakazawa and Sadao Kurohashi

Identifying Potential Adverse Drug Events in Tweets Using Bootstrapped Lexicons
Eric Benzschawel

Generating Natural Language Descriptions for Semantic Representations of Human Brain Activity
Eri Matsuo, Ichiro Kobayashi, Shinji Nishimoto, Satoshi Nishida and Hideki Asoh

Improving Twitter Community Detection through Contextual Sentiment Analysis
Alron Jan Lam

Significance of an Accurate Sandhi-Splitter in Shallow Parsing of Dravidian Languages
Devadath V V and Dipti Misra Sharma

Improving Topic Model Clustering of Newspaper Comments for Summarisation
Clare Llewellyn, Claire Grover and Jon Oberlander

Arabizi Identification in Twitter Data
Taha Tobaili

Robust Co-occurrence Quantification for Lexical Distributional Semantics
Dmitrijs Milajevs, Mehrnoosh Sadrzadeh and Matthew Purver

Singleton Detection using Word Embeddings and Neural Networks
Hessel Haagsma

A Dataset for Joint Noun-Noun Compound Bracketing and Interpretation
Murhaf Fares

An Investigation on The Effectiveness of Employing Topic Modeling Techniques to Provide Topic Awareness For Conversational Agents
Omid Moradiannasab

Improving Dependency Parsing Using Sentence Clause Charts
Vincent Kríž and Barbora Hladka

No Day Set (continued)

Graph- and surface-level sentence chunking
Ewa Muszyńska

From Extractive to Abstractive Summarization: A Journey
Parth Mehta

Putting Sarcasm Detection into Context: The Effects of Class Imbalance and Manual Labelling on Supervised Machine Classification of Twitter Conversations
Gavin Abercrombie and Dirk Hovy

Unsupervised Authorial Clustering Based on Syntactic Structure
Alon Daks and Aidan Clark

Suggestion Mining from Opinionated Text
Sapna Negi

An Efficient Cross-lingual Model for Sentence Classification Using Convolutional Neural Network
Yandi Xia, Zhongyu Wei and Yang Liu

QA-It: Classifying Non-Referential It for Question Answer Pairs
Timothy Lee, Alex Lutz and Jinho D. Choi

Building a Corpus for Japanese Wikification with Fine-Grained Entity Classes
Davaajav Jargalsaikhan, Naoaki Okazaki, Koji Matsuda and Kentaro Inui

A Personalized Markov Clustering and Deep Learning Approach for Arabic Text Categorization
Vasu Jindal

Controlled and Balanced Dataset for Japanese Lexical Simplification

Tomonori Kodaira   **Tomoyuki Kajiwara**   **Mamoru Komachi**

Tokyo Metropolitan University

Hino City, Tokyo, Japan

{kodaira-tomonori, kajiwara-tomoyuki}@ed.tmu.ac.jp, komachi@tmu.ac.jp

Abstract

We propose a new dataset for evaluating a Japanese lexical simplification method. Previous datasets have several deficiencies. All of them substitute only a single target word, and some of them extract sentences only from newswire corpus. In addition, most of these datasets do not allow ties and integrate simplification ranking from all the annotators without considering the quality. In contrast, our dataset has the following advantages: (1) it is the first controlled and balanced dataset for Japanese lexical simplification with high correlation with human judgment and (2) the consistency of the simplification ranking is improved by allowing candidates to have ties and by considering the reliability of annotators.

1 Introduction

Lexical simplification is the task to find and substitute a complex word or phrase in a sentence with its simpler synonymous expression. We define complex word as a word that has lexical and subjective difficulty in a sentence. It can help in reading comprehension for children and language learners (De Belder and Moens, 2010). This task is a rather easier task which prepare a pair of complex and simple representations than a challenging task which changes the substitute pair in a given context (Specia et al., 2012; Kajiwara and Yamamoto, 2015). Construction of a benchmark dataset is important to ensure the reliability and reproducibility of evaluation. However, few resources are available for the automatic evaluation of lexical simplification. Specia et al. (2012) and De Belder and Moens (2010) created benchmark datasets for evaluating English lexical simplifica-

tion. In addition, Horn et al. (2014) extracted simplification candidates and constructed an evaluation dataset using English Wikipedia and Simple English Wikipedia. In contrast, such a parallel corpus does not exist in Japanese. Kajiwara and Yamamoto (2015) constructed an evaluation dataset for Japanese lexical simplification[1] in languages other than English.

However, there are four drawbacks in the dataset of Kajiwara and Yamamoto (2015): (1) they extracted sentences only from a newswire corpus; (2) they substituted only a single target word; (3) they did not allow ties; and (4) they did not integrate simplification ranking considering the quality.

Hence, we propose a new dataset addressing the problems in the dataset of Kajiwara and Yamamoto (2015). The main contributions of our study are as follows:

- It is the first controlled and balanced dataset for Japanese lexical simplification. We extract sentences from a balanced corpus and control sentences to have only one complex word. Experimental results show that our dataset is more suitable than previous datasets for evaluating systems with respect to correlation with human judgment.

- The consistency of simplification ranking is greatly improved by allowing candidates to have ties and by considering the reliability of annotators.

Our dataset is available at GitHub[2].

2 Related work

The evaluation dataset for the English Lexical Simplification task (Specia et al., 2012) was an-

---

[1] http://www.jnlp.org/SNOW/E4

[2] https://github.com/KodairaTomonori/EvaluationDataset

Proceedings of the 54th Annual Meeting of the Association for Computational Linguistics – Student Research Workshop, pages 1–7,
Berlin, Germany, August 7-12, 2016. ©2016 Association for Computational Linguistics

sentence	「技を出し合い、気分が**高揚する**のがたまらない」とはいえ、技量で相手を上回りたい気持ちも強い。						
	Although using their techniques makes you feel **exalted**, I strongly feel I want to outrank my competitors in terms of skill.						
paraphrase list	盛り上がる	高まる 高ぶる	上がる	高揚する	興奮する	熱を帯びる	活性化する
	come alive	raised, excited	up	exalted	excited	heated	revitalized

Figure 1: A part of the dataset of Kajiwara and Yamamoto (2015).

notated on top of the evaluation dataset for English lexical substitution (McCarthy and Navigli, 2007). They asked university students to rerank substitutes according to simplification ranking. Sentences in their dataset do not always contain complex words, and it is not appropriate to evaluate simplification systems if a test sentence does not include any complex words.

In addition, De Belder and Moens (2012) built an evaluation dataset for English lexical simplification based on that developed by McCarthy and Navigli (2007). They used Amazon's Mechanical Turk to rank substitutes and employed the reliability of annotators to remove outlier annotators and/or downweight unreliable annotators. The reliability was calculated on penalty based agreement (McCarthy and Navigli, 2007) and Fleiss' Kappa. Unlike the dataset of Specia et al. (2012), sentences in their dataset contain at least one complex word, but they might contain more than one complex word. Again, it is not adequate for the automatic evaluation of lexical simplification because the human ranking of the resulting simplification might be affected by the context containing complex words. Furthermore, De Belder and Moens' (2012) dataset is too small to be used for achieving a reliable evaluation of lexical simplification systems.

3 Problems in previous datasets for Japanese lexical simplification

Kajiwara and Yamamoto (2015) followed Specia et al. (2012) to construct an evaluation dataset for Japanese lexical simplification. Namely, they split the data creation process into two steps: substitute extraction and simplification ranking.

During the substitute extraction task, they collected substitutes of each target word in 10 different contexts. These contexts were randomly selected from a newswire corpus. The target word was a content word (noun, verb, adjective, or adverb), and was neither a simple word nor part of any compound words. They gathered substitutes from five annotators using crowdsourcing. These procedures were the same as for De Belder and

Moens (2012).

During the simplification ranking task, annotators were asked to reorder the target word and its substitutes in a single order without allowing ties. They used crowdsourcing to find five annotators different from those who performed the substitute extraction task. Simplification ranking was integrated on the basis of the average of the simplification ranking from each annotator to generate a gold-standard ranking that might include ties.

During the substitute extraction task, agreement among the annotators was 0.664, whereas during the simplification ranking task, Spearman's rank correlation coefficient score was 0.332. Spearman's score of this work was lower than that of Specia et al. (2012) by 0.064. Thus, there was a big blur between annotators, and the simplification ranking collected using crowdsourcing tended to have a lower quality.

Figure 1 shows a part of the dataset of Kajiwara and Yamamoto (2015). Our discussion in this paper is based on this example.

Domain of the dataset is limited. Because Kajiwara and Yamamoto (2015) extracted sentences from a newswire corpus, their dataset has a poor variety of expression. English lexical simplification datasets (Specia et al., 2012; De Belder and Moens, 2012) do not have this problem because both of them use a balanced corpus of English (Sharoff, 2006).

Complex words might exist in context. In Figure 1, even when a target word such as "高揚する (feel exalted)" is simplified, another complex word "技量 (skill)" is left in a sentence. Lexical simplification is a task of simplifying complex words in a sentence. Previous datasets may include multiple complex words in a sentence but target only one complex word. Not only the target word but also other complex words should be considered as well, but annotation of substitutes and simplification ranking to all complex words in a sentence produces a huge number of patterns, therefore takes a very high cost of annotation. For example, when three complex words

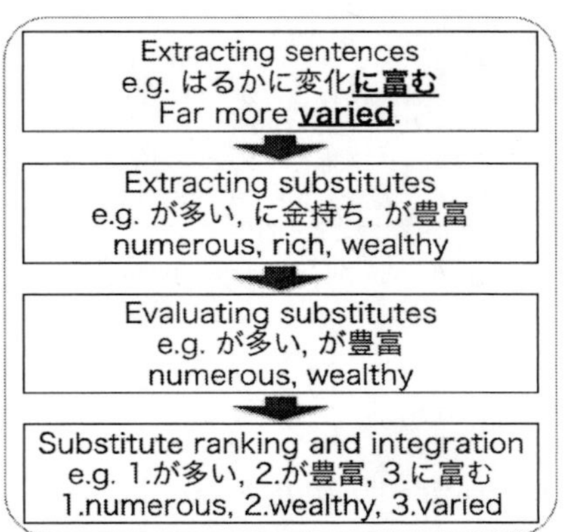

Figure 2: Process of constructing the dataset.

which have 10 substitutes each in a sentence, annotators should consider 10^3 patterns. Thus, it is desired that a sentence includes only simple words after the target word is substituted. Therefore, in this work, we extract sentences containing only one complex word.

Ties are not permitted in simplification ranking. When each annotator assigns a simplification ranking to a substitution list, a tie cannot be assigned in previous datasets (Specia et al., 2012; Kajiwara and Yamamoto, 2015). This deteriorates ranking consistency if some substitutes have a similar simplicity. De Belder and Moens (2012) allow ties in simplification ranking and report considerably higher agreement among annotators than Specia et al. (2012).

The method of ranking integration is naïve. Kajiwara and Yamamoto (2015) and Specia et al. (2012) use an average score to integrate rankings, but it might be biased by outliers. De Belder and Moens (2012) report a slight increase in agreement by greedily removing annotators to maximize the agreement score.

4 Balanced dataset for evaluation of Japanese lexical simplification

We create a balanced dataset for the evaluation of Japanese lexical simplification. Figure 2 illustrates how we constructed the dataset. It follows the data creation procedure of Kajiwara and Yamamoto's (2015) dataset with improvements to resolve the problems described in Section 3.

We use a crowdsourcing application, Lancers,[3]

Figure 3: Example of annotation of extracting substitutes. Annotators are provided with substitutes that preserve the meaning of target word which is shown bold in the sentence. In addition, annotators can write a substitute including particles.

to perform substitute extraction, substitute evaluation, and substitute ranking. In each task, we requested the annotators to complete at least 95% of their previous assignments correctly. They were native Japanese speakers.

4.1 Extracting sentences

Our work defines complex words as "High Level" words in the Lexicon for Japanese Language Education (Sunakawa et al., 2012).[4] The word level is calculated by five teachers of Japanese, based on their experience and intuition. There were 7,940 high-level words out of 17,921 words in the lexicon. In addition, target words of this work comprised content words (nouns, verbs, adjectives, adverbs, adjectival nouns, *sahen* nouns,[5] and *sahen* verbs[6]).

Sentences that include a complex word were randomly extracted from the Balanced Corpus of Contemporary Written Japanese (Maekawa et al., 2010). Sentences shorter than seven words or longer than 35 words were excluded. We excluded target words that appeared as a part of compound words. Following previous work, 10 contexts of occurrence were collected for each complex word. We assigned 30 complex words for each part of speech. The total number of sentences was 2,100 (30 words $\times$ 10 sentences $\times$ 7 parts of speech). We used a crowdsourcing application to annotate 1,800 sentences, and we asked university students majoring in computer science to annotate 300 sentences to investigate the quality of crowdsourcing.

4.2 Extracting substitutes

Simplification candidates were collected using crowdsourcing techniques. For each complex word, five annotators wrote substitutes that did not

---

[3] http://www.lancers.jp/

[4] http://jhlee.sakura.ne.jp/JEV.html

[5] Sahen noun is a kind of noun that can form a verb by adding a generic verb "suru (do)" to the noun. (e.g. "修理 repair")

[6] Sahen verb is a sahen noun that accompanies with "suru". (e.g. "修理する (do repair)")

Dataset	balanced	lang	sents.	noun (%)	verb (%)	adj. (%)	adv. (%)	outlier
De Belder and Moens (2012)	yes	En	430	100 (23.3)	60 (14.0)	160 (37.2)	110 (25.6)	excluded
Specia et al. (2012)	yes	En	2,010	580 (28.9)	520 (25.9)	560 (27.9)	350 (17.6)	included
Kajiwara and Yamamoto (2015)	no	Ja	2,330	630 (27.0)	720 (30.9)	500 (21.5)	480 (20.6)	included
This work	yes	Ja	2,010	570 (28.3)	570 (28.3)	580 (28.8)	290 (14.4)	excluded

Table 1: Comparison of the datasets. In this work, nouns include *sahen* nouns, verbs include *sahen* verbs, and adjectives include adjectival nouns.

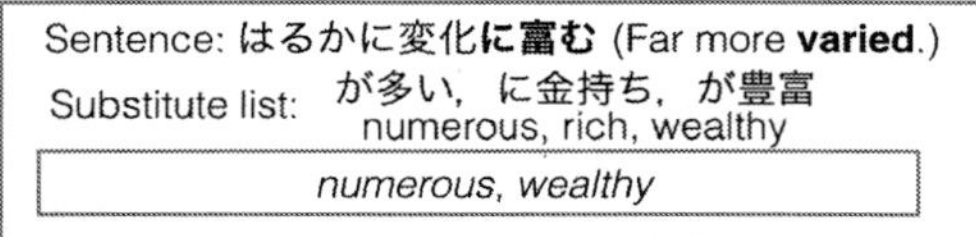

Figure 4: Example of annotation of evaluating substitutes. Annotators choose substitutes that fit into the sentence from substitutes list.

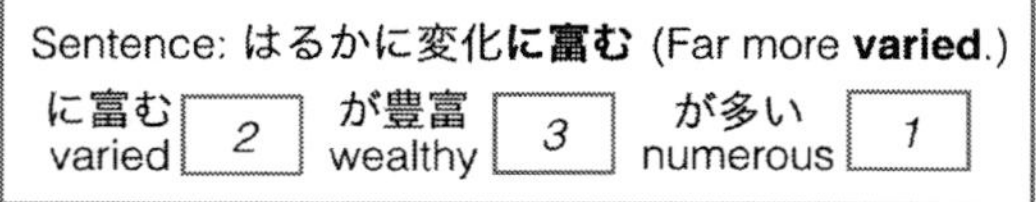

Figure 5: Example of annotation of ranking substitutes. Annotators write rank in blank. Additionally, they are allowed to write a tie.

change the sense of the sentence. Substitutions could include particles in context. Conjugation was allowed to cover variations of both verbs and adjectives. Figure 3 shows an example of annotation.

To improve the quality of the lexical substitution, inappropriate substitutes were deleted for later use, as described in the next subsection.

4.3 Evaluating substitutes

Five annotators selected an appropriate word to include as a substitution that did not change the sense of the sentence. Substitutes that won a majority were defined as correct. Figure 4 shows an example of annotation.

Nine complex words that were evaluated as not having substitutes were excluded at this point. As a result, 2,010 sentences were annotated, as described in next subsection.

4.4 Ranking substitutes

Five annotators arranged substitutes and complex words according to the simplification ranking. Annotators were permitted to assign a tie, but they could select up to four items to be in a tie because we intended to prohibit an insincere person from selecting a tie for all items. Figure 5 shows an ex-

ample of annotation.

4.5 Integrating simplification ranking

Annotators' rankings were integrated into one ranking, using a maximum likelihood estimation (Matsui et al., 2014) to penalize deceptive annotators as was done by De Belder and Moens (2012). This method estimates the reliability of annotators in addition to determining the true order of rankings. We applied the reliability score to exclude extraordinary annotators.

5 Result

Table 1 shows the characteristics of our dataset. It is about the same size as previous work (Specia et al., 2012; Kajiwara and Yamamoto, 2015). Our dataset has two advantages: (1) improved correlation with human judgment by making a controlled and balanced dataset, and (2) enhanced consistency by allowing ties in ranking and removing outlier annotators. In the following subsections, we evaluate our dataset in detail.

5.1 Intrinsic evaluation

To evaluate the quality of the ranking integration, the Spearman rank correlation coefficient was calculated. The baseline integration ranking used an average score (Kajiwara and Yamamoto, 2015). Our proposed method excludes outlier annotators by using a reliability score calculated using the method developed by Matsui et al. (2014).

$$\frac{1}{|P|} \sum_{p_1,p_2 \in P} \frac{p_1 \cap p_2}{p_1 \cup p_2} \qquad (1)$$

Pairwise agreement is calculated between each pair of sets ($p_1, p_2 \in P$) from all the possible pairings (P) (Equation 1). The agreement among annotators from the substitute evaluation phase was 0.669, and agreement among the students is 0.673, which is similar to the level found in crowdsourcing. This score is almost the same as that from Kajiwara and Yamamoto (2015). On the contrary,

sentence	最も安上りにサーファーを**装う**方法は，ガラムというインドネシア産のタバコを，これ見よがしに吸うことです．						
	The most simplest method that is **imitating** safer is pretentiously smoke that Garam which is Indonesian cigarette.						
paraphrase list	1. のふりをする professing	2. に見せかける counterfeiting	3. の真似をする, の振りをする playing, professing	4. を真似る playing	5. に成りすます pretending	6. を装う imitating	7. を偽る falsifying

Figure 6: A part of our dataset.

genre	PB	PM	PN	LB	OW	OT	OP	OB	OC	OY	OV	OL	OM	all
sentence	0	64	628	6	161	90	170	700	1	0	6	9	175	2,010
average of substitutes	0	4.12	4.36	5.17	4.41	4.22	3.9	4.28	4	0	5.5	4.11	4.45	4.3

Table 3: Detail of sentences and substitutes in our dataset. (BCCWJ comprise three main subcorpora: publication (P), library (L), special-purpose (O). PB = book, PM = magazine, PN = newswire, LB = book, OW = white paper, OT = textbook, OP =PR paper, OB = bestselling books, OC = Yahoo! Answers, OY = Yahoo! Blogs, OL = Law, OM = Magazine)

	baseline	outlier removal
Average	0.541	**0.580**

Table 2: Correlation of ranking integration.

the Spearman rank correlation coefficient of the substitute ranking phase was 0.522. This score is higher than that from Kajiwara and Yamamoto (2015) by 0.190. This clearly shows the importance of allowing ties during the substitute ranking task.

Table 2 shows the results of the ranking integration. Our method achieved better accuracy in ranking integration than previous methods (Specia et al., 2012; Kajiwara and Yamamoto, 2015) and is similar to the results from De Belder and Moens (2012). This shows that the reliability score can be used for improving the quality.

Table 3 shows the number of sentences and average substitutes in each genre. In our dataset, the number of acquired substitutes is 8,636 words and the average number of substitutes is 4.30 words per sentence.

Figure 6 illustrates a part of our dataset. Substitutes that include particles are found in 75 context (3.7%). It is shown that if particles are not permitted in substitutes, we obtain only two substitutes (4 and 7). By permitting substitutes to include particles, we are able to obtain 7 substitutes.

In ranking substitutes, Spearman rank correlation coefficient is 0.729, which is substantially higher than crowdsourcing's score. Thus, it is necessary to consider annotation method.

5.2 Extrinsic evaluation

In this section, we evaluate our dataset using five simple lexical simplification methods. We calcu-

	This work	K & Y	annotated
Frequency	**41.6**	35.8	41.0
# of Users	**32.9**	25.0	31.5
Familiarity	30.4	**31.5**	32.5
JEV	**38.2**	35.7	38.7
JLPT	**42.0**	40.9	43.3
Pearson	**0.963**	0.930	N/A

Table 4: Accuracy and correlation of the datasets.

late 1-best accuracy in our dataset and the dataset of Kajiwara and Yamamoto (2015). Annotated data is collected by our and Kajiwara and Yamamoto (2015)'s work in ranking substitutes task, and which size is 21,700 ((2010 + 2330) × 5) rankings. Then, we calculate correlation between the accuracies of annotated data and either those of Kajiwara and Yamamoto (2015) or those of our dataset.

5.2.1 Lexical simplification systems

We used several metrics for these experiments:

Frequency Because it is said that a high frequent word is simple, most frequent word is selected as a simplification candidate from substitutes using uni-gram frequency of Japanese Web N-gram (Kudo and Kazawa, 2007). This uni-gram frequency is counted from two billion sentences in Japanese Web text.

Number of Users Aramaki et al. (2013) claimed that a word used by many people is simple, so we pick the word used by the most of users. Number of Users were estimated from the Twitter corpus created by Aramaki et al. (2013). The corpus contains 250 million tweets from 100,000 users.

Familiarity Assuming that a word which is known by many people is simple, replace a target word with substitutes according to the familiarity score using familiarity data constructed by Amano and Kondo (2000). The familiarity score is an averaged score 28 annotators with seven grades.

JEV We hypothesized a word which is low difficulty for non-native speakers is simple, so we select a word using a Japanese learner dictionary made by Sunakawa et al. (2012). The word in dictionary has a difficulty score averaged by 5 Japanese teachers with their subjective annotation according to six grade system.

JLPT Same as above, but uses a different source called Japanese Language Proficient Test (JLPT). We choose the lowest level word using levels of JLPT. These levels are a scale of one to five.

5.2.2 Evaluation

We ranked substitutes according to the metrics, and calculated the 1-best accuracy for each target word. Finally, to compare two datasets, we used the Pearson product-moment correlation coefficient between our dataset and the dataset of Kajiwara and Yamamoto (2015) against the annotated data.

Table 4 shows the result of this experiment. The Pearson coefficient shows that our dataset correlates with human annotation better than the dataset of Kajiwara and Yamamoto (2015), possibly because we controlled each sentence to include only one complex word. Because our dataset is balanced, the accuracy of Web corpus-based metrics (Frequency and Number of Users) closer than the dataset of Kajiwara and Yamamoto (2015).

6 Conclusion

We have presented a new controlled and balanced dataset for the evaluation of Japanese lexical simplification. Experimental results show that (1) our dataset is more consistent than the previous datasets and (2) lexical simplification methods using our dataset correlate with human annotation better than the previous datasets. Future work includes increasing the number of sentences, so as to leverage the dataset for machine learning-based simplification methods.

References

Shigeaki Amano and Kimihisa Kondo. 2000. On the NTT psycholinguistic databases "lexical properties of Japanese". *Journal of the Phonetic Society of Japan 4(2)*, pages 44–50.

Eiji Aramaki, Sachiko Maskawa, Mai Miyabe, Mizuki Morita, and Sachi Yasuda. 2013. Word in a dictionary is used by numerous users. In *Proceeding of International Joint Conference on Natural Language Processing*, pages 874–877.

Jan De Belder and Marie-Francine Moens. 2010. Text simplification for children. In *Proceedings of the SIGIR Workshop on Accessible Search Systems*, pages 19–26.

Jan De Belder and Marie-Francine Moens. 2012. A dataset for the evaluation of lexical simplification. In *Proceedings of the 13th International Conference on Computational Linguistics and Intelligent Text Processing*, pages 426–437.

Colby Horn, Cathryn Manduca, and David Kauchak. 2014. Learning a lexical simplifier using Wikipedia. In *Proceedings of the 52nd Annual Meeting of the Association for Computational Linguistics (Volume 2: Short Papers)*, pages 458–463.

Tomoyuki Kajiwara and Kazuhide Yamamoto. 2015. Evaluation dataset and system for Japanese lexical simplification. In *Proceedings of the ACL-IJCNLP 2015 Student Research Workshop*, pages 35–40.

Taku Kudo and Hideto Kazawa. 2007. Japanese Web N-gram Version 1. *Linguistic Data Consoritium.*

Kikuo Maekawa, Makoto Yamazaki, Takehiko Maruyama, Masaya Yamaguchi, Hideki Ogura, Wakako Kashino, Toshinobu Ogiso, Hanae Koiso, and Yasuharu Den. 2010. Design, compilation, and preliminary analyses of balanced corpus of contemporary written Japanese. In *Proceedings of the Seventh International Conference on Language Resources and Evaluation*, pages 1483–1486.

Toshiko Matsui, Yukino Baba, Toshihiro Kamishima, and Hisashi Kashima. 2014. Crowdordering. In *Proceedings of the 18th Pacific-Asia Conference on Knowledge Discovery and Data Mining*, pages 336–347.

Diana McCarthy and Roberto Navigli. 2007. Semeval-2007 task 10: English lexical substitution task. In *Proceedings of the 4th International Workshop on Semantic Evaluations*, pages 48–53.

Serge Sharoff. 2006. Open-source corpora: Using the net to fish for linguistic data. *Journal of Corpus Linguistics, 11(4)*, pages 435–462.

Lucia Specia, Sujay Kumar Jauhar, and Rada Mihalcea. 2012. SemEval-2012 task 1: English lexical simplification. In *Proceedings of the 6th International Workshop on Semantic Evaluation*, pages 347–355.

Yuriko Sunakawa, Jae-ho Lee, and Mari Takahara.
2012. The construction of a database to support the
compilation of Japanese learners dictionaries. *Journal of the Acta Linguistica Asiatica 2(2)*, pages 97–
115.

Dependency Forest based Word Alignment

Hitoshi Otsuki[1], Chenhui Chu[2], Toshiaki Nakazawa[2], Sadao Kurohashi[1]

[1]*Graduate School of Informatics, Kyoto University*
[2]*Japan Science and Technology Agency*

{otsuki, kuro}@nlp.ist.i.kyoto-u.ac.jp, {chu,nakazawa}@pa.jst.jp

Abstract

A hierarchical word alignment model that searches for k-best partial alignments on target constituent 1-best parse trees has been shown to outperform previous models. However, relying solely on 1-best parses trees might hinder the search for good alignments because 1-best trees are not necessarily the best for word alignment tasks in practice. This paper introduces a dependency forest based word alignment model, which utilizes target dependency forests in an attempt to minimize the impact on limitations attributable to 1-best parse trees. We present how k-best alignments are constructed over target-side dependency forests. Alignment experiments on the Japanese-English language pair show a relative error reduction of 4% of the alignment score compared to a model with 1-best parse trees.

1 Introduction

In statistical machine translation (SMT), word alignment plays an essential role in obtaining phrase tables (Och and Ney, 2004; Koehn et al., 2003) or syntactic transformation rules (Chiang, 2007; Shen et al., 2008). IBM models (Brown et al., 1993), which are based on word sequences, have been widely used for obtaining word alignments because they are fast and their implementation is available as GIZA++.[1]

Recently, a hierarchical alignment model (whose implementation is known as Nile[2]) (Riesa et al., 2011), which performs better than IBM models, has been proposed. In the hierarchical alignment model, both source and target con-

---

[1] http://www.statmt.org/moses/giza/GIZA++.html
[2] http://jasonriesa.github.io/nile/

stituency trees are used for incorporating syntactic information as features, and it searches for k-best partial alignments on the target constituent parse trees. It achieved significantly better results than the IBM Model4 in Arabic-English and Chinese-English word alignment tasks, even though the model was trained on only 2,280 and 1,102 parallel sentences as gold standard alignments. However, their models rely only on 1-best source and target side parse trees, which are not necessarily good for word alignment tasks.

In SMT, forest-based decoding has been proposed for both constituency and dependency parse trees (Mi et al., 2008; Tu et al., 2010). A forest is a compact representation of n-best parse trees. It provides more alternative parse trees to choose from during decoding, leading to significant improvements in translation quality. In this paper, we borrow this idea to build an alignment model using dependency forests rather than 1-best parses, which makes it possible to provide the model with more alternative parse trees that may be suitable for word alignment tasks. The motivation of using dependency forests instead of constituency forests in our model is that dependency forests are more appropriate for alignments between language pairs with long-distance reordering, such as the one we study in this paper. This is because they are more suitable for capturing the complex semantic relations of words in a sentence (Kahane, 2012).

We conducted alignment experiments on the Japanese-English language pair. Experimental results show a relative error reduction of 4% of the alignment score compared to the model with 1-best parse trees.

2 Model Description

2.1 Dependency Forest

We first briefly explain dependency forests that are used in our model before describing the alignment

Proceedings of the 54th Annual Meeting of the Association for Computational Linguistics – Student Research Workshop, pages 8–14,
Berlin, Germany, August 7-12, 2016. ©2016 Association for Computational Linguistics

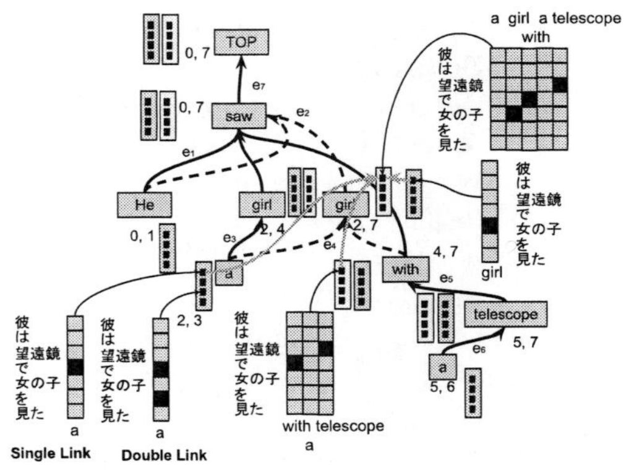

Figure 1: Bottom-up search for alignments over target-side dependency forest (This forest encodes 2-best parse trees for the sentence "he saw a girl with a telescope." The source sentence is "彼 (He) は望遠鏡 (telescope) で (with) 女の子 (girl) を見た (saw)". There are two interpretations for this sentence; either "with a telescope" depends on "saw" or "boy.")

Input : n-best dependency parses $\{T_i\}_{i=1}^n$ of a sentence
Score of T_i $Score_i$
Output: A forest F of $\{T_i\}_{i=1}^n$

1   $F = $
    `CreateForestStructure`$(\{T_i\}_{i=1}^n)$
2   $edgeScores = \{\}$
3   $minScore = Min(\{Score_i\}_{i=1}^n)$
4   **for** $i = 1$ **to** n **do**
5      $Score_i- = minScore$
6   **for** $edge \in T_i$ **do**
7         $edgeScores\,[edge] + = \frac{1}{n}Score_i$
8   **end**
9   **end**
10   **for** $hyperEdge \in F$ **do**
11   **for** $edge \in hyperEdge$ **do**
12         $hyperEdge.score+ =$
         $edgeScores\,[edge]$
13   **end**
14   **end**

Algorithm 1: Computation of a hyperedge score

construction method. A dependency forest is represented by a hypergraph $\langle V, E \rangle$, where V is a set of nodes and E is a set of hyperedges.

A hyperedge e connects nodes in the forest and is defined to be a triple $\langle tails(e), head(e), score \rangle$, where $tails(e)$ is a set of dependents of e, $head(e)$ is the head of e, and $score$ is the score of e that is usually obtained by heuristics (Tu et al., 2010). For example, e_1 in Figure 1 is equal to $\langle (he_{0,1}, boy_{2,4}, with_{4,7}), saw_{0,7}, 1.234 \rangle$. In our model, we use Algorithm 1 to compute hyperedge scores. Edges in a hyperedge are defined to be the ones obtained by connecting each tail with the head (Line 11). Hyperedge score is the sum of all the scores of edges in it (Line 12). The score of an edge is the normalized sum of the scores of all parses which contain the edge (Line 7).

Every node in a dependency forest corresponds to a word attached with a **span**, which is a range of word indices covered by the node. Following (Tu et al., 2010), a span is represented in the form i, j, which indicates the node covers all the words from i-th to $(j - 1)$-th word. This requires dependency forests to be projective. Separate nodes are used for a word if the nodes in dependency trees have different spans. For example, in Figure 1 there are two nodes for the word "boy" because they have different spans (i.e., (2, 4) and (2, 7)).

The construction of a dependency forest from dependency trees is done by sharing the common nodes and edges (Line 1). The common nodes are those with the same span and part-of-speech (POS) . Note that the dependency forest obtained from this method does not necessarily encode exactly the dependency trees from which they are created. Usually there are more trees that can be extracted from the dependency forests (Boullier et al., 2009). In our experiment, when we use the term "a n-best dependency forest", we indicate a dependency forest that is created from n-best dependency trees.

2.2   Finding Alignments over Forest

Following the hierarchical alignment model (Riesa et al., 2011), our model searches for the best alignment by constructing partial alignments (hypotheses) over target dependency forests in a bottom-up manner as shown in Figure 1.

The algorithm for constructing alignments is shown in Algorithm 2. Note that source dependency forests are included in the input to the algorithm. This is optional but can be included for richer features. Each node in the forest has partial alignments sorted by alignment scores. Because it is computationally expensive to keep all possible partial alignments for each node, we keep a beam size of k. A partial alignment for a node is an alignment matrix for target words that are covered by the node. In Figure 1, each partial alignment is represented as a black square. Scores of the partial alignments are a linear combination of features. There are two types of features: local and non-local features. A feature f is defined to be local if and only if it can be factored among the local productions in a tree, and non-local otherwise (Huang, 2008).

We visit the nodes in the topological order, to guarantee that we visit a node after visiting all its tail nodes (Line 1). For each node, we first generates partial alignments, which are one column alignment matrices for its word. Because of time complexity, we only generates null, single link and double link alignment (Line 5). A single and double link alignment refer to a column matrix having exactly one and two alignments, respectively, as shown in Figure 1. For each partial alignment, we compute its score using local features (Line 7) and pushed to a priority queue B_v (Line 8). These partial alignments are represented by black squares in a blue container in Figure 1. Then, we compute partial alignments for the target words covered by the node, by combining tails' partial alignments and one column alignments for its word using non-local features (Line 10 - 14), which is represented by the orange arrows in Figure 1. k-best combined partial alignments are put in Y_v (Line 14). They are represented by black squares in a yellow container in Figure 1. Here, we use cube pruning (Chiang, 2007) to get the approximate k-best combinations. Note that in the search over constituency parse trees, one column alignment matrices are generated only on the leaf node (Riesa et al., 2011), whereas we generate them also on non-leaf nodes in the search over dependency forests.

2.3 Features

The features we used include those used in Nile except for the automatically extracted rule and constellation features. This is because these features are not easily applicable to dependency forests. As shown in our experiments, these features have a contribution to the alignment score. However, our primary purpose is to show the effect of using forests on alignment quality.

Several features in Nile such as source-target POS local feature and coordination feature have to be customized for dependency forests, because it is possible that there are multiple nodes that correspond to the same word. We decided to consider all nodes corresponding to a word by counting the frequency of each POS tag of a node, and normalizing it with the total frequency of POS tags in the forest. For example, suppose there are four nodes which correspond to the same word, whose POS tags are JJ, VBG, JJ, VGZ. In this case the features "src-tgt-pos-feature-JJ=0.5", "src-tgt-pos-feature-VBG=0.25" and "src-tgt-pos-feature-VBZ=0.25" are activated.

Besides the features used in Nile, our model uses a contiguous alignment local feature and a hyperedge score non-local feature. The contiguous alignment feature fires when a target word is aligned to multiple source words, and these words are contiguous on a forest. Preliminary experiments showed, however, that none of these features contributed to the improvement of the alignment score.

3 Experiments

3.1 Experimental Settings

We conducted alignment experiments on the Japanese-English language pair. For dependency

---

Input : Source and target sentence $\mathbf{s}, \mathbf{t}$
Dependency forest F_s over $\mathbf{s}$
Dependency forest F_t over $\mathbf{t}$
Set of feature functions $\mathbf{h}$
Weight vector $\mathbf{w}$
Beam size k
Output: A k-best list of alignments over $\mathbf{s}$ and $\mathbf{t}$

```
1  for v ∈ TopologicalSort (F_t) do
2      links = ∅
3      B_v = ∅
4      i = word-index-of (v)
5      links = {(0,i)} ∪ SingleLinks (i)
       ∪ DoubleLinks (i)
6      for link ∈ links do
7          score = w · h(links, v, s, t, F_s, F_t)
8          Push (B_v, ⟨score, link⟩, k)
9      end
10     for hyperEdge ∈ InHyperEdges (v)
       do
11         c = hyperEdge.tail
12         Push (α_v, ⟨Y_{c_1}, · · · , Y_{c_{|c|}}, B_v⟩)
13     end
14     Y_v = CubePruning (α_v, k, w, h, v, s,
       t, F_s, F_t)
15 end
```

Algorithm 2: Construction of alignments

parsers, we used KNP (Kawahara and Kurohashi, 2006) for Japanese and Berkeley Parser (Petrov and Klein, 2007) for English. We converted constituent parse trees obtained by Berkeley Parser to dependency parse trees using rules.[3] We used 300, 100, 100 sentences from ASPEC-JE[2] for training, development and test data, respectively.[4] Our model as well as Nile has a feature called third party alignment feature, which activates for an alignment link that is presented in the alignment of a third party model. The beam size k was set to 128. We used different number of parse trees to create a target forest, e.g., 1, 10, 20, 50, 100 and 200.[5] The baseline in this experiment is a model with 1-best parse trees on the target side. For reference, we also experimented on Nile[6], the Bayesian subtree alignment model (Nakazawa model) (Nakazawa and Kurohashi, 2011) and IBM Model4.[7] We used Nile without automatically extracted rule features and constellation features to make a fair comparison with our model.

3.2 Results

Table 1 shows the alignment results evaluated on precision, recall and F-score for each experimental setting. The first row shows the names of different experimental settings. Each number in the row shows the number of n-best parse trees used to create target forests.

We can observe that using forests improves the score. However, the improvement does not monotonically increase with the number of trees on the target side. When 100-best is used in target side, it achieved the highest error reduction of 4% compared to the baseline model. [8]

We also conducted experiments on different number of beam size k, e.g, 200 and 300, from the insight that a larger number of trees encoded in a forest indicates that more noisy partial alignments are generated, using the same k as the 1-best model is not sufficient. However, we could not observe significant improvements.

[3] The conversion program is available at
https://github.com/hitochan777/mt-tools/releases/tag/1.0.1
[4] http://lotus.kuee.kyoto-u.ac.jp/ASPEC/
[5] In the experiments, we used 1-best parse trees for the source side. Although our model also allows to use forests on the source side, preliminary experiments showed that using forests on the source side does not improve the alignment score.
[6] Note that Nile uses 1-best constituency parse tree
[7] The alignments from Nakazawa model and IBM Model 4 were symmetrized with the grow-diag-final heuristic.
[8] $(82.39 - 81.66) / (100 - 81.66) \approx 4\%$

4 Discussion

We observed the improvement of alignments by using forests. We checked whether good parse trees were chosen when higher F-scores were achieved. It turned out that better parse trees led to higher F-scores, as shown in Figure 2a, but it was not always the case.

Figure 2a shows an improved example by using 100-best trees on the target side. In the figure, we can observe that "の" and "of" are correctly aligned. We observe that the English 1-best parse tree is incorrect, whereas 100-best model were able to choose a better tree.

Figure 2b shows a worsened example by using 200-best trees on the target side. We can see that the 200-best model aligned many words unnecessarily and the wrong tree is chosen even though the 1-best parse is good. There were many cases in which forests are harmful for alignments. There are two possible reasons. Firstly, most of the features in our model comes from Nile, but they are not informative enough to choose better parses from forests. Secondly, our model is likely to suffer from the data sparseness because using forests generates more noise than 1-best parses.

For our model to benefit from forests we have to consider the following: Firstly, our model's feature is based on the assumption that source and target forests contain trees with similar structures to each other. However the projectivity of forests prohibits our model from generating (choosing) target trees that are similar to the ones in source forests. Secondly, we observed the cases where no parse in forests captures the correct root and the difference of n-best parses are mainly POS tags of words.

Our model performs on par with Nile because our model is based on Nile. However, our model outperforms the Nakazawa model and IBM Model4. This is because our model is supervised but these models are unsupervised. The Nakazawa model outperformed IBM Model4 because it utilizes dependency trees, which provide richer information.

5 Related Work

Studies have been conducted to make use of more alternatives to cope with the unreliability of 1-best results. Liu et al. (2009) proposed a structure called weighted alignment matrix, which encodes the distribution over all possible alignments.

Model	1	10	20	50	100	150	200	Nile	Nakazawa	IBM Model 4
Precision	82.56	82.90	83.51	83.28	**83.77**	83.34	83.39	83.26	70.59	63.21
Recall	80.79	80.88	80.62	80.75	81.05	80.66	80.75	81.52	**82.67**	74.25
F-score	81.66	81.87	82.04	81.99	**82.39**	81.98	82.05	82.38	76.16	68.29

Table 1: Precision, Recall and F-score for ASPEC-JE. The numbers in the first row refer to the number of k-best parse trees used to generate forests.

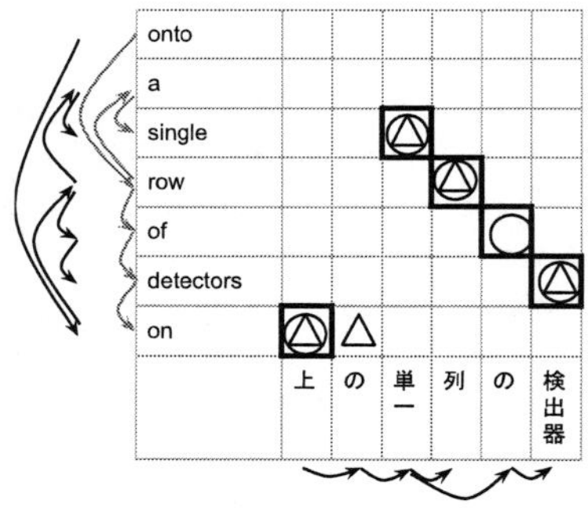

(a) 1-best and 100-best model comparison in the alignment of "onto a single row of detectors on" and "上 (on) の (of) 単一 (single) 列 (row) の (of) 検出器 (detectors)"

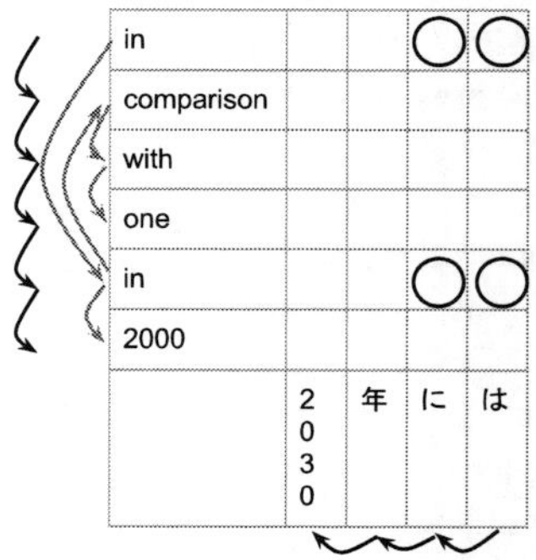

(b) 1-best and 200-best model comparison in the alignment of "in comparison with one in 2000" and "2030(2030) 年 (year) には (in)"

Figure 2: Alignment result: Black boxes represent golden alignments. Triangles represent 1-best model alignments. Circles represent the alignments of proposed model. Black and red arcs represent 1-best parses and chosen parses respectively.

They introduced a way to extract phrase pairs and estimate their probabilities. Their proposed method outperformed the baseline which uses n-best alignments. Venugopal et al. (2008) used n-best alignments and parses to generate fraction counts used for machine translation downstream estimation. While their approaches are to use n-best alignments already obtained from some alignment models, our model finds k-best list of alignments for given sentences.

Mi et al. (2008) and Tu et al. (2010) used packed constituency forests and dependency forests respectively for decoding. The best path that is suitable for translation is chosen from the forest during decoding, leading to significant improvement in translation quality. Note that they do not use forests for obtaining word alignments.

The approaches for modeling word alignment can be divided into two categories: discriminative models (Dyer et al., 2011; Setiawan et al., 2010) and generative models (Brown et al., 1993; Nakazawa and Kurohashi, 2011). Generative models such as the IBM models (Brown et al., 1993) have the advantage that they do not require golden alignment training data annotated by humans. However, it is difficult to incorporate arbitrary features in these models. On the other hand, discriminative models can incorporate arbitrary features such as syntactic information, but they generally require gold training data, which is hard to obtain in large scale. For discriminative models, word alignment models using deep neural network have been proposed recently (Tamura et al., 2014; Songyot and Chiang, 2014; Yang et al., 2013).

6 Conclusion

In this work, we proposed a hierarchical alignment model based on dependency forests, which advanced an alignment model that uses constituency parse trees (Riesa et al., 2011) to allow to use more suitable parse trees for word alignment. Experimental results on the Japanese-English language pair show a relative error reduction of 4% of the alignment score compared to a model with 1-best parse trees that using forest on the target side.

Our future work will involve the implementation of missing features, because the automatic translation rule features had a large contribution to the improvement of alignment quality in Nile.

The experimental results show that Nile, which uses 1-best constituency parses , had almost the same F-score as our proposed method with 100-best parse trees. It will be interesting to see the effect of using forests in Nile.

Moreover, we are considering to investigate the efficacy of our model with different parsers and language pairs.

Finally, we are also considering using training data with richer information such as the one described in (Li et al., 2010).

Acknowledgements

We thank Graham Neubig for his valuable comments during a pre-submission mentoring program, which had greatly improved the quality of the manuscript. We also thank the anonymous reviewers for their helpful comments.

References

Pierre Boullier, Alexis Nasr, and Benoît Sagot. 2009. Constructing parse forests that include exactly the n-best pcfg trees. In *Proceedings of the 11th International Conference on Parsing Technologies (IWPT'09)*, pages 117–128, Paris, France, October. Association for Computational Linguistics.

Peter F Brown, Vincent J Della Pietra, Stephen A Della Pietra, and Robert L Mercer. 1993. The mathematics of statistical machine translation: Parameter estimation. *Computational linguistics*, 19(2):263–311.

David Chiang. 2007. Hierarchical phrase-based translation. *Computational Linguistics*, 33(2):201–228.

Chris Dyer, Jonathan Clark, Alon Lavie, and Noah A Smith. 2011. Unsupervised word alignment with arbitrary features. In *Proceedings of the 49th Annual Meeting of the Association for Computational Linguistics: Human Language Technologies-Volume 1*, pages 409–419. Association for Computational Linguistics.

Liang Huang. 2008. Forest reranking: Discriminative parsing with non-local features. In *Association for Computational Linguistics*, pages 586–594.

Sylvain Kahane. 2012. Why to choose dependency rather than constituency for syntax: a formal point of view. *J. Apresjan, M.-C. L' Homme, M.-C. Iomdin, J. Milicevic, A. Polguère, and L. Wanner, editors, Meanings, Texts, and other exciting things: A Festschrift to Commemorate the 80th Anniversary of Professor Igor A. Mel' cuk*, pages 257–272.

Daisuke Kawahara and Sadao Kurohashi. 2006. A fully-lexicalized probabilistic model for japanese syntactic and case structure analysis. In *Proceedings of the Human Language Technology Conference of the NAACL, Main Conference*, pages 176–183, New York City, USA, June. Association for Computational Linguistics.

Philipp Koehn, Franz Josef Och, and Daniel Marcu. 2003. Statistical phrase-based translation. In *Proceedings of the 2003 Conference of the North American Chapter of the Association for Computational Linguistics on Human Language Technology-Volume 1*, pages 48–54. Association for Computational Linguistics.

Xuansong Li, Niyu Ge, Stephen Grimes, Stephanie Strassel, and Kazuaki Maeda. 2010. Enriching word alignment with linguistic tags. In *Language Resources and Evaluation Conference*.

Yang Liu, Tian Xia, Xinyan Xiao, and Qun Liu. 2009. Weighted alignment matrices for statistical machine translation. In *Proceedings of the 2009 Conference on Empirical Methods in Natural Language Processing: Volume 2-Volume 2*, pages 1017–1026. Association for Computational Linguistics.

Haitao Mi, Liang Huang, and Qun Liu. 2008. Forest-based translation. In *Association for Computational Linguistics*, pages 192–199.

Toshiaki Nakazawa and Sadao Kurohashi. 2011. Bayesian subtree alignment model based on dependency trees. In *International Joint Conference on Natural Language Processing*, pages 794–802.

Franz Josef Och and Hermann Ney. 2004. The alignment template approach to statistical machine translation. *Computational Linguistics*, 30(4):417–449.

Slav Petrov and Dan Klein. 2007. Improved inference for unlexicalized parsing. In *Human Language Technologies 2007: The Conference of the North American Chapter of the Association for Computational Linguistics; Proceedings of the Main Conference*, pages 404–411, Rochester, New York, April. Association for Computational Linguistics.

Jason Riesa, Ann Irvine, and Daniel Marcu. 2011. Feature-rich language-independent syntax-based alignment for statistical machine translation. In *Proceedings of the Conference on Empirical Methods in Natural Language Processing*, pages 497–507. Association for Computational Linguistics.

Hendra Setiawan, Chris Dyer, and Philip Resnik. 2010. Discriminative word alignment with a function word reordering model. In *Proceedings of the 2010 Conference on Empirical Methods in Natural Language Processing*, pages 534–544. Association for Computational Linguistics.

Libin Shen, Jinxi Xu, and Ralph Weischedel. 2008. A new string-to-dependency machine translation algorithm with a target dependency language model. In *Proceedings of ACL-08: HLT*, pages 577–585, Columbus, Ohio, June. Association for Computational Linguistics.

Theerawat Songyot and David Chiang. 2014. Improving word alignment using word similarity. In *Empirical Methods in Natural Language Processing*, pages 1840–1845. Citeseer.

Akihiro Tamura, Taro Watanabe, and Eiichiro Sumita. 2014. Recurrent neural networks for word alignment model. In *Antenna Measurement Techniques Association*, pages 1470–1480.

Zhaopeng Tu, Yang Liu, Young-Sook Hwang, Qun Liu, and Shouxun Lin. 2010. Dependency forest for statistical machine translation. In *Proceedings of the 23rd International Conference on Computational Linguistics*, pages 1092–1100. Association for Computational Linguistics.

Ashish Venugopal, Andreas Zollmann, Noah A Smith, and Stephan Vogel. 2008. Wider pipelines: N-best alignments and parses in mt training. In *Proceedings of Antenna Measurement Techniques Association*, pages 192–201. Citeseer.

Nan Yang, Shujie Liu, Mu Li, Ming Zhou, and Nenghai Yu. 2013. Word alignment modeling with context dependent deep neural network. In *Antenna Measurement Techniques Association*, pages 166–175.

Identifying Potential Adverse Drug Events in Tweets Using Bootstrapped Lexicons

Eric Benzschawel
Brandeis University
`ericbenz@brandeis.edu`

Abstract

Adverse drug events (ADEs) are medical complications co-occurring with a period of drug usage. Identification of ADEs is a primary way of evaluating available quality of care. As more social media users begin discussing their drug experiences online, public data becomes available for researchers to expand existing electronic ADE reporting systems, though non-standard language inhibits ease of analysis. In this study, portions of a new corpus of approximately 160,000 tweets were used to create a lexicon-driven ADE detection system using semi-supervised, pattern-based bootstrapping. This method was able to identify misspellings, slang terms, and other non-standard language features of social media data to drive a competitive ADE detection system.

1 Background

Pharmacovigilance is tasked with detecting, assessing, understanding, and preventing adverse effects or other drug-related medical problems (Organization, 2002). Adverse effects in post-approval drugs constitute a major public health issue, representing the fourth leading cause of death in the United States and an overall treatment cost higher than those of cardiovascular and diabetes care combined (Chee et al., 2011). In the United States alone, over 700,000 yearly hospital admissions—between 2 and 5% of total admissions—result from moderate to severe adverse effects (Honigman et al., 2001), underscoring the need to identify and prevent these serious medical complications.

Adverse effects from drug usage are broken down further into two categories—*adverse drug events* (ADEs) and *adverse drug reactions* (ADRs). ADRs are a subset of ADEs, where causality between a drug treatment program and negative medical reaction has been established such that the negative reactions occur in within standard dosages (Organization, 1972). ADEs more loosely define any overlapping period of drug treatment and adverse medical effects. Importantly, ADEs do not imply causation between the drug use and co-occurring negative event (Eriksson et al., 2013). Timely, accurate identification of these medical complications therefore facilitates improvements in patient health and helps decrease both manpower and monetary costs to a healthcare system and is considered a key quality of medical care (Honigman et al., 2001).

Existing systems of ADE documentation typically rely on automatic reporting systems hosted by national or international public health organizations, electronic health records, or data from other high-quality resources. Social media was an untapped resource until recently, despite evidence that suggests nearly 31% of patients suffering from chronic illness and 38% of medical caregivers consult drug reviews posted online to various social media sites (Harpaz et al., 2014).

Twitter has recently been used as an ADR detection resource in numerous research studies within the last five years, with methodologies ranging from lexicon matching to supervised machine learning (Sarker et al., 2015). Tweets can be used to supplement existing electronic ADE/ADR monitoring systems by providing real-world, real-time clinical narratives from users posted in the public domain. Because many electronic monitoring systems underreport the prevalence of minor ADEs/ADRs, typically due to their absence from medical records and clinical studies (Eriksson et al., 2013), Twitter presents a valuable resource for providing data on a wide range of negative medi-

Proceedings of the 54th Annual Meeting of the Association for Computational Linguistics – Student Research Workshop, pages 15–21,
Berlin, Germany, August 7-12, 2016. ©2016 Association for Computational Linguistics

cal events.

Social media data presents unique challenges to clinical NLP studies in ways analogous to electronic medical records—non-standard syntax, jargon, and misspellings handicap many existing NLP systems (Eriksson et al., 2013). Handling these areas of non-standard language usage complicates lexicon-based attempts at retrieving Tweets containing potential ADEs/ADRs. Many recently published systems handle this by mapping annotated ADEs/ADRs to entries in medical ontologies (Sarker et al., 2015). Annotation is a time-consuming process and limits the size of training data sets. Many problems with non-standard language usage can be addressed with semi-supervised, pattern-based bootstrapping which, after sufficient analysis, yields high-quality lexicons with competitive ADE/ADR detection capabilities.

2   Data

The largest existing publicly available dataset for this domain is Arizona State University's DIEGO Lab data, containing over 7,500 tweets annotated for presence or absence of an ADR (Ginn et al., 2014; Nikfarjam et al., 2015). Roughly 2,000 of the tweets contain annotated ADR relations. This data set has been used in both machine learning and lexicon-based approaches to ADR detection in social media (O'Connor et al., 2014).

In order to take advantage of semi-supervised learning methods and real-time data, Twitter-Drugs, a new corpus of 166,551 tweets, was generated from public tweets mined from mid-January to mid-February 2016 using 334 different drugs. Drugs were compiled from those used in the DIEGO data and supplemented with the New York State Department of Health's *150 Most Frequently Prescribed Drugs*[1], and those listed in Chemical and Engineering News' *Top 50 Drugs of 2014*[2].

After collecting approximately 700K query results, each tweet was heuristically screened for relevance. Tweets were considered irrelevant if they contained an external URL, any of a set of 16 salesmanship terms such as *promo* or *free shipping*, and whether the tweet text itself contained the queried drug string. Screening removed roughly 76.1% of mined tweets. The corpus is

---

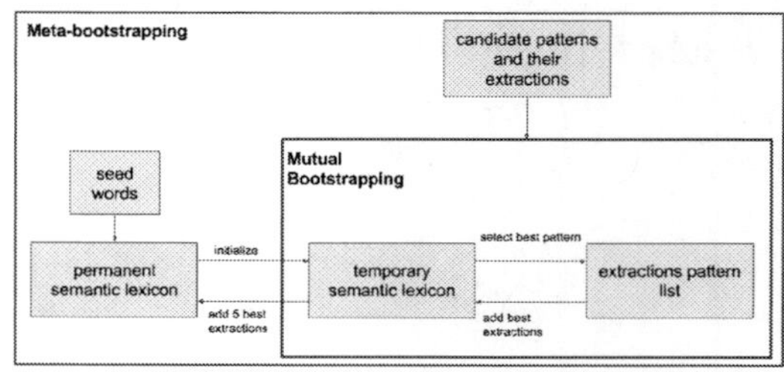

Figure 1:   Riloff and Jones (1999)'s meta-bootstrapping algorithm

available online[3] for future use or expansion and represents the largest available data set for Twitter-based clinical NLP tasks.

3   Methodology

Identifying potential ADEs required extraction of both drug mentions and negative medical events, for instance `oxycontin` and `made me dizzy`. Novel mentions were identified using a set of extraction patterns and a lexicon. Extraction patterns are flexible regular expressions capable of identifying both known and novel mentions. For instance, the pattern `took three <DRUG>` might identify `oxycontin`, `ibuprofen`, or `benzos`. `made me <REACTION>`, similarly, might identify `dizzy`, `hungry`, or `throw up`. Newly identified items are added to lexicons which are in turn used to identify new items.

Two separate lexicons for drugs and medical events were generated using the *meta-bootstrapping* algorithm detailed in Riloff and Jones (1999), which uses a pre-defined set of patterns to identify novel lexicon items occurring in similar environments as known lexicon items. To identify novel mentions, the algorithm relies on an initial set of extraction patterns and a small number of seed words to define the semantic category of interest, as seen in Figure 1. Though bootstrapped lexicons contain noise, manually screening for relevant items results in robust, automatically generated lexicons well suited to the task of identifying potential ADEs. Importantly, this method does not require expensive manual annotation and is capable of handling the colloquial terms and misspellings commonly found in social media data even though it is not specifically tailored for non-standard usage.

---

[1] `apps.health.ny.gov/pdpw`
   `/DrugInfo/DrugInfo.action`
[2] `CEN-supplement092014.pdf`

[3] `github.com/ericbenz/TwitterDrugs`

Meta-bootstrapping first identifies relevant extraction contexts from an input corpus and lists of known category items. This, in turn, results in a list of context patterns. Contexts were generated by taking combinations of one to three words preceding or following the known category item. Table 1 shows how known drug names and medical events present in each context pattern were anonymized with regular expressions capable of extracting one or many words.

Table 1: Extraction patterns and possible matches

Candidate Pattern	Extracted Entities
`took (\S+) tablet`	*ibuprofen, xanax, one, 25mg*
`made me (\S\s+)+`	*throw up, feel like dying, super happy*

Each candidate pattern was subsequently scored on the basis of how many new category items it extracts relative to the number of existing lexicon items. Scoring is initially spurred by the relatedness of extracted entities to a handful of seed words defining the semantic category of interest. Each pattern is scored with the function

$$score(pattern) = R * \log_2 F \qquad (1)$$

where F is the number of unique entities generated by the pattern which are already present in the semantic lexicon and $R = \frac{F}{N}$, where N is the total number of words the pattern extracted. R is high when patterns extract numerous items that are already contained in the semantic lexicon, as this reflects a high likelihood that all entities produced by this pattern are semantic category items.

This scoring function, however, is incapable of appropriately addressing the robustness of multiword medical events. In some cases, an extracted entity contains multiple unique reactions, such as

`gave me vertigo and really bad nausea`

where `vertigo` and `nausea` should be considered independently. Judging the above example based on the whole string as an indivisible entity will score it too low to be considered semantically relevant. This is because the string as an indivisible whole is unlikely to ever occur again or bear strong semblance to the provided seed words or existing lexicon items. Only portions of this string are important potential category items and are likely to be included in seed words or easily identified by patterns extracting single words.

Reranking this pattern to favor extractions containing these two substrings can allow the the entire extraction to enter the medical event lexicon where each relevant bit can be manually identified in post-processing. To do this, the scoring function was modified as

$$score(pattern) = \lambda(R * \log_2 F) \qquad (2)$$

where F is re-evaluated as the number of relevant substrings, and λ is a penalty term where $\lambda = \frac{c}{\log_2(avg\_words)}$, where c is a constant and avg_words is the average number of tokens per extraction per pattern. All other terms remain the same between both scoring functions.

Because the F values grow increasingly large as the semantic lexicons grow, the λ penalty is introduced to control the balance of single and multiple word entities. Shorter strings containing more relevant entities are penalized less than longer ones potentially containing lots of noise. The c constant must grow in proportion to the number of data instances being used in the training set. Too small a c value will result in lexicons comprised mostly of single-word extractions. Too large a c value will result in lexicons comprised mostly of multi-word extractions.

Following the scoring of each pattern, each entity is evaluated with the scoring function

$$score(entity) = \sum_{k=1}^{N} 1 + (0.1 * score(pattern_k)) \qquad (3)$$

where N is the number of different patterns which found the entity being scored. This function scores each entity on the basis of how many patterns were able to identify it, as words extracted by numerous patterns are more likely to be true members of the semantic lexicon. The five highest scoring patterns are added to the semantic lexicon, serving as additional seed words for subsequent bootstrapping iterations. This process continues until end conditions are reached.

4   Results

Six different training sets were used in the bootstrapping tasks to explore the influence of unannotated data during lexicon generation. Each training set contained the full DIEGO Lab training corpus and an increasingly large amount of non-overlapping TwitterDrugs data. The bootstrapping procedure outlined above continued until lexicons contained maximally $5000+i$ items, where i is the number of seed words. Bootstrapping terminated early if new items were not added for five consecutive iterations.

The resulting lexicons were used to flag tweets in held-out test sets where an extracted drug co-occurred with an extracted reaction. The DIEGO test set was used to compare flagged tweets using this methodology to O'Connor et al. (2014), which utilized a different lexicon-based ADR detection algorithm on the same DIEGO data set. Tweets flagged using bootstrapped lexicons increased precision, recall, and F_1 in most cases, suggesting the viability of this method.

4.1 Generating Drug Lexicons

Drug lexicons were generated using 10-20 seed words. As the number of training instances increased, additional seed words were required to spur the bootstrapping algorithm to add lexicon items in early iterations. Seed words were taken from the most frequently occurring drugs in the DIEGO training corpus.

Using only the DIEGO training data resulted in 1907 candidate patterns, 1312 extracted entities, and 113 relevant identified drugs. The best performing training set added 5K tweets from TwitterDrugs to those in the DIEGO training set, resulting in 355 relevant extracted entities of which nearly 60% were neither in the DIEGO data nor the list of drugs used to generate the TwitterDrugs corpus. Included in these lexicons are numerous misspellings, slang terms, and hashtags.[4]

4.2 Generating Medical Event Lexicons

Due to the challenges associated with multi-word extractions, only three training sets were explored for reaction extraction. 30 seed word were used for all bootstrapping procedures, taken from the most frequent annotated ADRs in the DIEGO dataset provided they were less than five words long.

Using only the DIEGO training data resulted in 32,879 candidate patterns, producing a lexicon with 1321 items. To balance single and multi-word expressions, where $c = 0.25$ for this small dataset. Manual analysis of each lexicon item

yielded 500 medical events after complex, multi-word entities were broken down. The largest lexicon contained 783 medical events extracted from 177,494 patterns generated by appending 5K tweets from TwitterDrugs to the DIEGO training set. $c = 0.75$ in this case. Over 87% of this lexicon contained novel entities.

4.3 Identifying Potential ADEs

Tweets were flagged as 'potentially containing an ADE' by identifying those in which a term from a drug lexicon co-occurred with one from a medical event lexicon. The effects of increasing the amount of training data can be seen in Table 2, which shows that an increasing proportion of tweets are flagged as the amount of training data increases. This suggests that the composition of the resulting lexicons contains drugs and reactions that more frequently co-occur.

The low proportion of flagged tweets is unsurprising, as most Twitter users rarely discuss the physical effects of their drug use. It is important to emphasize that the proportion of true ADEs is not identical to the proportion flagged. Discussion of drug indications—why a drug was taken—and beneficial effects are much more common than ADEs or ADRs. Of the proportion of flagged tweets, roughly 25.2% contained obvious ADEs. This is roughly 16% more than the 9.3% captured in the O'Connor et al. (2014) study which used only the DIEGO data.

In order to better evaluate the composition of flagged tweets using the bootstrapped lexicons, results were directly compared to the O'Connor et al. (2014) study using the 317 tweets distributed in the DIEGO Lab test set. O'Connor et al. (2014) reported precision, recall, and F_1 scores of 0.62, 0.54, and 0.58, respectively. In nearly all cases, bootstrapped lexicons have higher precision and F_1 score as Table 3 shows.

Adding small amounts of data helped increase performance mostly through increases in precision. Larger datasets hurt performance because the bootstrapped lexicons were tuned more appropriately to the composition of drugs and reactions present in the TwitterDrugs corpus which are not guaranteed to overlap exactly with the DIEGO data despite the shared source (Twitter).

Flagged tweets must be manually reviewed for potential ADE/ADR relations. Because flagged tweets were simply captured by mere co-

---

[4]Twitter permits the use of the # 'hashtag' to prefix strings for searching, indexing, and statistical analysis such as in #adderall or #mighthaveaheartattack

Table 2: Proportions of flagged tweets as 'potentially containing ADE relation' increases as larger amounts of TwitterDrugs data is used for bootstrapping.
(*—lexicon generated from DIEGO +5K TD dataset)

Training Corpus	Held-out Test Set	#Drugs	# ADEs	Num. Flagged	% Flagged
DIEGO	TwitterDrugs (TD)	113	500	7,993/166,551	4.80%
DIEGO +1K TD	165K TD	235	702	22,981/165,868	13.85%
DIEGO +5K TD	160K TD	355	783	25,135/161,868	15.53%
DIEGO +10K TD	155K TD	343	783*	24,661/156,868	15.72%
DIEGO +25K TD	140K TD	311	783*	22,668/141,868	15.98%
DIEGO +50K TD	115K TD	287	783*	19,091/116,868	16.34%

Table 3: Precision, recall, and F_1 score for bootstrapped lexicons using different training set combinations using larger portions of TwitterDrugs data, best results in **bold**

Med.Event Train Set		Drug Train Set					
		DIEGO	+1K	+5K	+10K	+25K	+50K
DIEGO		$P = .7321$	.7182	.7297	.7156	.7170	.7142
		$R = .5125$	.4938	.5062	.4875	.4750	.4688
		$F_1 = .6029$	.5852	.5978	.5799	.5714	.5660
+1K		**.7419**	.7177	.7280	.7154	.7167	.7167
		.5750	.5563	.5688	.5500	.5375	.5373
		.6479	.6267	.6386	.6219	.6143	.6142
+5K		.7368	.7130	.7241	.7105	.7112	.7112
		.5250	.5125	.5250	.5063	.4938	.4938
		.6131	.5964	.6087	.5912	.5830	.5830

occurrence of terms, numerous captured tweets contain discussions of beneficial effects or why a drug was taken. For instance, no obvious ADE/ADR exists in the flagged tweet

```
That ibuprofen 800 knocked my
        headache right out
```

Contrast this with

```
  took this vicodin and it is
seriously hard to breathe all of
           a sudden
```

which clearly documents a potentially dangerous co-occurrence of Vicodin® and breathing difficulties. Untangling beneficial effects and drug indications remains a problem area for automatic ADE/ADR detection especially given that similar language is used for both.

5   Discussion

Though social media represents a rich source of data, ADE detection with lexicon-based methods remains vulnerable to data sparsity—a low percentage of tweets containing drug names actually include ADEs. However, the results discussed above show that bootstrapping can increase the proportion of true ADEs in returned datasets. Meta-bootstrapped lexicons do not require extensive manual annotation unlike other recent lexicon-based systems. Because of the scoring function, bootstrapped lexicons are able to easily capture variations in spelling and slang phrases provided they occur in contexts similar to the words present in the growing semantic lexicon.

In the drug lexicon, several misspellings or slang variations of numerous drugs were identified, such as bendaryl (Benadryl®) or xannies (Xanax®), addressing a problem area for social media data. If one were to simply apply existing drug lexicons against this dataset, any slang terms or misspellings would be missed without additional processing. Meta-bootstrapping can easily retrieve this data, with the only post-processing being quick manual sifting of generated lexicons for relevant category items.

Medical event lexicons tended to robustly include slang descriptions for medical issues ranging from intoxication (tweakin, turnt up, smashed) to mental states (got me up like zombies), to descriptions of body processes and fluids (barf, urine contains blood). These cannot be identified with existing medical ontologies and several are liable to change dramatically as drug users modify the ways they describe their experiences. Importantly, manual analysis can easily capture these potential ADE indications without robust medical training.

Taken together, misspellings and common slang descriptions can be used to identify potentially severe ADEs, such as

```
The ER gave me percs and
flexeril, I'm high af lmao
```

where `percs` is a slang term for Percocet®, and `high` a common generic description for any number of abnormal sensory events. Percocet® and Flexeril® have a high potential for drug interaction causing drowsiness, lightheadedness, confusion, dizziness, and vision problems[5]—all potential adverse events contained within the generic slang term. Within slang-driven social media data, this drug interaction and its associated side effect would be difficult to capture without the flexible lexicons generated by the bootstrapping procedure.

Because the bootstrapped lexicons require manual pruning of irrelevant results, meta-bootstrapping is unlikely to save large amounts of time compared to existing research methods. However, the ease at which novel, relevant, non-standard lexicon items are identified and added to the lexicon and the competitive abilities of known-ADE identification in a small test set emphasizes the applicability of this approach for this task.

6 Future Work

The lexicons generated by meta-bootstrapping provide numerous opportunities for research extension. For instance, lexicons may be easily applied across a drug class, allowing for fast identification of ADE discussion in social media across a particular class of interest, such as the ongoing crisis surrounding the abuse of prescription-only narcotic painkillers. After flagging a tweet containing an ADE/ADR resulting from opioid use, researchers could utilize tweet metadata to help crisis managers identify demographic areas of interest for more targeted care.

Outside pharmacovigilance, the lexicons can also be used to 'bootstrap' corpus generation. Because novel extractions represented roughly 60% of the generated drug lexicon, these new entries

can be used to expand the search query set, returning a more diverse set of tweets than the original 334 drug names. This, in turn, is likely to lead to identification of more novel items, allowing the process to be repeated. Doing so allows for easy identification of slang terms as they are created and enter common use.

Lastly, the TwitterDrugs corpus represents a rich resource for subsequent research. It may be easily annotated for supervised techniques, or can be explored with different semi- and unsupervised methods for lexicon generation, relation extraction, or ADE/ADR classification. The bootstrapping procedure itself can be modified to include additional standardization techniques which may diminish the number of patterns by simplifying linguistic complexities. Lemmatization would be highly effective here, allowing patterns differentiated by only inflectional morphology to be combined. However, many of these standardization techniques still perform poorly on the non-standard language found in social media data.

Acknowledgments

Special thanks to Prof. Nianwen Xue, the advisor for this work, which presents a portion of a masters thesis on the same topic titled *Identifying Adverse Drug Events in Twitter Data Using Semi-Supervised Bootstrapped Lexicons* and available electronically at the Brandeis Institutional Repository[6]. Thanks also to Prof. Sanda Harabagiu (UT-Dallas), Prof. James Pustejovsky, Dr. Marc Verhagen, Dr. Keith Plaster, and Nikhil Krishnaswamy for additional help and input.

References

Brant W Chee, Richard Berlin, and Bruce Schatz. 2011. Predicting adverse drug events from personal health messages. In *AMIA Annual Symposium Proceedings*. American Medical Informatics Association.

Robert Eriksson, Peter Bjødstrup Jensen, Sune Frankild, Lars Juhl Jensen, and Søren Brunak. 2013. Dictionary construction and identification of possible adverse drug events in Danish clinical narrative text. *Journal of the American Medical Informatics Association*, 20(5):947–953.

Rachel Ginn, Pranoti Pimpalkhute, Azadeh Nikfarjam, Apurv Patki, Karen O'Connor, Abeed Sarker, Karen

---

[5] `umm.edu/health/medical /drug-interaction-tool`

[6] `bir.brandeis.edu/handle/10192/32253`

Smith, and Graciela Gonzalez. 2014. Mining twitter for adverse drug reaction mentions: a corpus and classification benchmark. In *Proceedings of the fourth workshop on building and evaluating resources for health and biomedical text processing*.

Rave Harpaz, Alison Callahan, Suzanne Tamang, Yen Low, David Odgers, Sam Finlayson, Kenneth Jung, Paea LePendu, and Nigam H Shah. 2014. Text mining for adverse drug events: the promise, challenges, and state of the art. *Drug Safety*, 37(10):777–790.

Benjamin Honigman, Patrice Light, Russel M Pulling, and David W Bates. 2001. A computerized method for identifying incidents associated with adverse drug events in outpatients. *International Journal of Medical Informatics*, 61(1):21–32.

Azadeh Nikfarjam, Abeed Sarker, Karen O'Connor, Rachel Ginn, and Graciela Gonzalez. 2015. Pharmacovigilance from social media: mining adverse drug reaction mentions using sequence labeling with word embedding cluster features. *Journal of the American Medical Informatics Association*, 22(3):671–681.

Karen O'Connor, Pranoti Pimpalkhute, Azadeh Nikfarjam, Rachel Ginn, Karen L Smith, and Graciela Gonzalez. 2014. Pharmacovigilance on twitter? mining tweets for adverse drug reactions. In *AMIA Annual Symposium Proceedings*. American Medical Informatics Association.

World Health Organization. 1972. International drug monitoring: the role of national centres. *World Health Organization Technical Report Series*, 498:1–25.

World Health Organization. 2002. The importance of pharmacovigilance.

Ellen Riloff and Rosie Jones. 1999. Learning dictionaries for information extraction by multi-level bootstrapping. In *AAAI/IAAI*, pages 474–479.

Abeed Sarker, Rachel Ginn, Azadeh Nikfarjam, Karen O'Connor, Karen Smith, Swetha Jayaraman, Tejaswi Upadhaya, and Graciela Gonzalez. 2015. Utilizing social media data for pharmacovigilance: a review. *Journal of biomedical informatics*, 54:202–212.

Generating Natural Language Descriptions for Semantic Representations of Human Brain Activity

Eri Matsuo
Ichiro Kobayashi

Ochanomizu University

g1220535@is.ocha.ac.jp
koba@is.ocha.ac.jp

Shinji Nishimoto
Satoshi Nishida

Center for Information and Neural Networks,
National Institute of Information and
Communications Technology

nishimoto@nict.go.jp
s-nishida@nict.go.jp

Hideki Asoh

Artificial Intelligence Research Center,
National Institute of Advanced
Industrial Science and Technology

h.asoh@aist.go.jp

Abstract

Quantitative analysis of human brain activity based on language representations, such as the semantic categories of words, have been actively studied in the field of brain and neuroscience. Our study aims to generate natural language descriptions for human brain activation phenomena caused by visual stimulus by employing deep learning methods, which have gained interest as an effective approach to automatically describe natural language expressions for various type of multi-modal information, such as images. We employed an image-captioning system based on a deep learning framework as the basis for our method by learning the relationship between the brain activity data and the features of an intermediate expression of the deep neural network owing to lack of training brain data. We conducted three experiments and were able to generate natural language sentences which enabled us to quantitatively interpret brain activity.

1 Introduction

In the field of brain and neuroscience, analyzing semantic activities occurring in the human brain is an area of active study. Meanwhile, in the field of computational linguistics, the recent evolution of deep learning methods has allowed methods of generating captions for images to be actively studied. Combining these backgrounds, we propose a method to quantitatively interpret the states of the human brain with natural language descriptions, referring to prior methods developed in the fields of both brain and neuroscience and computational linguistics. Because it is difficult to prepare a large-scale brain activity dataset to train a deep neural model of generating captions for brain activity from scratch, therefore, to handle this problem, we instead reuse a model trained to generate captions for images as the basis for our method. We apply brain activity data, instead of images, to the image caption-generation frameworks proposed by Vinyals et al.(2015) and Xu et al.(2015) to generate natural language descriptions expressing the contents of the brain activity. In this way, we aim to achieve a quantitative analysis of brain activities through language representation.

2 Related Studies

2.1 Language representation estimated from brain activity

In recent years, in the field of brain and neuroscience, the quantitative analysis of what a human recalls using brain activity data observed via functional magnetic resonance imaging (fMRI) while he or she watches motion pictures has been actively studied (Mitchell et al., 2008; Nishimoto et al., 2011; Pereira et al., 2013; Huth et al., 2012; Stansbury et al., 2013; Horikawa et al., 2013). Huth et al. (2012) created a map for semantic representation at the cerebral cortex by revealing the corresponding relationships between brain activities and the words of WordNet (Miller, 1995), thus representing objects and actions in motion pictures. Stansbury et al. (2013) employed Latent Dirichlet Allocation (LDA) (Blei et al., 2003) to assign semantic labels to still pictures using natural language descriptions synchronized with the pictures and discussed the resulting relationship between the visual stimulus evoked by the still pictures and brain activity. Based on these relationships, they have built a model that classifies brain activity into semantic categories, revealing the areas of the brain that deal with particular categories. Cukur et al. (2013) estimated how a human being

Proceedings of the 54th Annual Meeting of the Association for Computational Linguistics – Student Research Workshop, pages 22–29,
Berlin, Germany, August 7-12, 2016. ©2016 Association for Computational Linguistics

semantically changes his or her recognition of objects from the brain activity data in cases where he or she pays attention to objects in a motion picture. As mentioned above, Statistical models analyzing semantic representation in human brain activity have attracted considerable attention as appropriate models to explain higher order cognitive representations based on human sensory or contextual information.

Furthermore, Nishida et al.(2015) demonstrated that skip-gram, employed in the framework of word2vec proposed by Mikolov (2013), is a more appropriate model than the conventional statistical models used for the quantitative analysis of semantic representation in human brain activity under the same experimental settings as the prior studies. Moreover, they showed that there is a correlation between the distributed semantics, obtained by employing skip-gram to build distributed semantic vectors in the framework of word2vec with the Japanese Wikipedia corpus, and brain activity observed through blood oxygen level dependent (BOLD) contrast imaging via fMRI.

Prior studies have attempted to quantitatively analyze the relationship between semantic categories and human brain activity from the perspective of language representation, especially, the semantic categories of words. In this study, we aim to take a step further toward quantitatively analyzing this relationship by expressing brain activity with natural language descriptions.

2.2 Caption generation from images

Many previous studies on image caption generation have been based on two principal approaches. The first approach is to retrieve existing captions from a large database for a given image by ranking the captions (Kuznetsova et al., 2012; Kuznetsova et al., 2014; Vendrov et al., 2016; Yagcioglu et al., 2015). The second approach is to fill sentence templates based on the features extracted from a given image, such as objects and spatial relationships (Elliott and Keller, 2013; Elliott and Vries, 2015; Kulkarni et al., 2013; Mitchell et al., 2012). Although these approaches can produce accurate descriptions, they are neither flexible nor natural descriptions such as the ones written by humans. Recently, multiple methods proposed for generating captions for images have been developed based on the encoder-decoder (enc-dec) framework (Cho et al., 2014; Cho et al., 2015), which is typically used for media transformation (Chorowski, 2015), e.g., machine translation (Sutskever et al., 2014; Cho et al., 2014; Kiros et al., 2014; Bahdanau et al., 2015), to generate captions for images (Donahue et al., 2015; Kiros et al., 2015; Mao et al., 2014; Vinyals et al., 2015).

In the enc-dec framework, by combining two deep neural network models functioning as an encoder and a decoder, the enc-dec model first encodes input information into an intermediate expression and then decodes it into an expression in a different modality than that of the input information. Vinyals et al. (2015) achieved caption generation for images by building a enc-dec network employing GoogLeNet (Ioffe and Szegedy, 2015), which works effectively to extract the features of images, as the encoder, and Long Short-Term Memory Language Model (LSTM-LM) (Hochreiter and Schmidhuber, 1997; Sutskever et al., 2014), which is a deep neural language model, as the decoder. Xu et al. (2015) proposed a model using the Attention Mechanism (Cho et al., 2015) and demonstrated that the model achieved high precision when generating captions. Attention Mechanism is a system that automatically learns to pay attention to different parts of the input for each element of the output (Bahdanau et al., 2015; Cho et al., 2015; Yao et al., 2015).

In our study, we provide an enc-dec network with brain activity data as input, instead of an image, and attempt to generate natural language descriptions for this data.

3 Proposed Method

First, the process to generate captions for images using deep neural networks, employed in Vinyals et al.(2015) and Xu et al.(2015), works as follows:

Step 1. *Encoder: Extraction of features using VGGNet*
The encoder VGGNet (Simonyan and Zisserman, 2015), a pre-trained deep convolutional network, extracts the features from the input image. In the case with Attention Mechanism, the output of the encoder is $512 \times 14 \times 14$ dimensional data from the intermediate convolutional layer of VGGNet. In the case without Attention Mechanism, the output is 4,096 dimensional data from the last fully-connected layer of VGGNet.

Step 2. *Process for intermediate expression*
In the case with Attention Mechanism, the weighted sum of the set of the intermediate expressions calculated in Step 1 is computed as the input for the decoder. The weighted coefficients are learned by means of a multi-layered perceptron based on the hidden states of the decoder at the previous time step and 512 intermediate expressions. In the case without Attention Mechanism, the output of the encoder from Step 1 is just the input of the decoder in Step 3.

Step 3. *Decoder: Word estimation by LSTM-LM*
The LSTM-LM decoder predicts the next word from the intermediate expression produced in Step 2 and the hidden states of LSTM at the previous time step.

Step 4. *Caption generation by iterative word estimation*
A caption is generated by estimating the words one-by-one repeating Steps 2 and 3 until either the length of the sentence exceeds the predefined maximum or the terminal symbol of a sentence is output.

This study aims to generate natural language sentences that describe the events a human being calls to mind from the human brain activity input data observed by fMRI via the above caption-generation process. Figures 1 and 2 show overviews of our methods with and without Attention Mechanism, respectively. In essence, we train a simple model, a 3-layered perceptron (multi-layered perceptron; MLP) or ridge regression model, to learn the corresponding relationships between the cerebral nerve activity data stimulated by the input images and the features of the same image extracted by VGGNet, namely, the intermediate expression as for the image caption generator. The model replaces VGGNet as the encoder when brain activity data are used as input information instead of images. Then, the rest of the process to generate captions is the same as that of the above image caption generator. The process of the proposed method is as follows:

Step 1. *Encode brain activity to an intermediate expression*
The model, which is pre-trained to learn the mapping from the brain activity data stimulated by an image to the features extracted from the same image by VG-GNet, maps the input brain data to an intermediate expression.

Step 2 ∼ 4. The rest of the process is the same as above.

4 Experiments

In this study, we conducted three experiments, under the conditions shown in Table 2, using the model of caption generation for images and the model to learn the corresponding relationships between the brain activity data and the features obtained from VGGNet. The model for Exp.1 is illustrated in Figure 1, and the models for both Exps.2 and 3 are illustrated in Figure 2.

4.1 Experimental settings

We employed Chainer[1] as the deep-learning framework. We used Microsoft COCO[2], which contains 414,113 pairs of data with still pictures

---

[1] http://chainer.org/
[2] http://mscoco.org/

and natural language descriptions of their contents, as the training data for the building caption-generation model. In this study, we have so far been able to train the network with 168,000 pairs of the total dataset in the below experiments.

Table 2: The experimental setting.

Exp.	Image to Caption	Brain to Intermediate
Exp.1	Attention Mechanism	3-layered MLP
Exp.2	Without	(Neural Network)
Exp.3	Attention Mechanism	Ridge regression

We employed the brain activity data of a subject being stimulated by motion pictures (Nishimoto et al., 2011) as the data for training and evaluation. In the experiments, we used BOLD signals observed every 2s via fMRI while the subject was watching motion pictures as the brain activity data, and the still pictures extracted from the motion pictures were synchronized with the brain data. The brain activity data were observed throughout the brain and were recorded in $100(x) \times 100(y) \times 32(z)$ voxels. We employed 30,662 voxels corresponding to only the cerebral cortex region, which is the area of the whole brain, in the above observed voxels as input brain data (see, Figure 3). In the Exp.1, the multi-layered perceptron learns the corresponding relationships between the input 30,662 dimensional brain data and the $14 \times 14 \times 512 = 100,352$ dimensional data of the intermediate layer of VGGNet. In Exps.2 and 3, the 4,096 dimensional feature vector output by VGGNet is the target that needs to be correlated with the brain activity data. We have only 3,600 training brain activity data which are too small to train deep neural networks, so we have applied a pre-trained deep neural image caption generator to the task for describing brain activity caused by visual stimulation.

4.2 Exp.1: With Attention Mechanism and 3-layered MLP

First, we confirmed that our caption-generation model with the Attention Mechanism was well trained and had learned "attention" by generating captions and visualizing the attention for two pictures randomly selected from the COCO test dataset, as shown in Figure 4. Figure 5 shows two sets of still pictures and the generated descriptions for the brain activity data selected from the test dataset. Table 3 shows the perplexity of the generated captions for the COCO images and the

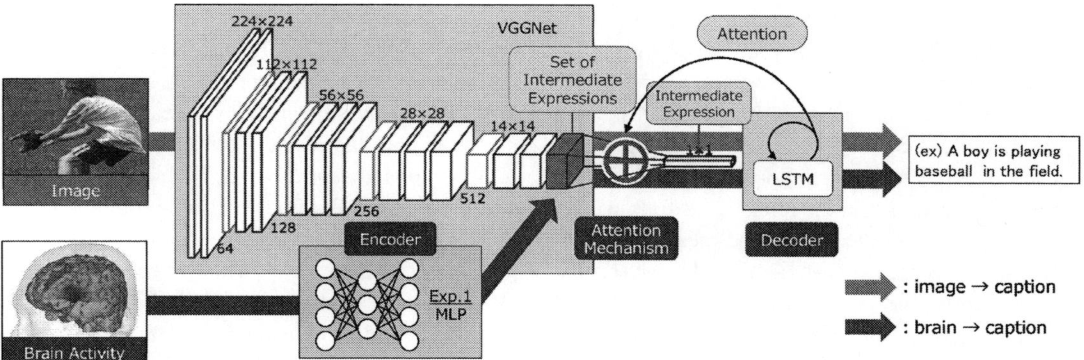

Figure 1: Overview of our approach (Exp.1: With Attention Mechanism and 3-Layered MLP).

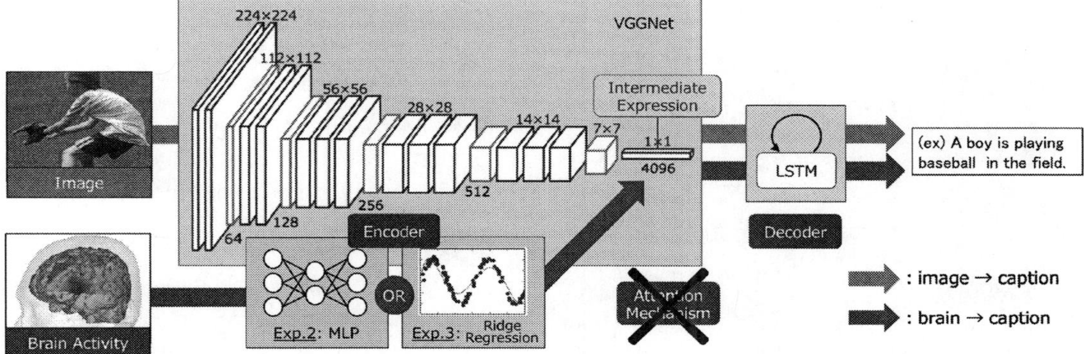

Figure 2: Overview of our approach (Exps.2 and 3: Without Attention Mechanism and with 3-Layered MLP or Ridge regression).

Table 2: Details of the experimental settings.

	Exp.1: Image to Caption with Attention	Exps.2 and 3: Image to Caption without Attention	Exp.1: Brain to Intermediates 3-Layered MLP	Exp.2: Brain to Intermediate 3-Layered MLP	Exp.3: Brain to Intermediate 3 Ridge regression
Dataset	Microsoft COCO		brain activity data		
Hyper-parameters	learning rate : 1.0 ($\times$ 0.999) gradient norm threshold : 5 L2-norm : 0.005		learning rate : 0.01 gradient norm threshold : 5 L2-norm : 0.005		L2-norm : 0.5
Learned parameters	Attention & LSTM initialized in [-0.1,0.1]	LSTM initialized in [-0.1,0.1]	weight in 3-Layered MLP initialized in [-0.2,0.2]		parameters in Ridge reg. initialized to 0
Units per layer	196 units	1,000 units	30,662 - 1,000 - 100,352	30,662 - 1,000 - 4,096	-
Vocabulary	Frequent 3,469 words (512-dim vector)		-		
Algorithm	stochastic gradient descent		stochastic gradient descent		ridge regression
Loss function	cross entropy		mean squared error		

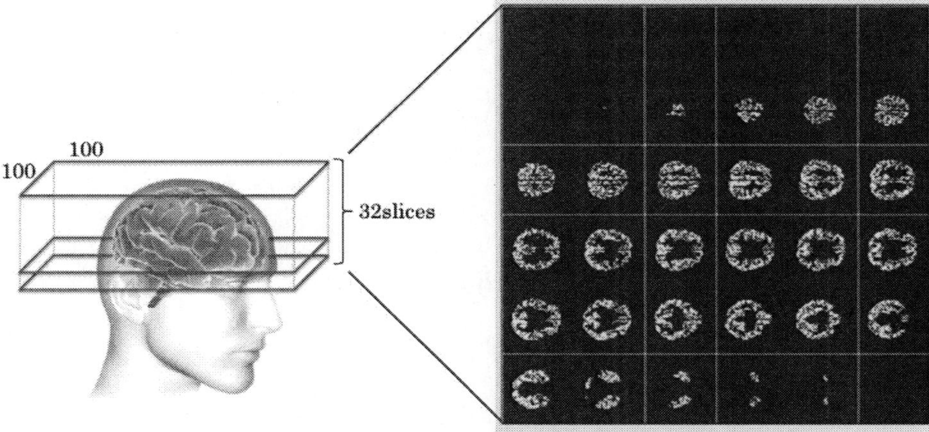

Figure 3: 30,662 voxels observed as the cerebral cortex region.

mean square error in the training process of the 3-layered MLP; the decreasing values of both quantities indicates the training progress.

The generated sentences for Exp.1 are not grammatically correct – they primarily comprise unsuitable meaningless prepositions and do not explain the contexts of the images. As for the evaluation of learning the model, the mean square error did not decrease sufficiently. This is probably caused by the fact that the output dimensions (100,352) are too large compared with the input dimensions (30,662) to learn the corresponding relationships between the brain activity data and the set of intermediate expressions.

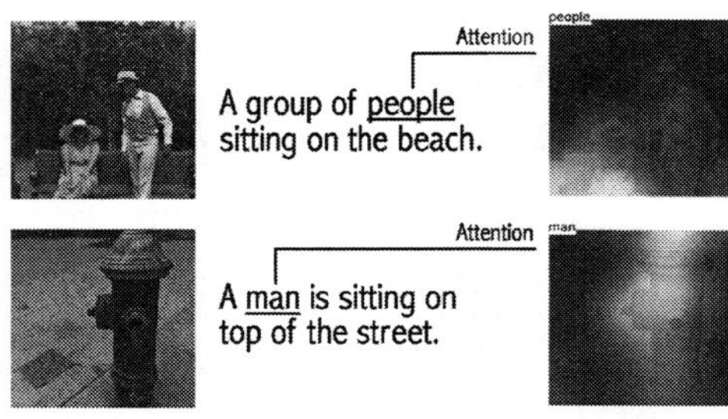

Figure 4: Caption generation with Attention Mechanism: target picture (left), generated caption (center), and attention (right).

Figure 5: Exp.1:Presented stimuli and the descriptions generated from the evoked brain activity.

Table 3: Exp.1: Training evaluation.

Num. of data	Perplexity	Iteration	MSE
14000	88.67	1	118.32
42000	66.24	5	116.44
84000	60.40	10	114.31
126000	60.10	15	112.36
168000	60.32	16	112.01

4.3 Exp.2: Without Attention Mechanism and with 3-Layered MLP

Using the same procedure as Exp.1, we confirmed that our caption-generation model without Attention Mechanism was well trained by generating captions for two pictures.

Figure 6 shows two sets of still pictures and the generated descriptions for the brain activity data. Table 4 shows the perplexity of the generated image captions and the mean square error of MLP.

Relative to the result of Exp.1, the meaningless prepositions disappear and the generated words seem to depict the image, that is, our model acquires more appropriate expressions, both syntactically and semantically. This is probably because MLP could learn the relationship better by reducing the output dimension from 100,352 to 4,096; we can confirm this by looking at the decrease in the mean square error.

Figure 6: Exp.2:Presented stimuli and the descriptions generated from the evoked brain activity.

Table 4: Exp.2: Training evaluation.

Num. of data	Perplexity	Iteration	MSE
14000	96.50	1	28.95
42000	47.87	5	22.70
84000	47.22	10	17.19
126000	47.37	15	13.37
168000	46.30	20	10.76

4.4 Exp.3: Without Attention Mechanism and with Ridge regression

Figure 7 shows two sets of pictures and descriptions for the brain activity data selected from the test data. The perplexity of the generated captions for the images is the same as in Exp.2, and the mean square error using ridge regression is 8.675.

The generated sentences are syntactically established, that is, prepositions, e.g., "in" and "on," and articles, e.g., "an," are precisely used. Compared with the results of Exps.1 and 2, we can see that the grammar of the descriptions has considerably improved. Except for the subjects in the descriptions, the contents of the images are correctly described. In particular, in the descriptions of the second image, an appropriate description of the image is generated, as we see that the person and umbrella are both recognized and their relationship is correctly described. In addition, Exp.3 had the lowest mean square error.

In these three experiments, we confirmed that the methods without Attention Mechanism perform better than that with Attention Mechanism and that ridge regression produces better results than 3-layered perceptron. Therefore, we can conclude that a simple method that can avoid overfitting the data is more appropriate for noisy and small data, such as brain activity data. However, in Exp.2, if we trained the network with more datasets, this result might be changed because we have observed that the mean square error of MLP has been decreasing.

A man is sitting on top of the table.

A man is in the back of an umbrella.

Figure 7: Exp.3:Presented stimuli and the descriptions generated from the evoked brain activity.

5 Conclusions

We proposed a method to generate descriptions of brain activity data by employing a framework to generate captions for still pictures using deep neural networks and by learning the corresponding relationships between the brain activity data and the features of the images extracted by VGGNet. We conducted three experiments to confirm our proposed method. We found that the model without Attention Mechanism using ridge regression performed the best in our experimental settings. In the future, we aim to increase the accuracy of our method to generate captions by revising the parameter settings, using additional training data and introducing evaluation measures, such as BLEU and METEOR. Moreover, we will further consider ways to learn the relationship between brain activity data and the intermediate expression and will introduce Bayesian optimization to optimize the parameter settings.

References

D. Bahdanau, K. Cho, and Y. Bengio. 2015. *Neural machine translation by jointly learning to align and translate*. In ICLR'15.

D. Blei, A. Ng, and M. Jordan. 2003. *Latent Dirichlet allocation*. Journal of Machine Learning Research, 3:993-1022.

K. Cho, B. van Merrienboer, C. Gulcehre, F. Bougares, H. Schwenk, and Y. Bengio. 2014. *Learning phrase representations using RNN encoder-decoder for statistical machine translation*. In EMNLP'14.

K. Cho, A. Courville, Y. Bengio. 2015. *Describing Multimedia Content using Attention based Encoder Decoder Networks*. Multimedia, IEEE Transactions on, 17(11): 1875-1886.

J. Chorowski, D. Bahdanau, D. Serdyuk, K. Cho, and Y. Bengio 2015. *Attention-based models for speech recognition*. In arXiv preprint arXiv: 1506.07503.

T. Cukur, S. Nishimoto, A. G. Hut, and J. L. Gallant. 2013. *Attention during natural vision warps semantic representation across the human brain*. Nature Neuroscience 16, 763-770.

J. Donahue, L. A. Hendricks, S. Guadarrama, M. Rohrbach, S. Venugopalan, K. Saenko, and T. Darrell. 2015 *Long-term Recurrent Convolutional Networks for Visual Recognition and Description*. In CVPR'15.

D. Elliott and F. Keller. 2013. *Image description using visual dependency representations*. In EMNLP'13.

D. Elliott and A. P. de Vries. 2015. *Describing Images using Inferred Visual Dependency Representations*. In ACL'15.

S. Hochreiter and J. Schmidhuber. 1997 *Long Short-Term Memory*. Neural Computation 9(8).

T. Horikawa, M. Tamaki, Y. Miyawaki, Y. Kamitani. 2013. *Neural Decoding of Visual Imagery During Sleep*. SCIENCE VOL 340.

A. G. Huth, S. Nishimoto, A. T. Vu, J. L. Gallant. 2012. *A continuous semantic space describes the representation of thousands of object and action categories across the human brain*. Neuron, 76(6):1210-1224.

S. Ioffe and C. Szegedy. 2015 *Batch normalization: Accelerating deep network training by reducing internal covariate shift*. In arXiv preprint arXiv:1502.03167.

R. Kiros, R. Salakhutdinov, and R. Zemel. 2014. *Multimodal neural language models*. In ICML'14.

R. Kiros, R. Salakhutdinov, and R. Zemel. 2015. *Unifying visual-semantic embeddings with multimodal neural language models*. In NIPS'15 Deep Learning Workshop.

G. Kulkarni, V. Premraj, V. Ordonez, S. Dhar, S. Li, Y. Choi, A. C. Berg, T. L. Berg. 2013. *Babytalk: Understanding and generating simple image descriptions*. Pattern Analysis and Machine Intelligence, IEEE Transactions on, 35(12): 2891-2903.

P. Kuznetsova, V. Ordonez, A. C. Berg, T. L. Berg, and Y. Choi. 2012. *Collective generation of natural image descriptions*. In ACL'12.

P. Kuznetsova, V. Ordonez, T. Berg, and Y. Choi. 2014. *TREETALK: Composition and compression of trees for image descriptions*. In ACL'14.

J. Mao, W. Xu, Y. Yang, J. Wang, Z. Huang, A. Yuille. 2014. *Deep Captioning with Multimodal Recurrent Neural Networks (m-RNN)*. In ICLR'14.

T. Mikolov, I. Sutskever, K. Chen, G. Corrado, J. Dean. 2013. *Distributed Representations of Words and Phrases and their Compositionality*. In NIPS'13.

G. A. Miller. 1995. *WordNet: a lexical database for English*. Communications of the ACM, Volume 138, Pages 39-41.

T. M. Mitchell, S. V. Shinkareva, A. Carlson, K. M. Chang, V. L. Malave, R. A. Mason, M. A. Just. 2008. *Predicting Human Brain Activity Associated with the Meanings of Nouns*. Science 320, 1191.

M. Mitchell, X. Han, J. Dodge, A. Mensch, A. Goyal, A. Berg, K. Yamaguchi, T. Berg, K. Stratos, and H. Daume III. 2012. *Midge: Generating image descriptions from computer vision detections. In European Chapter of the Association for Computational Linguistics*. In ACL'12.

S. Nishida, A. G. Huth, J. L. Gallant, S. Nishimoto. 2015. *Word statistics in large-scale texts explain the human cortical semantic representation of objects, actions, and impressions*. Society for Neuroscience Annual Meeting 2015 333.13.

S. Nishimoto, A. T. Vu, T. Naselaris, Y. Benjamini, B. Yu, J. L. Gallant. 2011. *Reconstructing visual experiences from brain activity evoked by natural movies*. Current Biology, 21(19):1641-1646.

F. Pereira, G. Detre, and M. Botvinick, 2011. *Generating text from functional brain images*. Frontiers in Human Neuroscience, Volume 5, Article 72.

F. Pereiraa, M. Botvinicka, G. Detre, 2013. *Using Wikipedia to learn semantic feature representations of concrete concepts in neuroimaging experiments*. Artificial Intelligence, Volume 194, January 2013, Pages 240-252.

K. Simonyan, and A. Zisserman. 2015. *Very deep convolutional networks for large-scale image recognition*. In ICLR'15.

D. E. Stansbury, T. Naselaris, and J. L. Gallant. 2013. *Natural Scene Statistics Account for the Representation of Scene Categories in Human Visual Cortex*. Neuron 79, Pages 1025-1034, September 4, 2013, Elsevier Inc.

I. Sutskever, O. Vinyals, Q. V. Le. 2014. *Sequence to sequence learning with neural networks.* In NIPS'14.

I. Vendrov, R. Kiros, S. Fidler, R. Urtasun. 2016. *Order-Embeddings of Images and Language.* In ICLR'16.

O. Vinyals, A. Toshev, S. Bengio, and D. Erhan. 2015. *Show and tell: A neural image caption generator.* In CVPR'15.

K. Xu, J. Ba, R. Kiros, A. Courville, R. Salakhutdinov, R. Zemel, and Y. Bengio. 2015. *Show, attend and tell: Neural image caption generation with visual attention.* In ICML'15.

S. Yagcioglu, E. Erdem, A. Erdem, R. Cakici. 2015. *A Distributed Representation Based Query Expansion Approach for Image Captioning.* In ACL'15.

L. Yao, A. Torabi, K. Cho, N. Ballas, C. Pal, H. Larochelle, and A. Courville. 2015. *Describing videos by exploiting temporal structure.* In ICCV'15.

Improving Twitter Community Detection through Contextual Sentiment Analysis of Tweets

Alron Jan Lam

College of Computer Studies
De La Salle University
2401 Taft Avenue, Malate, Manila, Philippines
`alron_lam@dlsu.edu.ph`

Abstract

Works on Twitter community detection have yielded new ways to extract valuable insights from social media. Through this technique, Twitter users can be grouped into different types of communities such as those who have the same interests, those who interact a lot, or those who have similar sentiments about certain topics. Computationally, information is represented as a graph, and community detection is the problem of partitioning the graph such that each community is more densely connected to each other than to the rest of the network. It has been shown that incorporating sentiment analysis can improve community detection when looking for sentiment-based communities. However, such works only perform sentiment analysis in isolation without considering the tweet's various contextual information. Examples of these contextual information are social network structure, and conversational, author, and topic contexts. Disregarding these information poses a problem because at times, context is needed to clearly infer the sentiment of a tweet. Thus, this research aims to improve detection of sentiment-based communities on Twitter by performing contextual sentiment analysis.

1 Introduction

Twitter, as a micro-blogging platform, has become an avenue for people to voice out their opinions online. This gives concerned entities, like policy-makers or brand managers, the chance to hear people out in an unprecedented way. However, to effectively utilize this source of information, the massive amount of tweets must first be processed to be more easily understood (Kavanaugh et al., 2012).

One such way to achieve this is through community detection, which is a domain-independent, graph-based problem that can be applied to many different disciplines including social media analysis. Its definition is that it is the problem of looking for groups of vertices that are more densely connected to each other than to the rest of the graph (Papadopoulos et al., 2012; Tang and Liu, 2010). Hence, due to its domain-independence, setting up the input graph properly according to the desired application is important (Darmon et al., 2014). When applied to Twitter, a wide array of communities can be found, such as communities of users with similar interests (Lim and Datta, 2012b; Lim and Datta, 2012a), communities of users who interact frequently (Amor et al., 2015), communities of geographically-nearby users (Bakillah et al., 2015), or communities of users with similar sentiments towards a certain topic (Cao et al., 2015), among many other possibilities.

Finding these communities can yield insights like (1) the different kinds of conversations going on, (2) who participates in them, and (3) what they are talking about. These kinds of insights could be valuable to entities such as policy-makers (Amor et al., 2015).

However, most works on Twitter community detection are focused on finding communities within social networks based on explicit relationships between users, such as following-follower relationships (Java et al., 2007), or mention/retweet relationships (Pearce et al., 2014; Zhang et al., 2012). An often-overlooked source of information are the actual contents of the users' tweets. In some cases, this may not be important. But when looking for communities of users who share similar sentiments, this could potentially improve

Proceedings of the 54th Annual Meeting of the Association for Computational Linguistics – Student Research Workshop, pages 30–36,
Berlin, Germany, August 7-12, 2016. ©2016 Association for Computational Linguistics

community detection (Deitrick and Hu, 2013).

The work of Deitrick and Hu (2013) utilized sentiment analysis to improve community detection. In addition to the usual graph edges representing follower-following relations, they added more edge weights between users who expressed the same sentiments towards the same topic. That is, whenever two users tweet with the same sentiment polarity (positive or negative) containing the same hashtag (treated as the topic), their edge weight is incremented, indicating a stronger relationship between these users. They showed that doing this technique improves community detection according to the modularity score, and this in turn, facilitates better sentiment analysis.

However, works like that of Deitrick and Hu (2013) perform sentiment analysis of a tweet in an isolated manner. That is, various contextual information available for a tweet are totally disregarded. Examples of these include conversational (tweets preceding the target tweet in the conversation thread), author (tweets recently posted by the author preceding the target tweet) and topic (recent tweets about the same topic posted before the target tweet) context (Ren et al., 2016; Vanzo et al., 2014). Another example of contextual information is social network structure, wherein connections between users help determine sentiment polarities by utilizing social theories such as balance theory ("an enemy of my enemy is my friend") and homophily ("birds of the same feather flock together") (West et al., 2014; Tan et al., 2011). The aforementioned studies have shown that incorporating contextual information can improve sentiment analysis.

Thus, in looking for sentiment-based Twitter communities wherein there are stronger connections between users having similar sentiments, it may be beneficial to take a contextual approach to sentiment analysis.

2 Twitter Community Detection

This section compares and contrasts different works on Twitter community detection. Table 1 is a summary of all reviewed works and a comparison of these works in terms of desired community type and edge construction scheme. The community detection algorithms and evaluation metrics used by these works are also discussed in this section.

It can be observed in Table 1 that different re-

Year	Authors	Community Types	Edge Construction
2013	Deitrick & Wu	Social Network-based, Sentiment-based	Based on follow, mention, and re-tweet relationships, and on tweets having the same hashtags and same sentiment polarity
2014	Darmon et al.	Interaction-based, Topic-based	Based on mention and re-tweet relationships, and on tweets having the same hashtags
2015	Bakillah et al.	Interaction-based, Topic-based	Based on follow, mention, and re-tweet relationships, and on tweets having the same URLs and similar tweet content
2015	Amor et al.	Social Network-based, Interaction-based	Based on follow, mention, and re-tweet relationships
2015	Cao et al.	Sentiment-based	Based on difference between users' sentiment trends over time

Table 1: Twitter Community Detection Works and their Desired Community Types, and Edge Construction Scheme

search works aimed to identify different types of communities. These communities are: (1) social network-based (who are in the same social groups?), (2) interaction-based (who frequently interact with each other through re-tweets and mentions?), (3) topic-based (who talk about the same things?), and (4) sentiment-based (who feel the same way about certain topics?).

It is important to note the different types of communities the works aimed to extract, because they largely influence how the community detection problem is set-up. Since community detection is a domain-independent problem that applies to any graph structure, performing Twitter community detection requires that relevant information be represented appropriately through the vertices and edges in a graph. With the input graph laid out, researchers can then select appropriate community detection algorithms to be used. Lastly, researchers can then choose appropriate metrics for evaluating their approach. These three aspects are discussed in more detail in the following subsections.

2.1 Edge Construction

As previously mentioned, the desired community types largely influence the representation of information as a graph, consisting of vertices and edges. Although in theory this might not always be the case, most reviewed works used vertices to represent users, and consequently, edges to represent relationships between the users. The works only differed in terms of what kind of relationships the edges represented.

For works that aimed to identify social groups, that is, communities of people who generally followed each other within their own communities, edges have generally been used to represent a "follow" relationship (Amor et al., 2015; Lim and Datta, 2012b; Lim and Datta, 2012a). On Twitter, users "follow" other users to "subscribe" to their tweets and be able to see them as they get published. It is important to note that the "follow" relationship is not necessarily two-way. That is, if user A follows user B, it is possible that user B does not follow user A. Given the explicit "follow" relationships on Twitter, some works have represented "follow" networks on Twitter in a straightforward manner by using directed edges to represent these "follow" relationships. As discussed earlier, the goal of these works is usu-

ally to find social groups or cliques within the graph that represent social circles (since people who are friends in real life tend to follow each other) or people with similar interests (since people also follow users they may not know personally, but whom they are interested in). This type of edge construction, since it is straightforward and based on explicit "follow" relationships, is usually used in combination with other edge construction schemes, wherein the "follow" relationships determine the existence of edges, while other information are used to increment edge weights (Deitrick and Hu, 2013).

For works that aimed to identify communities of people that interacted with each other frequently, main relationships involved are the "re-tweet" and "mention" relationships (Amor et al., 2015; Darmon et al., 2014; Bakillah et al., 2015). When user A re-tweets a tweet by user B, user A is essentially re-publishing the said tweet and propagating it to his/her own followers. On the other hand, a mention happens when user A tags user B in a tweet. This either happens when user A simply wants to call user B's attention to his/her tweet, or when user A is replying to one of user B's tweets. Note that it is possible for users to mention multiple users in a single tweet. Having said that, mentions or re-tweets between users have been used to either increment existing edge weights (Amor et al., 2015; Darmon et al., 2014), or to establish the existence of new edges altogether (Bakillah et al., 2015) in works that sought interaction-based communities. An example of such a work is that of Amor et al. (2015), where they found what they called conversation communities: groups of conversations with people talking about a topic of interest.

For works that aimed to identify communities of people who were interested in similar topics (Bakillah et al., 2015; Darmon et al., 2014; Deitrick and Hu, 2013), hashtags have been used to establish or strengthen edges between users. Hashtags are a way for Twitter users to tag their tweet as talking about a certain topic. These are arbitrarily defined and purely user-generated tags in the form '#hashtag'. Users sometimes tend to copy other hashtags instead of creating their own, resulting into popular, trending hashtags. With this in mind, the idea of topic-based community detection is to look for communities of users who talk about similar topics identified through the hashtags. For example, if user A tweets with the hashtag '#ClimateChange', and user B also tweets with the same hashtag, then either more weight is added to an existing edge between them (Darmon et al., 2014; Deitrick and Hu, 2013), or a new edge between the users is created on this basis (Bakillah et al., 2015).

For works that aimed to identify communities of people sharing similar sentiments, the idea is to establish stronger relationships between users who feel the same sentiment polarity toward the same topic (identified through the hashtag) (Cao et al., 2015; Deitrick and Hu, 2013). For example, if user A tweets "We are in a bad situation. #ClimateChange" and user B tweets "Our world is dying. #ClimateChange", then user A and user B's edge should be added more weight because their tweets both express negative sentiments about climate change (Deitrick and Hu, 2013).

In summary, different community types warrant different edge construction schemes. However, it is important to note that works on Twitter community detection do not necessarily utilize just one of the aforementioned schemes. Rather, researchers oftentimes experiment with and combine different edge construction and weighting schemes to see which configuration produces the best output (Bakillah et al., 2015; Deitrick and Hu, 2013).

2.2 Algorithms

The reviewed works on community detection have used a variety of algorithms, each being appropriate to different scenarios or constraints. For example, some of the algorithms can handle directed and weighted graphs (Xie, 2012; Rosvall and Bergstrom, 2008; Lancichinetti et al., 2011), while some can detect overlapping communities (Xie, 2012; Lancichinetti et al., 2011), while some execute relatively quickly for large graphs (Xie, 2012; Rosvall and Bergstrom, 2008). These are examples of factors that the researchers took into consideration when choosing their algorithms. A more detailed discussion of each work follows.

Deitrick and Hu (2013) chose the Speaker Listener Propagation Algorithm, or SLPA, (Xie, 2012) and the Infomap algorithm (Rosvall and Bergstrom, 2008) for community detection as they both work with weighted and directed graphs, and they both execute relatively quickly on large graphs. In addition, SLPA can identify overlapping communities.

Darmon et al. (2014) chose the Order Statistics Local Optimization Method, or OSLOM, (Lancichinetti et al., 2011) for community detection because of its ability to work with weighted and directed graphs, and its ability to identify overlapping communities.

Bakillah et al. (2015) chose the Fast-Greedy Optimization of Modularity, or FGM, (Clauset et al., 2004) for its ability to handle complex social graphs from Twitter, and the Varied Density-Based Spatial Clustering of Applications with Noise, or VDBSCAN, (Liu et al., 2007) for its ability to obtain spatial clusters at certain points in time.

Amor et al. (2015) chose the Markov Stability (Delvenne et al., 2010) due to its mechanism of modeling information flow. The primary goal of their research was to understand the Twitter discussion on the care.data program in terms of information flow and the roles that Twitter users play. Hence, their selection of Markov Stability fits their goals.

Lastly, Cao et al. (2015) chose to use Heirarchical Agglomerative Clustering (Jain and Dubes, 1988) based on sentiment distance. Since they were focused on looking for communities with similar sentiments, the clustering method is appropriate for this task.

2.3 Evaluation

To evaluate their approaches, researchers of related works have used quantitative and/or qualitative analysis. Quantitative analysis usually entails optimizing some metric, like the well-known modularity score (Newman, 2006), which indicates how well-formed the communities are as opposed to randomly generated communities. Other works have also performed experiments in which they pre-determined the communities beforehand, treating the community detection problem as a "classification" problem of placing vertices in their proper communities. As such, these works have used precision and recall to evaluate their approach (Bakillah et al., 2015). However, the manual pre-determination of communities beforehand can be a difficult task, so this kind of evaluation methodology is not too popular, making metric optimization as the more common evaluation approach. Exact numerical results of these studies are not discussed here because direct comparison of results is not appropriate due to differences in datasets and types of communities being detected.

Year	Authors	Level of Sentiment Analysis	Contextual Information Used
2016	Ren et al.	Document-level (tweet)	Conversational, Author, Topic Context
2014	Vanzo et al.	Document-level (tweet)	Conversational Context
2014	West et al.	User-level (towards another user)	Social Network Structure
2011	Tan et al.	User-level (towards a topic)	Social Network Structure

Table 2: Contextual Sentiment Analysis Works and their Levels of Sentiment Analysis and Contextual Information Used

On the other hand, researchers also use qualitative analyses in the form of case studies. Usually, this comes in the form of a discussion on the insights acquired from the community detection approach. For example, Amor et al. (2015) discussed in their work how their approach was able to reveal insights into who were concerned about the care.data program in the UK (political activists, media, UK healthcare professionals, and US healthcare professionals) and what they were concerned about (data privacy, impact on patient welfare, etc). Other works like that of Cao et al. (2015) also involved interviewing domain experts and asking them to evaluate whether community detection results would be useful to them or others in the field whose tasks involve analyzing social media data.

3 Contextual Sentiment Analysis

This section compares and contrasts different works on Contextual Sentiment Analysis. Shown in Table 2 is a summary of reviewed works and a comparison of these works in terms of level of sentiment analysis and context types considered. The algorithms and evaluation metrics used by these works are also discussed in the section.

3.1 Sentiment Analysis Types

It can be seen in Table 2 that for the reviewed works, there are two levels of sentiment analy-
sis: document-level and person-level. A document is essentially a collection of sentences. In the case of Ren et al. (2016), Vanzo et al. (2014), and Tan et al. (2011), having Twitter as the domain, a document refers to a tweet. While in the case of West et al. (2014) with Wikipedia discussions and US Congress speeches as the domain, a document refers to a person's post and speech respectively. Document-level sentiment analysis usually involves utilizing lexical information found in the text.

On the other hand, person-level sentiment analysis focuses on determining the overall sentiment of a person towards a particular person on topic, as opposed to focusing on each individual document a person generates. For example, say it is desirable to determine user A's sentiment towards Obama based on his/her tweets. Person-level sentiment analysis would then require consideration of all user A's tweets about Obama, instead of just determining the conveyed sentiment in each tweet. For most related works, document-level sentiment analysis is performed as a sub-task of person-level sentiment analysis (West et al., 2014; Tan et al., 2011).

3.2 Context Types

In addition to using textual information for sentiment analysis, the reviewed works utilized a variety of contextual information. The principle is that these provide more knowledge needed to perform more accurate sentiment analysis.

For document-level sentiment analysis (tweet-level in this case), context types used by Ren et al. (2016) and Vanzo et al. (2014) are conversational, author and topic. Having Twitter as the domain, conversational context was defined as the most recent l tweets preceeding a target tweet in the conversation it belongs to. Author context was defined by Ren et al. (2016) as the most recent l tweets posted by a user before the target tweet. Lastly, topic context was defined by Ren et al. (2016) as the most recent l tweets posted before the target tweet that shares at least one hashtag with the target tweet. The rationale is that the textual information found in a single tweet may be ambiguous, and thus, insufficient to clearly determine its sentiment polarity. Therefore, taking into account the aforementioned contexts can fill in the said gap.

For person-level sentiment analysis, social network structure has been used by West et al. (2014) and Tan et al. (2011) as contextual information. These works rely on theories about social behavior such as balance theory ("an enemy of my enemy is my friend") and homophily ("birds of the same feather flock together") to complement document-level sentiment analysis based on the document text. The idea is that information gained from people's connections or interactions can help determine a person's sentiment towards a topic (Tan et al., 2011) or another user (West et al., 2014).

3.3 Metholodgy

Ren et al. (2016), with document-level sentiment analysis as the goal, represented words found in the target tweet and in contextual tweets (conversational, author, and topic, as explained in the previous sub-section) through word embeddings. They then train a convolutional neural network to classify the target tweet's sentiment polarity given these input features.

Vanzo et al. (2014), with document-level sentiment analysis as the goal, use a Markovian formulation of the Support Vector Machine model to classify a target tweet given the preceding tweets in its conversational context. They represent tweets through bag of words, a distributed lexical semantic model, a user sentiment inclination profile, and various combinations of these three.

West et al. (2014), with person-level sentiment analysis (towards another person) as the goal, use a scheme they call "triangle balance" in which they minimize a cost function that applies penalties for going against the sentiment model and for going against the social theories they used. The setting of cost parameters was done through machine learning.

Tan et al. (2011), with person-level sentiment analysis (towards a topic) as the goal, use a factor-graph model for estimating the probability of each polarity for a given person. They experiment on learning and no-learning approaches in setting the necessary parameters.

Since the determination of sentiment polarities is generally a classification problem, most of the reviewed works evaluated their results through metrics common to classification tasks like precision, recall, F-measure, accuracy, and ROC.

4 Conclusion

Based on the review of related works, it can be seen that the desired community types largely dictate the edge construction scheme used in the input graphs. Furthermore, it has been shown that using sentiment analysis to modify edge weights when performing community detection can improve the detection of sentiment-based communities (Deitrick and Hu, 2013). The idea is that users who feel the same about a particular topic should have a stronger connection.

However, one possible improvement over the work of (Deitrick and Hu, 2013) is to perform contextual sentiment analysis. This is because various contextual information, such as conversational, author, and topic context, along with social network structure, have been shown to improve sentiment analysis (Ren et al., 2016; Vanzo et al., 2014; West et al., 2014; Tan et al., 2011). The assumption is that the improvement in sentiment analysis will improve the modification of edge weights (and therefore, the representation of connection between users) and consequently, improve sentiment-based community detection. Evaluation can be through quantitative analysis by using well-known metrics in community detection, such as modularity, or through qualitative analysis by performing case studies. Analysis of the results can provide insight on which contextual information provide the most improvement in the task of sentiment-based community detection on Twitter.

References

B Amor, S Vuik, Ryan Callahan, Ara Darzi, Sophia N Yaliraki, and Mauricio Barahona. 2015. Community detection and role identification in directed networks: understanding the twitter network of the care. data debate. *arXiv preprint arXiv:1508.03165*.

Mohamed Bakillah, Ren-Yu Li, and Steve HL Liang. 2015. Geo-located community detection in twitter with enhanced fast-greedy optimization of modularity: the case study of typhoon haiyan. *International Journal of Geographical Information Science*, 29(2):258–279.

Nan Cao, Lu Lu, Yu-Ru Lin, Fei Wang, and Zhen Wen. 2015. Socialhelix: visual analysis of sentiment divergence in social media. *Journal of Visualization*, 18(2):221–235.

Aaron Clauset, Mark EJ Newman, and Cristopher Moore. 2004. Finding community structure in very large networks. *Physical review E*, 70(6):066111.

David Darmon, Elisa Omodei, and Joshua Garland. 2014. Followers are not enough: A question-oriented approach to community detection in online social networks. *arXiv preprint arXiv:1404.0300*.

William Deitrick and Wei Hu. 2013. Mutually enhancing community detection and sentiment analysis on twitter networks.

J-C Delvenne, Sophia N Yaliraki, and Mauricio Barahona. 2010. Stability of graph communities across time scales. *Proceedings of the National Academy of Sciences*, 107(29):12755–12760.

Anil K Jain and Richard C Dubes. 1988. *Algorithms for clustering data*. Prentice-Hall, Inc.

Akshay Java, Xiaodan Song, Tim Finin, and Belle Tseng. 2007. Why we twitter: understanding microblogging usage and communities. In *Proceedings of the 9th WebKDD and 1st SNA-KDD 2007 workshop on Web mining and social network analysis*, pages 56–65. ACM.

Andrea L Kavanaugh, Edward A Fox, Steven D Sheetz, Seungwon Yang, Lin Tzy Li, Donald J Shoemaker, Apostol Natsev, and Lexing Xie. 2012. Social media use by government: From the routine to the critical. *Government Information Quarterly*, 29(4):480–491.

Andrea Lancichinetti, Filippo Radicchi, José J Ramasco, and Santo Fortunato. 2011. Finding statistically significant communities in networks. *PloS one*, 6(4):e18961.

Kwan Hui Lim and Amitava Datta. 2012a. Finding twitter communities with common interests using following links of celebrities. In *Proceedings of the 3rd international workshop on Modeling social media*, pages 25–32. ACM.

Kwan Hui Lim and Amitava Datta. 2012b. Following the follower: detecting communities with common interests on twitter. In *Proceedings of the 23rd ACM conference on Hypertext and social media*, pages 317–318. ACM.

Peng Liu, Dong Zhou, and Naijun Wu. 2007. Vdbscan: varied density based spatial clustering of applications with noise. In *Service Systems and Service Management, 2007 International Conference on*, pages 1–4. IEEE.

Mark EJ Newman. 2006. Modularity and community structure in networks. *Proceedings of the national academy of sciences*, 103(23):8577–8582.

Symeon Papadopoulos, Yiannis Kompatsiaris, Athena Vakali, and Ploutarchos Spyridonos. 2012. Community detection in social media. *Data Mining and Knowledge Discovery*, 24(3):515–554.

Warren Pearce, Kim Holmberg, Iina Hellsten, and Brigitte Nerlich. 2014. Climate change on twitter: Topics, communities and conversations about the 2013 ipcc working group 1 report. *PloS one*, 9(4):e94785.

Yafeng Ren, Yue Zhang, Meishan Zhang, and Donghong Ji. 2016. Context-sensitive twitter sentiment classification using neural network. AAAI.

Martin Rosvall and Carl T Bergstrom. 2008. Maps of random walks on complex networks reveal community structure. *Proceedings of the National Academy of Sciences*, 105(4):1118–1123.

Chenhao Tan, Lillian Lee, Jie Tang, Long Jiang, Ming Zhou, and Ping Li. 2011. User-level sentiment analysis incorporating social networks. In *Proceedings of the 17th ACM SIGKDD international conference on Knowledge discovery and data mining*, pages 1397–1405. ACM.

Lei Tang and Huan Liu. 2010. Community detection and mining in social media. *Synthesis Lectures on Data Mining and Knowledge Discovery*, 2(1):1–137.

Andrea Vanzo, Danilo Croce, and Roberto Basili. 2014. A context-based model for sentiment analysis in twitter. In *COLING*, pages 2345–2354.

Robert West, Hristo S Paskov, Jure Leskovec, and Christopher Potts. 2014. Exploiting social network structure for person-to-person sentiment analysis. *arXiv preprint arXiv:1409.2450*.

Jierui Xie. 2012. *Agent-based dynamics models for opinion spreading and community detection in large-scale social networks*. Ph.D. thesis, Rensselaer Polytechnic Institute.

Yang Zhang, Yao Wu, and Qing Yang. 2012. Community discovery in twitter based on user interests. *Journal of Computational Information Systems*, 8(3):991–1000.

Significance of an Accurate Sandhi-Splitter in Shallow Parsing of Dravidian Languages

Devadath V V   **Dipti Misra Sharma**

Language Technology Research Centre

International Institute of Information Technology - Hyderabad, India.

`devadathv.v@research.iiit.ac.in`

`dipti@iiit.ac.in`

Abstract

This paper evaluates the challenges involved in shallow parsing of Dravidian languages which are highly agglutinative and morphologically rich. Text processing tasks in these languages are not trivial because multiple words concatenate to form a single string with morpho-phonemic changes at the point of concatenation. This phenomenon known as *Sandhi*, in turn complicates the individual word identification. Shallow parsing is the task of identification of correlated group of words given a raw sentence. The current work is an attempt to study the effect of *Sandhi* in building shallow parsers for Dravidian languages by evaluating its effect on Malayalam, one of the main languages from Dravidian family. We provide an in-depth analysis of effect of *Sandhi* in developing a robust shallow parser pipeline with experimental results emphasizing on how sensitive the individual components of shallow parser are, towards the accuracy of a sandhi splitter. Our work can serve as a guiding light for building robust text processing systems in Dravidian languages.

1 Introduction

Identification of individual words is crucial for the computational processing of a text. In Dravidian languages, word identification becomes complex because of *Sandhi*. *Sandhi* is a phenomenon of concatenation of multiple words or characters to form a single complex string, with morpho-phonemic changes at the points of concatenation (VV et al., 2014). The morphological units that can be concatenated in a *Sandhi* operation can belong to any linguistic class: a noun joins with

a verb or a postposition or particle, a verb joins with other verbs, auxiliaries, connectives, adverbs combining with verbs and so on. The phenomenon is different from a noun compound multi-word expression in that the noun-compound concatenations are semantics-driven. Whereas *Sandhi* is not semantically driven but phonologically driven. This leads to misclassification of classes of words by pos-tagger which eventually affects parsing. Hence making shallow parsers for Dravidian languages is a challenging task.

Shallow parsing (Abney, 1992) is a task of automatic identification of correlated group of words (chunks) which reduces the computational effort at the level of full parsing by assigning partial structure to a sentence. To be precise, chunks are correlated group of words which contain only the head or content word and its modifiers. Shallow parser is not a single module but is a set of modules (Hammerton et al., 2002) with tokeniser, parts-of-speech tagger (pos-tagger) and chunker put in a pipeline. It has been experimentally proved that shallow parsers are useful in both text (Collins, 1996), (Buchholz and Daelemans, 2001) and speech processing domains (Wahlster, 2013).

The current work aims to give an in-depth analysis on the effect of *Sandhi* in shallow parsing of Dravidian languages with a focus on Malayalam, the most agglutinative language (Sankaran and Jawahar, 2013) in the Dravidian family. For the purpose of analysis, we chose to create our own pos-tagger and chunker trained on a new 70k words annotated corpus with word internal features of morpho-phonological nature particularly because *Sandhi* evolved out of morpho-phonological reasons.

In this paper, for the first time in the literature, we evaluate the impact of *Sandhi* and the resultant error propagation in shallow parser for Dravidian languages. In this work, we compare the

Proceedings of the 54th Annual Meeting of the Association for Computational Linguistics – Student Research Workshop, pages 37–42,
Berlin, Germany, August 7-12, 2016. ©2016 Association for Computational Linguistics

performances of pos-tagger, and chunker on a gold standard sandhi-split test data and how the error of a sandhi-splitting tool propagates to other components of shallow parsing pipeline. We have released the 70k annotated data and the trained models of pos-agger, chunker and shallow parser described in this paper[1].

2 Sandhi in Dravidian languages

Sandhi is a very common phenomenon in Sanskrit and Dravidian languages. Even though many languages exhibit agglutinative properties in morphemes, in these languages, this goes beyond the morphemes and agglutinates words with morpho-phonemic change. For example,

(1) **avanaareyaaN snEhikkunnath ?**
    'avan_ aare aaN snEhikkunnath ?
    'he whom is loving ?
    'whom he is loving?

Example 1 is a valid sentence from Malayalam. There are two strings, *avanaareyaaN* and *snEhikkunnath*. Here second string is a single word but first string, *avanaareyaaN* is a combination of 3 sub-strings or words; *avan_*, *aare* and *aaN*. The last character "*n_*" of *avan_* is a pure consonant which can stand alone without the help of a vowel. When this word joins with the next word *aare*, "*n_*" of *avan_* becomes a normal consonant by joining with the first character "*aa*" of *aare*. When *aare* joins with the word *aaN*, an insertion of an additional character "*y*" happens, and together they form *avanaareyaaN*.

$$avan\_ + aare + aaN \rightarrow ava\mathbf{n}aar\mathbf{e}yaaN$$

Sandhi happens in Dravidian languages at two levels. One is at morpheme level and other is at word level. In morpheme level, stem or root(s) join with the affixes to create a word along with morpho-phonemic changes as explained above. This is considered as *Internal Sandhi*. *Sandhi* between words as in example (1) is known as *External Sandhi*. For this work, *External Sandhi* is the matter of concern because this makes the individual word identification difficult.

<hr>

[1]Data and Models created during this project can be found in this link https://github.com/Devadath/Malayalam-Shallow-Parser

3 Sandhi-Splitter

Sandhi-splitter is a tool which splits a string of conjoined words into a sequence of individual words, where each word in the sequence has the capacity to stand alone as a single word. To be precise, sandhi-splitter facilitates the task of individual word identification within such a string of conjoined words.

To the best of our knowledge, only 2 works have been published on Malayalam sandhi-splitter with proper empirical results (VV et al., 2014), (Kuncham et al., 2015). For all the experiments, we used the former sandhi splitter since the accuracy is better than the latter one. This method applies Bayesian methods at character level to find out the precise split points and used hand-crafted rules to induce morpho-phonemic changes. The remaining sections of this paper focus on an in-depth analysis of effect of *Sandhi* in shallow parsing in the language of Malayalam.

4 Effect of *Sandhi* in Shallow Parsing

4.1 An overview of Shallow Parser pipeline

A typical architecture of a shallow parser has three main modules namely sandhi-splitter, pos-tagger and chunker. Input to the shallow parser is a raw sentence and the output is a chunked text with its pos and chunk information of every word present in it. The diagram of the architecture is given in Figure 1.

Figure 1: Pipeline Architecture

4.2 Effect of *Sandhi* in POS-Tagging

As mentioned in Section 1, *Sandhi* happens between words from different grammatical categories.

(2) **addEhamoraddhyaapakanaaN**
    'addEhaM oru addhyaapakan_ aaN
    'He one teacher(male) is
    'He is a teacher

Example 2 is a sentence in Malayalam with 4 words in it. Here first word *addEhaM* is a pronoun, second word *oru* is quantifier, third word *addhyaapakan_* is a noun and fourth word *aaN* is a copula. But these words are agglutinated to become a string of words *addEhamoraddhyaapakanaaN*, making the system incapable of identifying individual words, consequently resulting in an erroneous POS tagging.

   (3) **varumen_kil_**
         'varuM en_kil_'
         'come.FUT if'
         'if comes'

In example 3, there are 2 different words from different grammatical classes. *varuM* is a finite verb whereas *en_kil_* is a conjunction and they are agglutinated together to form *varumen_kil_* which should not be tagged by a single pos-tag.

Because of the morphological richness, morphological features like root, prefix and suffix information are helpful features in identifying the grammatical category of a word. In order to evaluate the effect of *Sandhi* we decided to create a pos-tagger which uses both word-external (context) and word-internal features (morphological features) because a word is a result of *Sandhi* between morphemes like prefix, suffix, root, stem etc. For incorporating these features we used CRF (Lafferty et al., 2001) for building pos-tagger. We created a pos-annotated news corpus of 70k words by manual efforts along with bootstrapping. The pos information is incorporated after splitting and validating the *Sandhi*. The Tag-set we used to annotate is BIS tag-set[2], specially designed for Indian languages. Since morph analyzers are not available for Malayalam, in order to capture the prefix and suffix information, certain number of characters from the beginning and end of a word are used as features for POS Tagging. Table 1 shows the features used for pos-tagging.

Features
W_{-1}, W_0, W_1,
W[0], W[0:2], .., W[0:5],
W[-5], W[-5:-3], .., W[-5:EOW]

Table 1: Features for our POS Tagger. W is Word and W[l:m] refers to character at indexes. W_x refers to word at relative position of x with respect to current position. 'EOW' refers to End Of Word.

4.3 Effect of *Sandhi* in Chunking

Chunks are identified based on the pos-tags of words. Since a chunk is a group of a head word

---

2http://tinyurl.com/hhllsky

and its modifiers, they are meaningful subsets of a sentence. But if the individual words are not correctly identified, inappropriate pos-tags will be assigned and meaningless chunks will be created. There are 4 words and 3 chunks in example 2. [*addEhaM* PRP]NP, [*oru* QT *addhyaapakan_* NN]NP, and [*aaN* VM]VP. If the *Sandhi* is not identified and individual words are not extracted, system will fail to identify the meaningful sub-parts of a sentence like chunk/phrase/constituents. Similarly in example 3, the string *varumen_kil_* has two words and two chunks [*varuM* VM]VP and [*en_kil_* CC]CCP. Hence processing *Sandhi* in the first stage is extremely important in any NLP task for Dravidian languages.

For evaluating the effect of *Sandhi* in chunker, we decided to create a chunker. We incorporated chunk information using IIIT-tagset (Bharati, 2006) in the data annotated for pos-tagging, which is a corpus of 70k words. Table 2 shows the features we used for the chunker. Each feature is composed of a word and its corresponding POS tag.

Features
W_{-2}/POS_{-2},..,W_0/POS_0,..,W_2/POS_2

Table 2: Features for our Chunker. W is Word and POS refers to POS tag.

5 End to End Shallow parser

Shallow parser is a set of modules comprising of sandhi-splitter, pos-tagger and chunker in order. A raw text will be given as the input and the sandhi-splitter identifies individual words, pos-tagger assigns pos-tags to each word and chunker groups them to chunks and outputs the chunked sentence as shown in Figure 2.

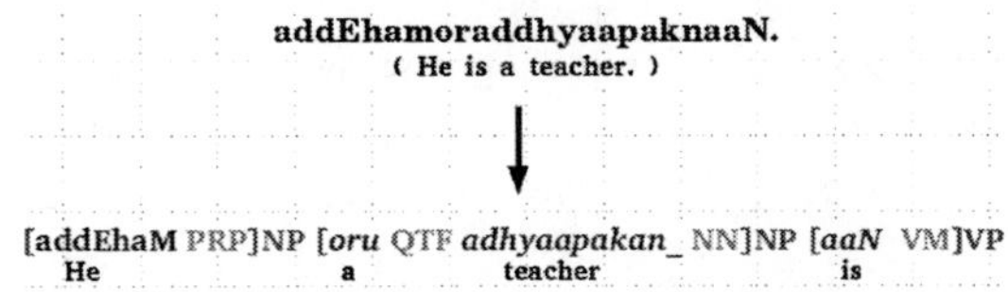

Figure 2: Example of a raw input and the subsequent chunked output

5.1 Data

We have used the manually created 70k pos and chunk annotated corpus which we have already mentioned in 4.2 and 4.3. Out of 70k data, 8k data has been taken as test data and remaining 62k as training data for pos-tagging and chunking. Since creating training data for sandhi-splitter is a laborious task, we used the sandhi-annotated training data of size 2k words used by (VV et al., 2014). Whereas test data will be the same 8k data which were employed for pos tagging and chunking.

5.2 Experiments

Two types of experiments have been conducted to evaluate the error propagation of the Malayalam shallow parser pipeline. In the first type of experiments, individual modules in the pipeline are considered as independent of the output of previous modules. In the second type of experiment individual modules are considered as dependent on the output of previous modules.

5.2.1 Experiment Type - 1

In this experiment, input to each module will not be affected by the performance of its previous modules. This experiment evaluates the performance of all the individual modules with respect to the current train and test data. Table 3 presents the results.

Module	P	R	F-1	A
Sandhi Splitter	91.77	62.95	74.68	88.46
POS tagger	90.45	90.49	90.47	90.45
Chunker	88.47	91.55	89.98	92.92

Table 3: Results of Experiment Type- 1 : Results of individual modules where each module will not be affected by the performance of its previous modules. Here, 'P' refers to Precision, 'R' to Recall, 'F-1' to F-Measure and 'A' to Accuracy

5.2.2 Experiment Type - 2

In these experiments, output of one module will be given as input to the next module, hence the performance of the previous module affects the next module. These experiments are to evaluate the error propagation from each module which eventually affects the final output. Here the evaluation of the pos-tagger is done based on the number of words which got correctly identified by the sandhi-splitter and then got the correct pos-tags by the pos-tagger. A chunk can be a word or a group of words. Hence a chunk is considered as correct only when there are exact number of words in the

chunk where all the words in it should meet the criteria for the evaluation of pos-tagger. Shallow Parser pipeline evaluation scores are given in Table 4.

S	S+P	P+C	S+P+C
88.46	79.87	81.88	71.38

Table 4: Results of Experiment Type- 2: Pipeline accuracies where the performance of previous modules affect the subsequent modules. Here 'S' refers to sandhi splitter, 'P' to pos-tagger and 'C' to chunker. "+" indicates that the output of the previous module is given as the input to the next module.

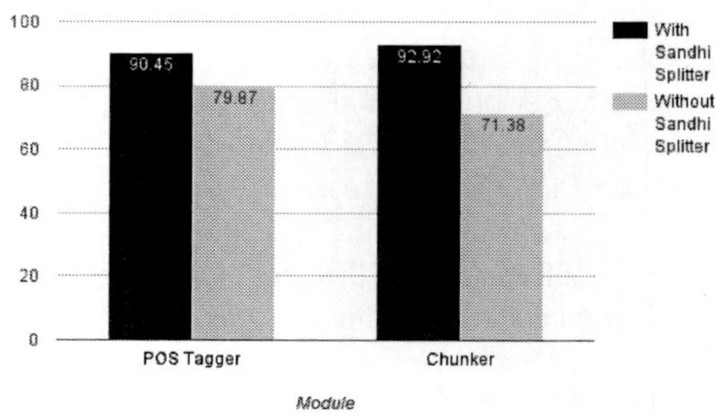

Figure 3: Comparison of accuracies of POS tagger and Chunker with and without Sandhi splitter

Error propagation due to the performance of sandhi-splitter is very high when compared to other modules. Accuracy of the pos-tagger, came down to 79% from 90% due to the errors caused by sandhi-splitter and further this brought down the accuracy of chunker to 71% from 92%.

6 Analysis of Experiment Type-2 Results In Various Modules

6.1 Sandhi-Splitter

We have 2 types of errors created by the sandhi splitter.

1. Not splitting a token which has to be split into words.

2. Splitting a token which should not have been split.

In this experiment, error 1 is more prevalent than error 2. For example, *aRivilla* (no knowledge) should have been split into *aRiv* (knowledge) and *illa* (no). But the system failed to do so. The mentioned problem is due to the lack of diverse patterns in training data. When it comes to error 2, split occurs either between a root and its suffix or just splits in common sandhi split points like *ya, va* or *ma*. The word *aTiccamaRtti* (suppressed) got split into *aTiccaM* and *aRtti* where both the words are meaningless. This problem is also due to the lack of diverse patterns in training data. Another cause of errors are rules employed in Sandhi Splitter for inducing morpho-phonemic changes after split. Though the system correctly identified "n" as split point for *kaalinuLLa (which is for leg)*, but when the rules got applied, this became *kaalin_+uLLa*, where it should have been simply "*n*" which represents a dative case suffix. Whereas *kaalin_* which is meaningless in that context.

6.2 POS-Tagger

The errors in sandhi splitting will eventually affect the performance of pos-tagger in two ways along with sole errors created by pos tagger. Precisely the errors from sandhi splitter has been propagated to pos-tagger, along with errors from pos-tagger. Since it is in a pipeline, wrongly split tokens given to the pos-tagger will have unknown patterns which make the system unable to predict the tag accurately since the pos-tagger uses the morphological features defined based on characters. Subsequently, this will have an impact at the word level context as well. One such instance is where the string *raajaavaaN* (is king) got split into *raajaa* and *aaN*, where it should have been *raajaav* and *aaN*. Here *raajaa* (king) got tagged as adjective and *aaN* (is) ideally a verb but got tagged as a noun, since the previous word got tagged as an adjective.

6.3 Chunker

Errors from both sandhi-splitter and pos-tagger affect the performance of chunker. Errors together from sandhi-splitter and pos-tagger have been propagated to chunker. A chunk is tagged as incorrect when the words and number of words along with their respective pos-tags are not correct. Many instances have 2 or more words per chunk and the chunk-tag is decided based on pos-tags of words. Since it is in a pipeline, two types of errors can propagate,

- Errors due to unidentified or wrongly identified words from sandhi-splitter.

- Errors from pos-tagger, which was affected or unaffected by the errors from sandhi-splitter.

There are many instances where sandhi-splitter could not identify individual words from a token like *aRivilla* (no knowledge). Ideally *aRiv* and *illa*, where the first word is a noun and the other is a verb. Hence there should be a noun chunk (NP) and a verb chunk (VP). Since individual words are not available, pos-tags and chunk-tags will be wrongly identified. Similar would be the case of wrongly identified words.

7 Conclusion and Future Works

In this work we have discussed about experiments conducted to evaluate the significance of an accurate sandhi-splitter in shallow parsing of Dravidian languages, with a focus on Malayalam. We evaluated the performance of individual modules and pipeline with gold standard sandhi-split test data and how the error of a sandhi-splitting tool propagates to other components of shallow parsing pipeline. From the evaluation we found that *Sandhi* severely affects the performance of individual modules and hence the performance of shallow parser. This study validates the the need of a highly accurate sandhi-splitter for all Dravidian languages. As a future work, we propose to work in three main directions.

1. In order to reduce the error propagation in pipelined Shallow parser, joint modeling of a shallow parser is proposed.

2. Investigating further improvements in sandhi-splitting by formulating sandhi-splitting as a statistical machine translation task, where the raw text will be given as the source language and the target language will be the sentences with individual words identified.

3. Since manual creation of annotated data in huge amount is tedious, we plan to apply cross-lingual projection techniques to create Sandhi splitter for all Dravidian languages by exploiting their morphological similarity.

Acknowledgments

The authors are grateful to Pruthwik Mishra for the invaluable help and support during the work. We also would like to thank our colleagues for their critical and invaluable comments while writing the paper. This work has been done as the part of *Taruviithi*, a treebank creation project for Indian languages which is supported by the Department of Electronics and Information Technology (DEITY), India.

References

StevenP. Abney. 1992. Parsing by chunks. In RobertC. Berwick, StevenP. Abney, and Carol Tenny, editors, *Principle-Based Parsing*, volume 44 of *Studies in Linguistics and Philosophy*, pages 257–278. Springer Netherlands.

Akshar Bharati. 2006. Anncorra: Annotating corpora guidelines for pos and chunk annotation for indian languages.

S. Buchholz and W. Daelemans. 2001. Complex answers: A case study using a www question answering system. *Nat. Lang. Eng.*, 7(4):301–323, December.

Michael John Collins. 1996. A new statistical parser based on bigram lexical dependencies. In *Proceedings of the 34th annual meeting on Association for Computational Linguistics*, pages 184–191. Association for Computational Linguistics.

James Hammerton, Miles Osborne, Susan Armstrong, and Walter Daelemans. 2002. Introduction to special issue on machine learning approaches to shallow parsing. *The Journal of Machine Learning Research*, 2:551–558.

Prathyusha Kuncham, Kovida Nelakuditi, Sneha Nallani, and Radhika Mamidi. 2015. Statistical sandhi splitter for agglutinative languages. In *Computational Linguistics and Intelligent Text Processing*, pages 164–172. Springer.

John Lafferty, Andrew McCallum, and Fernando CN Pereira. 2001. Conditional random fields: Probabilistic models for segmenting and labeling sequence data.

Naveen Sankaran and CV Jawahar. 2013. Error detection in highly inflectional languages. In *Document Analysis and Recognition (ICDAR), 2013 12th International Conference on*, pages 1135–1139. IEEE.

Devadath VV, Litton J Kurisinkel, Dipti M Sarma, and Vasudeva Varma. 2014. Sandhi splitter for malayalam. In *Proceedings of International Conference On Natural Language Processing(ICON)*.

W. Wahlster. 2013. *Verbmobil: Foundations of Speech-to-Speech Translation*. Artificial Intelligence. Springer Berlin Heidelberg.

Won't somebody please think of the children?
Improving Topic Model Clustering of Newspaper Comments for Summarisation

Clare Llewellyn	**Claire Grover**	**Jon Oberlander**
School of Informatics	School of Informatics	School of Informatics
University of Edinburgh	University of Edinburgh	University of Edinburgh
Edinburgh, UK	Edinburgh, UK	Edinburgh, UK
`s1053147@sms.ed.ac.uk`	`grover@inf.ed.ac.uk`	`jon@inf.ed.ac.uk`

Abstract

Online newspaper articles can accumulate comments at volumes that prevent close reading. Summarisation of the comments allows interaction at a higher level and can lead to an understanding of the overall discussion. Comment summarisation requires topic clustering, comment ranking and extraction. Clustering must be robust as the subsequent extraction relies on a good set of clusters. Comment data, as with many social media datasets, contains very short documents and the number of words in the documents is a limiting factors on the performance of LDA clustering. We evaluate whether we can combine comments to form larger documents to improve the quality of clusters. We find that combining comments with comments that reply to them produce the highest quality clusters.

1 Introduction

Newspaper articles can accumulate many hundreds and sometimes thousands of online comments. When studied closely and analysed effectively they provide multiple points of view and a wide range of experience and knowledge from diverse sources. However, the number of comments produced per article can prohibit close reading. Summarising the content of these comments allows users to interact with the data at a higher level, providing a transparency to the underlying data (Greene and Cross, 2015).

The current state of the art within the comment summarisation field is to cluster comments using Latent Dirichlet Allocation (LDA) topic modelling (Khabiri et al., 2011; Ma et al., 2012; Llewellyn et al., 2014). The comments within each topic cluster are ranked and comments are typically extracted to construct a summary of the cluster. In this paper we focus on the clustering subtask. It is important that the clustering is appropriate and robust as the subsequent extraction relies on a good set of clusters. Research in a related domain has found that topical mistakes were the largest source of error in summarising blogs – (Mithun and Kosseim, 2009) a similar data type.

Comment data, as with many social media datasets, differs from other content types as each 'document' is very short. Previous studies have indicated that the number of documents and the number of words in the documents are limiting factors on the performance of topic modelling (Tang et al., 2014). Topic models built using longer documents and using more documents are more accurate. Short documents can be enriched with external data. In our corpus the number of comments on each newspaper article is finite and the topics discussed within each set have evolved from the original article. We therefore decided not to increase the set with data from external sources.

In this work we consider whether we can combine comments within a comments dataset to form larger documents to improve the quality of clusters. Combining comments into larger documents reduces the total number of comments available to cluster which may decrease the quality of the clusters. The contribution of this work is in showing that combining comments with their direct replies, their children, increases the quality of the clustering. This approach can be applied to any other task which requires clustering of newspaper comments and any other data which contains small documents linked using a thread like structure. Combining data in this way to improve the clustering reduces the need to import data from external sources or to adapt the underlying clustering algorithm.

43

Proceedings of the 54th Annual Meeting of the Association for Computational Linguistics – Student Research Workshop, pages 43–50,
Berlin, Germany, August 7-12, 2016. ©2016 Association for Computational Linguistics

2 Related Work

2.1 Summarisation

The summarisation domain is well developed. The earliest focus of the field was single document summarisation – for a survey paper see (Gupta and Lehal, 2010). This approach was extended into the summarisation of multiple documents on the same topic (Goldstein et al., 2000) and to summarising discussions such as email or Twitter conversations (Cselle et al., 2007; Sharifi et al., 2010; Inouye and Kalita, 2011).

The basic idea behind the summarisation of textual data is the grouping together of similar information and describing those groups (Rambow et al., 2004). Once these groups are formed they are described using either an extractive or abstractive approach. Extractive summarisation uses units of text, generally sentences, from within the data in the group to represent the group. Abstractive summarisation creates a description of the data in the group as a whole, analogous to the approach a human would take.

2.1.1 Comment Summarisation

Abstractive summarisation is a very complex task, and because comment summarisation is a relatively new task, current work mostly focuses on extractive approaches. The general task involves clustering the comments into appropriate topics and then extracting comments, or parts of comments to represent those topics (Khabiri et al., 2011; Ma et al., 2012). Ma et al. (2012) summarise discussion on news articles from Yahoo!News and Khabiri et al (2011) summarise comments on YouTube videos. Both studies agree on the definition of the basic task as: clustering comments into topics, ranking to identify comments that are key in the clusters, and evaluating the results through a human study. Both approaches focus on using LDA topic modelling to cluster the data. Ma et al. (2012) explored two topic models, one where topics are derived from the original news article and a second, extended version that allows new topics to be formed from the comments. They found that the extended version was judged superior in a user study. Khabiri et al. (2011) contrasted LDA topic models with k-means and found topic modelling superior. A study by Llewellyn et al. (2014) contrasted topic modelling, k-means, incremental one pass clustering and clustering on common unigrams and bi-grams. They found that the topic modelling approach was superior. Aker et al. (2016) looked at a graph based model that included information from DBpedia, finding that this approach out performed an un-optimised LDA model. They then labelled the clusters using LDA clustering and extracted keywords.

Other work has been conducted in related domains such as summarising blogs, microblogs and e-mail.

2.1.2 Blog Summarisation

Comments are similar to blogs in that they are generated by multiple individuals who exhibit a vast array of writing styles. Mithum and Koseim (2009) found that whereas news articles have a generalisable structure that can be used to aid summarisation, blogs are more variable. In particular they found that errors in blog summarisation are much higher than in news text summarisation. They determined that errors were often due to the candidate summary sentences being off topic and they suggest that blog summarisation needs to be improved in terms of topic detection. When investigating the summarisation of blogs and comments on blogs Balahur et al.(2009) found that it is very common to change topics between the original blog post and the comments, and from comment to comment. The research of Mithum and Koseim (2009) and Balahur et al. (2009) indicates that topic identification is a key area on which to concentrate efforts in the emerging field of comment summarisation.

2.1.3 Microblog Summarisation

A significant amount of work has been conducted in the area of Twitter summarisation. Many Twitter summarisation techniques exploit that tweets often include hashtags which serve as an indication of their topic. Duan et al.(2012) designed a summarisation framework for Twitter by defining topics and selecting tweets to represent those topics. The topics are defined using hashtags and are split when at high volume by specific time slices and word frequency. Rosa et al. (2011) also use hashtags to cluster tweets into topics, using them as annotated classes for training data. They focus on supervised machine learning, specifically SVM and K Nearest Neighbour, as they found the results from unsupervised clustering (LDA and k-means clustering) performed poorly when applied to Twitter data. In a further Twitter summarisation tool, TweetMotif, O'Connor et al. (2010) use language modelling to create summaries. They form topic clusters by identifying phrases that could define a topic, looking for those phrases in the corpus and merging sets of topics that are similar. Research on microblog summarisation indicates that when summarising comments it is possible but difficult to use unsupervised clustering and several rules have been suggested that can be followed to produce the most suitable clusters for summarisation.

2.1.4 E-mail Summarisation

E-mail and comments are similar in several respects: they both exhibit a thread-like structure, containing multiple participant conversations that occur along a variable time line, they may refer back to previous parts of the conversation and exhibit high variability in writing styles (Carenini et al., 2007). Topic identification is challenging in e-mail threads. Wan and Mckeown (2004) noted that several different tasks were conducted in email conversations: decision making, requests for action, information seeking and social interaction. Rambow et al. (2004) found that e-mail has an inherent structure and that this structure can be use to extract e-mail specific features for summarisation. This suggests that comments may have an inherent structure which can be used to assist in summarisation.

3 Methods

3.1 Data

The work reported here is based on comments from news articles taken from the online, UK version of the Guardian newspaper. It is composed of online comments that are created by readers who have registered and posted under a user-name. The site is moderated and comments can be removed. We harvested the comments once the comment section is closed and the data is no longer updated. The comment system allows users to view comments either in a temporal fashion, oldest or newest first, or as threads. Users are then able to add their own comments to the set by either posting directly or by replying to another user, adding their comments to any point in the thread. This develops a conversational style of interaction where users interact with each other and comment upon the comments of others. The topics discussed can therefore evolve from the topics of the original article.

In total we have gathered comments posted in response to thirteen articles. Each week a journalist from the Guardian summarises the comments on one particular article and we have selected data from these weekly summaries to provide a further point of comparison. A typical example is our comment set 5 where the initial article was titled 'Cutting edge: the life of a former London gang leader', the journalist had divided the comments into sets as follows:

- 40% criticised gang culture for creating a desire for fame and respect

- 33% would like to hear more from victims of gang violence

- 17% found Dagrou's story depressing

- 10% believed he should be praised for turning his life around

An example of a comment that fit into the journalist based classification scheme is: *"I'd love to see an in-depth article about a person whose life is made a complete misery by gangs. You know, maybe a middle-aged lady who lives on her own in a gang area, something like that."*

An example of a comment that does not fit into the classification scheme: *"So people who don't have to turn their lives around are ignored and not supported. These are the people who are sometimes homeless cause there is no help if you haven't been in prison or don't have kids".*

In this work we refer to all of the comments on a single article as a *comment set*. There is data that has been annotated by humans (the gold standard set) and data that has not. The gold standard data set contained three comment sets. It was produced by human(s) assigning all comments from a comment set to topic groups. For one comment set two humans assigned groups (Set 1) and for two comment sets (Sets 2 and 3) a single human assigned groups. No guidance was given as to the number of topics required, but the annotators were asked to make the topics as broad or as inclusive as they could.

In the set where both humans assigned topics the first annotator determined that there were 26 topics whereas the second annotator identified 45 topics. This difference in topic number was due to a variation in numbers of clusters with a single

Table 1: Comment Set Composition - A description of the data set

Set	1	2	3	4	5	6	7	8	9	10	11	12	13
Comments	160	230	181	51	121	169	176	205	254	328	373	397	661
Authors	67	140	112	28	65	105	103	111	120	204	240	246	420
Threads	54	100	82	21	53	71	67	80	95	132	198	164	319
Groups of siblings	126	186	154	45	108	139	148	160	205	256	314	320	553
Time Segment	77	113	68	33	72	110	76	117	142	160	124	119	203
Over 50 Words (%)	58	52	29	39	37	36	18	38	49	44	26	26	30
Mean number of words	80	81	45	58	53	45	38	69	72	61	40	43	48
Human topics	14	21	20	-	-	-	-	-	-	-	-	-	
Automatic topics	-	-	-	5	5	7	8	5	5	18	18	16	7

member. Once these were removed both annotators had created 14 clusters. The human-human F-Score was 0.607 including the single clusters and 0.805 without. It was felt that agreement at this level meant that double annotation was not required for the futher two sets. All annotated sets have the clusters with single members removed.

A further 10 sets of comments were collected which were not annotated. Table I shows the composition of these comment sets. We can see that the number of comments varies and that number of authors, threads, groups of siblings (comments that reply to the same comment) and time segments tend to increase with size. The number of words in a comment does not. The sets of comments, with annotations where available, can be found at (Llewellyn, 2016).

3.2 Data Manipulation

We have investigated methods for combining the individual comments into larger 'documents' using metadata features. The data is combined according to aspects extracted from the metadata; these are as follows:

- STANDARD: Comments are not combined in any way. This is a baseline result to which the other results can be compared.

- AUTHOR: Comments are grouped together if they have the same author. A common approach to increase the size of Twitter documents is to group tweets together that come from a single author on the assumption that authors stick to the same/similar topics. Here the same approach is tried with comments.

- TIME: Comments are grouped together within a ten minute segment. Comments may be on the same topics if they are posted at the same time (if the users are viewing comments through the newest first method).

It is hypothesised that there may be topical consistency within threads. The 'threadness' was identified in several ways:

- FULL THREAD: Comments were grouped together to reflect the full thread from the original root post and including all replies to that post and all subsequent posts in the thread.

- CHILDREN: A comment is grouped with all direct replies to that comment.

- SIBLINGS: A comment is grouped with its siblings, all other comments that reply to a specific comment.

All of the groups of related comments are combined together, according to the method, to form a single document for each group.

3.2.1 Short Documents

Previous work indicates that removing short documents from the data sets prior to topic modelling improves the quality of the topic models (Tang et al., 2014). We found, in an experiment into whether length of comments influenced the quality of clusters, that removing comments that contain few than 50 terms increases the ability of a topic model to classify documents that are longer than 50 terms but it does not increase the ability to classify all documents, especially shorter documents. If we deem it useful to have short comments in the clusters for the ranking and extraction phase of summarisation, then it is important that these shorter documents are retained in the model building stage, we therefore include them in our experiments detailed here.

3.3 Topic Modelling

The clustering method used in this work is Latent Dirichlet Allocation (LDA) topic modelling (Blei et al., 2003). It produces a generative model used to determine the topics contained in a text document. A topic is formed from words that often co-occur, therefore the words that co-occur more frequently across multiple documents most likely belong to the same topic. It is also true that each document may contain a variety of topics. LDA provides a score for each document for each topic. In this case we assign the document to the topic or topics for which it has the highest score.

This approach was implemented using the Mallet tool-kit (McCallum, 2002). The Mallet tool kit topic modelling implementation allows dirichlet hyper-parameter re-estimation. This means that although the hyper parameters are initially set it is possible to allow them to be re-estimated to better suit the data set being modelled. In these experiments, after previous optimisation tests, we initially set the sum of alpha across all topics as 4, beta as 0.08. We set the number of iterations at 1000, and we allow re-estimation of the dirichlet hyper-parameters every 10 iterations.

In order to cluster the comment data into topics an appropriate number of topics must be chosen. In choosing the number of topics we aim to pick a number which strikes a balance between producing a small number of broad topics or a large number of overly specific topics. We aim to echo a human like decision as to when something is on- or off-topic. Too few items in each topic is to be avoided, as is having a small number of topics (O'Connor et al., 2010).

In our data set, we choose the number of clusters by two methods. When data has been annotated by humans the number of topics identified by humans was chosen as the cluster number. When the data had not been annotated by humans the cluster number was identified using an automatic method of stability analysis. This method was proposed by Greene, O' Callaghan, and Cunningham (2014), and it assumes that if there is a 'natural' number of topics within a data set, then this number of topics will give the most stable result each time the data is re-clustered. Stability is calculated using a ranked list of most predictive topic words. Each time the data is modelled, the change in the members and ordering of that list is used to calculate a stability score. Green et. al (2014) used the top twenty features to form their ranked list of features. Here, as the length of the documents is shorter, we use the top ten.

The sets of documents as described in the previous sections are then used to build topic models and the comments are assigned to topical clusters using these models. Ten-fold cross-validation is used. As topic modelling is a generative process, the topics produced are not identical on each new run as discussed in more detail in (Koltcov et al., 2014). Therefore the process is repeated 100 times, so that an average score can be supplied.

3.4 Metrics

There are two main metrics that are exploited in this work: Perplexity and micro-averaged F-score. Perplexity is judged by building a model using training data, and then testing with a held out set to see how well the word counts of the test documents are represented by the word distributions represented in the topics in the model (Wallach et al., 2009). This score shows how perplexed the model is by the new data. Perplexity has been found to be consistent with other measures of cluster quality such as point-wise mutual information (Tang et al., 2014). PMI data is also available and can be supplied if requested.

It is difficult to judge when a perplexity score is 'good enough' as perplexity will continue to decrease as the number of clusters increases. Topic models that represent single comments are the least perplexed. Therefore a section of the dataset has been hand annotated and this is used to provide a micro-averaged F-score. This can be used to gauge if the perplexity scores are equivalent to human judgements. For more details on this metric see Sokolova and Lapalme (2009).

Table 2: Combined Data, Annotated, F-score (results that beat the standard baseline are in bold)

	1	2	3
Standard Baseline	0.59	0.36	0.33
Author	0.43	0.34	0.32
Children	**0.70**	**0.41**	**0.48**
Full Thread	**0.63**	**0.38**	**0.37**
Siblings	0.59	0.37	0.33
Time	0.38	0.31	0.24

Table 3: Combined Data - Perplexity Score (the best / least perplexed model is in bold)

Comment Set	1	2	3	4	5	6	7	8	9	10	11	12	13
Standard	**253**	671	520	343	555	444	531	960	1084	818	**659**	756	810
Author	572	644	525	422	555	582	518	1005	1224	908	669	766	761
Children	373	**608**	**405**	**274**	**427**	**406**	**434**	**673**	1019	**637**	712	**514**	**657**
Full Thread	707	764	477	394	496	499	567	1026	1490	991	933	753	875
Siblings	613	730	560	401	590	532	607	804	**1009**	734	759	649	813
Time	584	715	459	460	579	433	542	796	1090	965	776	720	716.05

Here we present scores in terms of micro-averaged F-score (when a gold standard is available for comparison), and by perplexity. A higher F-score indicates a more human like model and a lower perplexity score indicates a less perplexed model. Significance is tested using a Student's two tailed t-test and significant results are quoted when p<0.01 (Field, 2013).

4   Results and Discussion

First we will discuss the results from the 3 annotated data sets (1, 2 and 3). Using an F-score metric we find that, for all three annotated sets that grouping comments using the metadata features author and time does not improve topic clustering. Grouping comments using thread based features was more sucessful. We found that combining comments with their replies (the children) and combining comments within the full thread sets significantly beat the standard baseline (Table 2).

The results differ when judged by perplexity (Table 3). We found for two of the comment sets (2 and 3) the children data set gave models that were significantly less perplexed than the standard baseline but this was not the case for comment set 1. For comment set 1 no models beats the baseline using the perplexity metric.

When we look at all of the data, judged using a perplexity score (Table 3), we found that the combined children data sets consistently created models (for 10 out of the 13 sets) that are significantly less perplexed than a standard baseline. For one of the datasets the data combined with other replies to the same message, the siblings set, beats the baseline. For two of the sets no combination method beats the baseline.

The automated results and human results as indicated by perplexity and micro-averaged F-score are not in complete agreement, but there are some commonalities. Both sets of results indicate that the group that combines responses with comments (the children group) has the highest agreement with the human model, and it consistently produces the least perplexed model.

5   Conclusions

It is worth noting that although we focus here on newspaper comments, the need for summarisation applies to any web-based chat forum and the findings therefore have a wide applicability.

LDA topic modelling perfoms better with longer documents. Here we have investigated methods for combining newspaper comments into longer documents in order to improve LDA clustering and therefore provide a strong basis for subsequent comment summarisation. We found that combining comments using features derived from the thread structure of the commenting system was more successful than features from the comments metadata. We found that using a combination of a comment and its children provides 'documents' that produce models that can more accurately classify comments into topics than other document combination methods. It is likely that the method of grouping comments with their direct replies, their children, is the most successful because commentors interact with the other comments through the thread system (rather than newest or oldest first) and they add topically relevent information to the threads. It also indicates that topics in threads evolve, meaning that grouping the entire thread together into a single document works less well than grouping the immediate decendants - the children.

We found that these results were generally consistent, but not identical, across two metrics - perplexity and F-score. We therefore confirm that the perplexity measure is a useful metric in this domain when annotated data is not available.

References

Ahmet Aker, Emina Kurtic, AR Balamurali, Monica Paramita, Emma Barker, Mark Hepple, and Rob Gaizauskas. 2016. A graph-based approach to topic clustering for online comments to news. In *Advances in Information Retrieval*, pages 15–29. Springer.

Alexandra Balahur, Mijail Alexandrov Kabadjov, Josef Steinberger, Ralf Steinberger, and Andres Montoyo. 2009. Summarizing opinions in blog threads. In *PACLIC*, pages 606–613.

David M. Blei, Andrew Y. Ng, and Michael I. Jordan. 2003. Latent dirichlet allocation. 3:993–1022.

Giuseppe Carenini, Raymond T Ng, and Xiaodong Zhou. 2007. Summarizing email conversations with clue words. In *Proceedings of the 16th international conference on World Wide Web*, pages 91–100. ACM.

Gabor Cselle, Keno Albrecht, and Rogert Wattenhofer. 2007. BuzzTrack: topic detection and tracking in email. In *Proceedings of the 12th International Conference on Intelligent User Interfaces*, IUI '07, pages 190–197. ACM.

YaJuan DUAN, CHEN ZhuMin WEIF uRu, ZHOU Ming Heung, and Yeung SHUM. 2012. Twitter topic summarization by ranking tweets using social influence and content quality. In *Proceedings of the 24th International Conference on Computational Linguistics*, pages 763–780.

Andy Field. 2013. *Discovering statistics using IBM SPSS statistics*. Sage.

Jade Goldstein, Vibhu Mittal, Jaime Carbonell, and Mark Kantrowitz. 2000. Multi-document summarization by sentence extraction. In *Proceedings of the 2000 NAACL-ANLPWorkshop on Automatic Summarization - Volume 4*, NAACL-ANLP-AutoSum '00, pages 40–48. Association for Computational Linguistics.

Derek Greene and James P Cross. 2015. Unveiling the political agenda of the european parliament plenary: A topical analysis. *arXiv preprint arXiv:1505.07302*.

Derek Greene, Derek O'Callaghan, and Pádraig Cunningham. 2014. How many topics? stability analysis for topic models. In *Machine Learning and Knowledge Discovery in Databases*, pages 498–513. Springer.

Vishal Gupta and Gurpreet Singh Lehal. 2010. A survey of text summarization extractive techniques. 2(3).

David Inouye and Jugal K Kalita. 2011. Comparing twitter summarization algorithms for multiple post summaries. In *Privacy, Security, Risk and Trust (PASSAT) and 2011 IEEE Third Inernational Conference on Social Computing (Social-Com), 2011 IEEE Third International Conference on*, pages 298–306. IEEE.

Elham Khabiri, James Caverlee, and Chiao-Fang Hsu. 2011. Summarizing user-contributed comments. In *ICWSM*.

Sergei Koltcov, Olessia Koltsova, and Sergey Nikolenko. 2014. Latent dirichlet allocation: stability and applications to studies of user-generated content. In *Proceedings of the 2014 ACM conference on Web science*, pages 161–165. ACM.

Clare Llewellyn, Claire Grover, Jon Oberlander, and Ewan Klein. 2014. Re-using an argument corpus to aid in the curation of social media collections. In *LREC*, pages 462–468.

Clare Llewellyn. 2016. Guardian Comments data. `http://homepages.inf.ed.ac.uk/s1053147/data/comments_2016.html`. [Online; accessed 09-June-2016].

Zongyang Ma, Aixin Sun, Quan Yuan, and Gao Cong. 2012. Topic-driven reader comments summarization. In *Proceedings of the 21st ACM international conference on Information and knowledge management*, pages 265–274. ACM.

AK McCallum. 2002. MALLET: a machine learning for language toolkit.

Shamima Mithun and Leila Kosseim. 2009. Summarizing blog entries versus news texts. In *Proceedings of the Workshop on Events in Emerging Text Types*, pages 1–8. Association for Computational Linguistics.

Brendan O'Connor, Michel Krieger, and David Ahn. 2010. Tweetmotif: Exploratory search and topic summarization for twitter. In *ICWSM*.

Owen Rambow, Lokesh Shrestha, John Chen, and Chirsty Lauridsen. 2004. Summarizing email threads. In *Proceedings of HLT-NAACL 2004: Short Papers*, pages 105–108. Association for Computational Linguistics.

Kevin Dela Rosa, Rushin Shah, Bo Lin, Anatole Gershman, and Robert Frederking. 2011. Topical clustering of tweets. *Proceedings of the ACM SIGIR: SWSM*.

Beaux Sharifi, Mark-Anthony Hutton, and Jugal Kalita. 2010. Summarizing microblogs automatically. In *Human Language Technologies: The 2010 Annual Conference of the North American Chapter of the Association for Computational Linguistics*, pages 685–688. Association for Computational Linguistics.

Marina Sokolova and Guy Lapalme. 2009. A systematic analysis of performance measures for classification tasks. 45(4):427–437.

Jian Tang, Zhaoshi Meng, Xuanlong Nguyen, Qiaozhu Mei, and Ming Zhang. 2014. Understanding the limiting factors of topic modeling via posterior contraction analysis. In *Proceedings of The 31st International Conference on Machine Learning*, pages 190–198.

Hanna M Wallach, Iain Murray, Ruslan Salakhutdinov, and David Mimno. 2009. Evaluation methods for topic models. In *Proceedings of the 26th Annual International Conference on Machine Learning*, pages 1105–1112. ACM.

Stephen Wan and Kathy McKeown. 2004. Generating overview summaries of ongoing email thread discussions. In *Proceedings of the 20th international conference on Computational Linguistics*, page 549. Association for Computational Linguistics.

Arabizi Identification in Twitter Data

Taha Tobaili
Knowledge Media Institute
The Open University
taha.tobaili@open.ac.uk

Abstract

In this work we explore some challenges related to analysing one form of the Arabic language called *Arabizi*. Arabizi, a portmanteau of *Araby-Englizi*, meaning Arabic-English, is a digital trend in texting Non-Standard Arabic using Latin script. Arabizi users express their natural dialectal Arabic in text without following a unified orthography. We address the challenge of identifying Arabizi from multi-lingual data in Twitter, a preliminary step for analysing sentiment from Arabizi data. We annotated a corpus of Twitter data streamed across two Arab countries, extracted linguistic features and trained a classifier achieving an average Arabizi identification accuracy of 94.5%. We also present the percentage of Arabizi usage on Twitter across both countries providing important insights for researchers in NLP and sociolinguistics.

1 Introduction

Arabizi comprises a portion of the Arabic social media, thus any large dataset crawled from an Arabic public source may contain Modern-Standard Arabic (MSA), Non-Standard Arabic (NSA), Arabizi and other languages such as English and French. MSA is the formal Arabic that is mostly used in news broadcasting channels and magazines to address the entire Arab region. NSA is informal, dialectal and esoteric to each region. It varies among North Africa, Egypt, Levant, and the Arabian Gulf. Arabizi is a descendant of NSA, where dialectal words are expressed in Latin script such as حبيبي which means *darling* written as *7abibi*. Apart from being dialectal, people express

their natural voice in text without following a unified orthographical and grammatical regulations.

A. Bies et al. mention that the use of Arabizi is prevalent enough to pose a challenge for Arabic NLP research (2014). Basis Technology, a company that specializes in computational linguistics for digital forensics stated that Arabizi poses a problem for government analytics since it has no structure (2012). The way Arabs use Arabizi is a significant challenge for data scientists for the following reasons: it is written in Latin script, it varies among regions, it is not written in a unified orthographical, syntactical or grammatical structure, it could be mixed with other languages in a single sentence, and it often exist within multi-lingual datasets.

Identification of Arabizi advances the Arabic NLP, specifically in sentiment analysis for Arabic. Being able to identify and analyse Arabizi will fill an important gap in processing Arabic from social media data. Several researchers working on sentiment analysis for Arabic filter out Arabizi from their datasets, mainly due to the non-availablitiy of public resources such as word lexicons, stemmers, and POS taggers to process this type of text. In a recent survey about sentiment analysis for Arabic, S. Ahmed et al. mention that the use of dialect and Arabizi have not been addressed yet in existing literature (2013). In this paper we address the following questions: How frequent is the usage of Arabizi in Egypt and Lebanon on Twitter, and which methods could be used to automatically identify Arabizi within multi-lingual Twitter streams.

Public social media data, particularly Twitter, is important for sentiment analysis as it contains and reflects the public's opinion. The type of data in Twitter is large-scale and diverse, not biased to certain groups of people or topics. We collect Twitter data from Egypt and Lebanon, pre-

Proceedings of the 54th Annual Meeting of the Association for Computational Linguistics – Student Research Workshop, pages 51–57,
Berlin, Germany, August 7-12, 2016. ©2016 Association for Computational Linguistics

process it, and annotate sample datasets. First, we present the amount of Arabizi usage in each of Egypt and Lebanon by reporting the percentage of Arabic, English, and Arabizi tweets. Second, we extract some linguistic features using Langdetect[1] (Nakatani, 2010), a language detection library ported from Google's language-detection, and train an SVM classifier to identify Arabizi from multi-lingual Twitter data. We believe that being able to identify Arabizi from multi-lingual data on social media brings us closer to addressing sentiment analysis for Arabic, inclusive of NSA and Arabizi.

The rest of the paper is structured as follows: In Section II, we investigate what other researchers have done for analysing Arabizi. In Section III, we collect, pre-process and annotate Twitter data and present our approach of extracting linguistic features and training the classifier. In Section IV, we present the results and a discussion. In Section V, we conclude and add a future work plan.

2 Related Work

In this section we survey papers and present the efforts of other researchers on the percentage of Arabizi usage, the motive for analysing sentiment from Arabizi data, and related work in Arabic dialect and Arabizi detection.

2.1 Percentage of Arabizi Usage

Several sociolinguistic studies focus on the Arabizi phenomena, where the researchers tend to explore how this texting style developed and became a trend in the Arab region. S. Jaran and F. Al-Haq (Jaran and Al-Haq, 2015) presented how natives coin and trend Arabizi words by adopting an English word and conjugating it in their NSA such as: I miss you → *missak*, *ak* is a suffix added when referring to the pronoun *you* in the masculine form in several NSA dialects. In (Muhammed et al., 2011; Yaghan, 2008; Aboelezz, 2009; Alabdulqader et al., 2014; Gibson, 2015; Jaran and Al-Haq, 2015; Keong et al., 2015) the authors collected information about people who use Arabizi such as age, gender, and level of education and reported the frequency and context of Arabizi usage within certain groups of people. In Table 1 we present these studies that were conducted by monitoring mobile messaging, distributing surveys among university students, or analysing on-

---

line forum comments. The percentage of Arabizi usage varies in each of these studies depending on the year the study was conducted, the region, the medium, and the users. However, most of these studies are based on private mobile messages, we on the other hand report the percentage of Arabizi usage on a public social medium. We investigated Arabizi from Twitter data across 2 Arab countries, Egypt and Lebanon; our method can be applied to any other Arab country.

2.2 Arabizi in Sentiment Analysis

We point to few studies where researchers collected Arabic data for sentiment analysis but filtered out Arabizi, saying that their tools are incapable of handling Arabizi. M. Al-Kabi et al. carried out a research in sentiment analysis on a dataset of 1,080 NSA reviews collected from social and news websites filtering out Arabizi (2013; 2014). R. Duwairi and I. Qarqaz collected 500 Facebook comments in Arabic for sentiment analysis filtering out Arabizi as well (2014). R. Duwairi et al. also mention that Arabizi is common in Arab blogs, highlighting the fact that there are no Arabizi benchmark datasets nor sentiment lexicons available (2015).

2.3 Arabic Dialect Detection

Recent studies are focused on detecting dialectal Arabic from a given text. Most of these studies rely on annotated dialectal Arabic corpora and training a classifier with character and word n-gram features. O. Zaidan and C. Callison-Burch annotated over 100,000 sentences and trained an n-gram probabilistic classifier that detects the dialect of input sentences (2014). S. Malmasi et al. used 2 classifiers to predict whether a given sentence is dialectal or MSA (2015). First, a Conditional Random Field (CRF) classifier trained with word-level features using MADAMIRA (2014) and other tools. Second, a trained sentence level classifier covering dialectal statistics, writing style, and word relatedness features. Other recent efforts on dialect detection (Cotterell and Callison-Burch, 2014; Elfardy and Diab, 2013; Sadat et al., 2014; Al-Badrashiny et al., 2015) include creating dialectal corpora.

To the best of our knowledge, K. Darwish presented the only work on Arabizi detection in the literature (2014). However, his work focuses on word-level detection. He collected Arabizi words from tweets and trained a character-level language

---

¹https://goo.gl/xn1jJr

52

Reference	Year	Location	Participants	Data	Size of Data	Arabizi	English	Arabic
(Keong et al., 2015)	2015	Malysia	20 Arab Post Graduates	SMS	200 Messages	35%	50%	10%
(Bies et al., 2014)	2014	Egypt	26 Native Arabic Speakers	SMS	101,292 Messages	77%	-	23%
(Alabdulqader et al., 2014)	2014	Saudi Arabia	61 Students and Non-students	SMS, BBM, and Whatsapp	3236 Messages	15%	8%	74%
(Bianchi, 2012)	2012	Jordan	-	Online Forum	460,220 Posts	35.5%	17.5%	32%
(Al-Khatib and Sabbah, 2008)	2008	Jordan	46 Students	SMS	181 Messages	37%	54%	9%

Table 1: Percentage of Arabizi Usage in Related Work

model and a statistical sequence labelling algorithm. In our work, we extract sentence-level features using Langdetect and train a classifier to
identify Arabizi tweets.

3 The Approach

3.1 Data Collection and Annotation

We use geographic information[2] to stream tweets
coming from within Lebanon and Egypt, where
we specified the coordinates of each region separately. We collect two datasets, one from each
country, and split each into Arabic and Non-
Arabic, shown in Table 2. The Non-Arabic data
includes any tweet written in Latin script. We take
the Non-Arabic data segment, pre-process it, and
annotate a sample of 5,000 tweets to be used for
reporting the percentage of Arabizi usage and as a
training dataset for the Arabizi identification classifier.

Country	Tweets	Arabic Tweets	Non-Arabic Tweets
Lebanon	60,364	28,340	32,024
Egypt	249,149	174,821	74,328

Table 2: Distribution of Tweets

Twitter data contains a lot of noisy tweets such
as tweets that contain only URLs, hashtags, user
mentions, laughter, and spam. We pre-process
the data to maximize the number of textual tweets
in each of the Non-Arabic dataset. We filter out
URLs, hashtags, user mentions, laughter, exagger-
ation, and emojis from tweets. Though some of
these features can be used in an extended work for
sentiment analysis, for this task we only aim for
language identification. We filter out hashtags because most of them are in English. We filter out
laughter expressions and exaggerated words because Langdetect misdetects sentences containing
words with repetitive letters. From the resulting
data, we deleted tweets that contain no text and

[2]https://goo.gl/PFJj3H

duplicated tweets. We observed from our datasets
that many tweets aim to gather followers with expressions such as: *follow me*, *follow insta*, and *follow plz*. We consider such tweets as spam and filter out any tweet containing the word *follow*. Our
pre-processed Non-Arabic datasets lessened from
32,024 to 21,878 for Lebanon and from 74,328 to
36,970 for Egypt.

We extracted and annotated 5,000 tweets which
was done manually by one Arab native. Since
Arabizi users might switch between Arabizi
and English within a single sentence, we tag
Arabizi tweets if the number of Arabizi words
are sufficient to imply that the dominant language
used is Arabizi. To tag an Arabizi tweet it should
have more Arabizi words than English words and
the Arabizi words should consist of nouns and
verbs not just connectors and stop words. For
example:

Tweet: *honestly allah y3afeke (recovery wish)
that you still cant get over a story thats a year
not my fault ur ex boyfriend was a *** sara7a
(honestly)*
Arabizi Words < English Words
Tag: Not Arabizi

Tweet: *kel marra b2oul monday bade ballesh diet
bas emta ha yeje hayda lnhar/Everytime I plan
to start a diet on monday but when will this day
come*
Arabizi Words > English Words
Tag: Arabizi

Tweet: *eh (yes) God bless your mom w (and) your
family*
Tag: Not Arabizi

Out of each sample dataset, we tagged 465
Arabzi tweets from Lebanon and 955 Arabizi
tweets from Egypt. However, each sample dataset
is multi-lingual containing tweets in languages
other than English and Arabizi. The annotated

datasets can be found on project-rbz.com[3]

3.2 Arabizi Identification

We utilize Langdetect, a language detection library that detects one or more languages for each input sentence, and returns the language with the highest confidence score. Though it does not detect Arabizi sentences, it detects irrelevant languages when tested against Arabizi. It may detect 3 or more languages, or one irrelevant language with high confidence. We use those detections as input features to train a classifier to identify Arabizi from Twitter data. For example:

Tweet: *never been so scared for an exam*
Languages Detected: {en:0.99}

Tweet: *kan yom eswed yom ma 3reftk /It was a bad day I didn't recognize you*
Languages Detected: {so: 0.42, cy: 0.42, sv: 0.14}

We use the irrelevant languages detected, the number of irrelevant languages, and their confidence scores as input features for the Arabizi identification classifier.

3.2.1 Feature Selection

We extracted the following features during the streaming and pre-processing of tweets: Language detected by Twitter API, languages detected by Langdetect, location of the tweet, country of the user, language of the user, number of words per tweet, and count of word occurrences per tweet.

We extracted (language detected by Twitter API, tweet location, country and language of the user) from each tweet stream, for example:

id	twt	lang	twt_country	usr_id	usr_lang	usr_country
001468231	Hello World	EN	EGY	48933812	EN	EGY

We tested all the features on several classifiers and found that the best results are obtained from an SVM classifier using (languages detected by Langdetect, the language detected by Twitter API, and the count of word occurrences per tweet). The languages detected by Langdetect include: languages predicted, number of predicted languages, and the confidence score of each. Although, Langdetect is more accurate than Twitter API when tested against our data, adding the language detected by Twitter API to the set of features improved the overall accuracy of Arabizi identification. The count of word occurrences per tweet helps the classifier identify words that are frequently used in Arabizi. We disregarded the other features (location of the tweet, country and language of the user, and the number of words per tweet) because they did not have any effect on the classification results.

3.2.2 Classification

We run Langdetect against our annotated sample datasets; in Table 3 we present the distribution of languages detected with high confidence scores apart from the manual Arabizi annotation. We note that the other languages detected

Country	Dataset Size	English	Arabizi	French	Other
Lebanon	5,000	3,242	465	158	1,135
Egypt	5,000	2,868	955	0	1,177

Table 3: Distribution of Languages in Sample Data

are mainly Far-Eastern languages written in Latin script. Though there are very few tweets in Spanish and Dutch, they are negligible. Far-Eastern expatriates living and working in the Arab region constitute a large part of the population. Our findings show that most of the other languages detected in our Twitter datasets in Lebanon are Filipino, and Indian in Egypt. For this experiment we filter out all languages other than English and Arabizi that have confidence score of 0.7 or higher from our sample datasets. The annotated datasets are lessened to 3,707 tweets for Lebanon and 3,823 for Egypt. We note that the remaining datasets contain multi-lingual tweets however those tweets were not given high confidence scores by Langdetect.

We carry out two experiments, one with our annotated datasets that are filtered from other languages and another with balanced datasets. Since the ratio of English to Arabizi tweets is very high, we under-sample the annotated-filtered datasets to have an almost equal number of English to Arabizi tweets. We applied a 10-fold cross validation technique in which we split the data into 80% and 20% for training and testing respectively, and average the validation results for all folds.

[3]http://www.project-rbz.com/

4 Results and Discussion

4.1 Arabizi Usage

In Table 4 we present the percentage of Arabic vs Non-Arabic tweets in each country. In Table 5 we present the distribution of languages in each of the Non-Arabic sample dataset.

Country	Tweets	Arabic	Non-Arabic
Lebanon	60,364	47%	53%
Egypt	249,149	70%	30%

Table 4: Arabic vs Non-Arabic Tweets

Country	Tweets	English	Arabizi	French	Other
Lebanon	5,000	65%	9.3%	3%	22.7%
Egypt	5,000	57%	19%	-	23%

Table 5: Distribution of Languages in Non-Arabic Tweets

As it can be seen from the results, the percentage of Arabizi usage differs in each Arab country. In Lebanon, Arabic and Non-Arabic tweets are almost equal, however English is dominant in Non-Arabic tweets. On the other hand, Arabic is dominant in tweets from Egypt. The total Arabizi usage is 4.9% for Lebanon and 5.7% for Egypt. We also observed that not only do the percentage of Arabizi usage differs between countries but also they way it is used in text. In Egypt, most of the Non-English tweets are written either in English or in Arabizi rather than mixing both in single tweets as compared to Lebanon. Also, in Egypt people tend to abbreviate Arabizi words in many cases by avoiding to write the vowels. For example:

Tweet from Egypt:
na w nta hn3ml duet m3 b3d /me and you will perform a duet together
Abbreviations: ana → na, enta → nta, hane3mal → hn3ml, ma3 → m3, ba3d → b3d

Tweet from Lebanon:
bonsoir 7ewalit a3melik add 3ala fb bass i didnt find you can you give me your account /Morning I tried adding you on fb but...
Languages: English, French, and Arabizi.

4.2 Arabizi Identification

We filtered our sample datasets from languages other than English and Arabizi that were detected by Langdetect with high confidence scores. We selected an SVM classifier with the following features: Languages detected by Langdetect, the language detected by Twitter API, and the count of word occurrences per tweet. We present the averaged 10-fold cross validation results in Table 6.

Country	Tweets	Recall	Precision	F-Measure	Accuracy
Lebanon	3,707	91	88	88	93
Egypt	3,823	96	78	85	96

Table 6: Averaged K-Fold Validation Results for Sample Datasets

Since Arabizi is only 12% for Lebanon and 25% for Egypt from the Non-Arabic datasets that are filtered from other languages, shown in Table 3, these datasets are considered imbalanced. We balanced the datasets by undersampling the English tweets and repeated the experiment. We present the averaged validation results for the balanced datasets in Table 7.

Country	Tweets	Recall	Precision	F-Measure	Accuracy
Lebanon	1,150	97	97	97	97
Egypt	2,200	97	97	97	97

Table 7: Averaged Validation Results for Balanced Sample Datasets

4.3 Discussion

Our results show that the percentage of Arabizi usage in Twitter data across both Lebanon and Egypt is lower than the findings by other researchers in mobile messaging, as shown in Table 1. We hypothesize that people prefer to text in Arabizi on private mediums since Arabizi is generally perceived as an informal way of communication. However, 4.9% or 5.7% of a country's Twitter data is Arabizi, which is a large amount of data that might contain valuable information. Therefore it is important to generate NLP resources to identify, analyse, and process Arabizi data.

We found that most of the unidentified Arabizi tweets are tweets from Lebanon written in both English and Arabizi. Langdetect identifies most of such mixed tweets as English. As for the false identification, it was due to misidentification of Far-Eastern tweets. Neither Langdetect nor Twitter API was able to correctly identify all Far-Eastern tweets. The classifier could be enhanced to overcome those errors by extracting word-level features from tweets, such as TF-IDF, n-grams, word lengths, and vowel-consonant ratio, and by training it to classify mixed and Far-Eastern tweets.

The analysis of Arabizi usage on Twitter for different Arab countries provides an insight for researchers who tempt to analyse sentiment from Arabic data and for sociolinguistic researchers who study a language in relation to social factors such as region and dialect. We believe that creating tools to automatically identify Arabizi is a necessary step towards sentiment analysis over this type of text. Arabizi identification could be applied in automatic creation of an Arabizi corpus that could be used for classification tasks and in automatic language detection for machine translation tools.

Another aspect of research in Arabizi includes transliteration to Arabic. There are some tools available such as Yamli[4], Microsoft Maren[5], and Google Input Tools[6], however those tools are designed to help Arab speakers get MSA text by typing Arabizi. Using transliterators to convert the natural Arabizi text, such as tweets, may result in broken Arabic words. Some researchers are working on Arabizi transliteration as in (Bies et al., 2014; May et al., 2014; Chalabi and Gerges, 2012; Darwish, 2014).

5   Conclusion and Future Work

In this work we have studied the usage of Arabizi on Twitter and the creation of tools to automatically identify Arabizi from multi-lingual streams of data. We collected Twitter data from Lebanon and Egypt and presented the percentage of each language, particularly Arabizi, providing an important insight for researchers working on the analysis of natural text for the Arab region. We trained an Arabizi identification classifier by annotating sample datasets and extracting features using Langdetect, an existing language detection library. We achieved an average classification accuracy of 93% and 96% for Lebanon and Egypt datasets respectively. Our Arabizi identifi-

cation classifier relies on sentence-level features; it could be improved by extracting word-level features from text. Our aim is to advance the Arabic NLP research by facilitating analysis on social media data without the need to filter out complex or minority languages.

Several researchers have contributed to the analysis of MSA in the literature, which is useful for analysing formal blogs and news pages. However analysing the public's sentiment requires effort for NSA and Arabizi as most people from the Arab region express their opinion on social media using their mother tongue in text. Though NSA and Arabizi are written in different scripts, they can be addressed simultaneously since both share similar challenges. We plan to extend this work by exploring the usage of NSA and Arabizi across several regions, and by identifying dialect on social media. We follow by trying to extract sentiment from NSA and Arabizi which might require the creation of dialect sentiment lexicons and parsers to process the heterogeneous Arabic social data.

References

M Aboelezz. 2009. Latinised Arabic and connections to bilingual ability. In *Papers from the Lancaster University Postgraduate Conference in Linguistics and Language Teaching.*

Shehab Ahmed, Michel Pasquier, and Ghassan Qadah. 2013. Key issues in conducting sentiment analysis on Arabic social media text. In *9th International Conference on Innovations in Information Technology (IIT)*, pages 72–77. IEEE.

Mohamed Al-Badrashiny, Heba Elfardy, and Mona Diab. 2015. Aida2: A hybrid approach for token and sentence level dialect identification in Arabic. *CoNLL 2015*, page 42.

Mohammed Al-Kabi, Amal Gigieh, Izzat Alsmadi, Heider Wahsheh, and Mohamad Haidar. 2013. An opinion analysis tool for colloquial and standard Arabic. In *The 4th International Conference on Information and Communication Systems (ICICS).*

Mohammed N Al-Kabi, Izzat M Alsmadi, Amal H Gigieh, Heider A Wahsheh, and Mohamad M Haidar. 2014. Opinion mining and analysis for Arabic language. *International Journal of Advanced Computer Science and Applications (IJACSA)*, 5(5):181–195.

M. A. Al-Khatib and E. H. Sabbah. 2008. Language choice in mobile text messages among Jordanian university students. *SKY Journal of Linguistics*, 21:37–65.

---

⁴`http://www.yamli.com/`
⁵`https://goo.gl/3zLLOn`
⁶`http://www.google.com/inputtools/`

Ebtisam Alabdulqader, Majdah Alshehri, Rana Almurshad, Alaa Alothman, and Noura Alhakbani. 2014. Computer mediated communication: Patterns & language transformations of youth in Arabic-speaking populations. *Information Technology & Computer Science (IJITCS)*, 17(1):85.

Basis-Technology. 2012. The burgeoning challenge of deciphering Arabic chat.

R. M. Bianchi. 2012. 3arabizi-when local Arabic meets global nglish. *Acta Linguistica Asiatica*, 2(1):89–100.

Ann Bies, Zhiyi Song, Mohamed Maamouri, Stephen Grimes, Haejoong Lee, Jonathan Wright, Stephanie Strassel, Nizar Habash, Ramy Eskander, and Owen Rambow. 2014. Transliteration of Arabizi into Arabic orthography: Developing a parallel annotated Arabizi-Arabic script sms/chat corpus. *ANLP 2014*, page 93.

A. Chalabi and H. Gerges. 2012. Romanized Arabic Transliteration. In *24th International Conference on Computational Linguistics*, page 89.

R. Cotterell and C. Callison-Burch. 2014. A multidialect, multi-genre corpus of informal written Arabic. In *LREC*, pages 241–245.

K. Darwish. 2014. Arabizi Detection and Conversion to Arabic. *ANLP 2014*, page 217.

R. M. Duwairi and I. Qarqaz. 2014. Arabic sentiment analysis using supervised classification. In *International Conference on Future Internet of Things and Cloud (FiCloud)*, pages 579–583. IEEE.

RM Duwairi, Nizar A Ahmed, and Saleh Y Al-Rifai. 2015. Detecting sentiment embedded in Arabic social media–a lexicon-based approach. *Journal of Intelligent and Fuzzy Systems*.

H. Elfardy and M. T. Diab. 2013. Sentence Level Dialect Identification in Arabic. In *ACL (2)*, pages 456–461.

M. Gibson. 2015. A framework for measuring the presence of minority languages in cyberspace. *Linguistic and Cultural Diversity in Cyberspace*, page 61.

S. A. Jaran and F. A. Al-Haq. 2015. The use of hybrid terms and expressions in colloquial Arabic among Jordanian college students: A sociolinguistic study. *English Language Teaching*, 8(12):86.

Yuen Chee Keong, Othman Rahsid Hameed, and Imad Amer Abdulbaqi. 2015. The use of Arabizi in English texting by Arab postgraduate students at UKM. *The English Literature Journal*, 2(2):281–288.

Shervin Malmasi, Eshrag Refaee, and Mark Dras. 2015. Arabic dialect identification using a parallel multidialectal corpus. In *Proceedings of the 14th Conference of the Pacific Association for Computational Linguistics (PACLING 2015), Bali, Indonesia*, pages 209–217.

Jonathan May, Yassine Benjira, and Abdessamad Echihabi. 2014. An Arabizi-English Social Media Statistical Machine Translation System.

Randa Muhammed, Mona Farrag, Nariman Elshamly, and Nady Abdel-Ghaffar. 2011. Summary of Arabizi or Romanization: The dilemma of writing Arabic texts. In *Jil Jadid Conference*, pages 18–19. University of Texas at Austin.

S. Nakatani. 2010. Language Detection Library for Java.

Arfath Pasha, Mohamed Al-Badrashiny, Mona T Diab, Ahmed El Kholy, Ramy Eskander, Nizar Habash, Manoj Pooleery, Owen Rambow, and Ryan Roth. 2014. Madamira: A fast, comprehensive tool for morphological analysis and disambiguation of Arabic. In *LREC*, pages 1094–1101.

Fatiha Sadat, Farnazeh Kazemi, and Atefeh Farzindar. 2014. Automatic identification of Arabic language varieties and dialects in social media. *Proceedings of SocialNLP*.

M A Yaghan. 2008. ”arabizi”: A contemporary style of Arabic slang. *Design Issues*, 24(2):39–52.

O. F. Zaidan and C. Callison-Burch. 2014. Arabic Dialect Identification. *Computational Linguistics*, 40(1):171–202.

Robust Co-occurrence Quantification for Lexical Distributional Semantics

Dmitrijs Milajevs   **Mehrnoosh Sadrzadeh**   **Matthew Purver**

Queen Mary University of London

London, UK

{d.milajevs,m.sadrzadeh,m.purver}@qmul.ac.uk

Abstract

Previous optimisations of parameters affecting the word-context association measure used in distributional vector space models have focused either on high-dimensional vectors with hundreds of thousands of dimensions, or dense vectors with dimensionality of a few hundreds; but dimensionality of a few thousands is often applied in compositional tasks as it is still computationally feasible and does not require the dimensionality reduction step. We present a systematic study of the interaction of the parameters of the association measure and vector dimensionality, and derive parameter selection heuristics that achieve performance across word similarity and relevance datasets competitive with the results previously reported in the literature achieved by highly dimensional or dense models.

1 Introduction

Words that occur in similar context have similar meaning (Harris, 1954). Thus the meaning of a word can be modeled by counting its co-occurrence with neighboring words in a corpus. Distributional models of meaning represent co-occurrence information in a vector space, where the dimensions are the neighboring words and the values are co-occurrence counts. Successful models need to be able to discriminate co-occurrence information, as not all co-occurrence counts are equally useful, for instance, the co-occurrence with the article *the* is less informative than with the noun *existence*. The discrimination is usually achieved by weighting of co-occurrence counts. Another fundamental question in vector space design is the vector space dimensionality and what

neighbor words should correspond to them.

Levy et al. (2015) propose optimisations for co-occurrence-based distributional models, using parameters adopted from predictive models (Mikolov et al., 2013): *shifting* and *context distribution smoothing*. Their experiments and thus their parameter recommendations use high-dimensional vector spaces with word vector dimensionality of almost **200K**, and many recent state-of-the-art results in lexical distributional semantics have been obtained using vectors with similarly high dimensionality (Baroni et al., 2014; Kiela and Clark, 2014; Lapesa and Evert, 2014).

In contrast, much work on *compositional* distributional semantics employs vectors with much fewer dimensions: e.g. **2K** (Grefenstette and Sadrzadeh, 2011; Kartsaklis and Sadrzadeh, 2014; Milajevs et al., 2014), **3K** (Dinu and Lapata, 2010; Milajevs and Purver, 2014) or **10K** (Polajnar and Clark, 2014; Baroni and Zamparelli, 2010). The most common reason thereof is that these models assign tensors to functional words. For a vector space V with k dimensions, a tensor $V \otimes V \cdots \otimes V$ of rank n has k^n dimensions. Adjectives and intransitive verbs have tensors of rank 2, transitive verbs are of rank 3; for coordinators, the rank can go up to 7. Taking $k = $ **200K** already results in a highly intractable tensor of $\mathbf{8 \times 10^{15}}$ dimensions for a transitive verb.

An alternative way of obtaining a vector space with few dimensions, usually with just 100–500, is the use of SVD as a part of Latent Semantic Analysis (Dumais, 2004) or another models such as SGNS (Mikolov et al., 2013) and GloVe (Pennington et al., 2014). However, these models take more time to instantiate in comparison to weighting of a co-occurrence matrix, bring more parameters to explore and produce vector spaces with uninterpretable dimensions (vector space dimension interpretation is used by some lexical mod-

58

Proceedings of the 54th Annual Meeting of the Association for Computational Linguistics – Student Research Workshop, pages 58–64,
Berlin, Germany, August 7-12, 2016. ©2016 Association for Computational Linguistics

els, for example, McGregor et al. (2015), and the passage from formal semantics to tensor models relies on it (Coecke et al., 2010)). In this work we focus on vector spaces that directly weight a co-occurrence matrix and report results for SVD, GloVe and SGNS from the study of Levy et al. (2015) for comparison.

The mismatch of recent experiments with non-dense models in vector dimensionality between lexical and compositional tasks gives rise to a number of questions:

- To what extent does model performance depend on vector dimensionality?
- Do parameters influence 200K and 1K dimensional models similarly? Can the findings of Levy et al. (2015) be directly applied to models with a few thousand dimensions?
- If not, can we derive suitable parameter selection heuristics which take account of dimensionality?

To answer these questions, we perform a systematic study of distributional models with a rich set of parameters on SimLex-999 (Hill et al., 2014), a lexical *similairty* dataset, and test selected models on MEN (Bruni et al., 2014), a lexical *relatedness* dataset. These datasets are currently widely used and surpass datasets stemming from information retrieval, WordSim-353 (Finkelstein et al., 2002), and computational linguistics, RG65 (Rubenstein and Goodenough, 1965), in quantity by having more entries and in quality by attention to evaluated relations (Milajevs and Griffiths, 2016).

2 Parameters

2.1 PMI variants (`discr`)

Most co-occurrence weighting schemes in distributional semantics are based on *point-wise mutual information* (PMI, see e.g. Church and Hanks (1990), Turney and Pantel (2010), Levy and Goldberg (2014)):

$$\text{PMI}(x, y) = \log \frac{P(x, y)}{P(x)P(y)} \quad (1)$$

As commonly done, we replace the infinite PMI values,[1] which arise when $P(x, y) = 0$, with zeroes and use PMI hereafter to refer to a weighting with this fix.

---

[1] We assume that the probability of a single token is always greater than zero as it appears in the corpus at least once.

Parameter	Values
Dimensionality D	1K, 2K, 3K, 5K 10K, 20K, 30K, 40K, 50K
discr	PMI, CPMI, SPMI, SCPMI
freq	$1, n, \log n$
neg	0.2, 0.5, 0.7, 1, 1.4, 2, 5, 7
cds	*global*, 1, 0.75
Similarity	Cosine, Correlation

Table 1: **Model parameters and their values.**

An alternative solution is to increment the probability ratio by 1; we refer to this as *compressed PMI* (CPMI, see e.g. McGregor et al. (2015)):

$$\text{CPMI}(x, y) = \log \left(1 + \frac{P(x, y)}{P(x)P(y)} \right) \quad (2)$$

By incrementing the probability ratio by one, the PMI values from the segment of $(-\infty; 0]$, when the joint probability $P(x, y)$ is less than the chance $P(x)P(y)$, are compressed into the segment of $(0; 1]$. As the result, the space does not contain negative values, but has the same sparsity as the space with PMI values.

2.2 Shifted PMI (`neg`)

Many approaches use only *positive* PMI values, as negative PMI values may not positively contribute to model performance and sparser matrices are more computationally tractable (Turney and Pantel, 2010). This can be generalised to an additional cutoff parameter k (`neg`) following Levy et al. (2015), giving our third PMI variant (abbreviated as SPMI):[2]

$$\text{SPMI}_k = \max(0, \text{PMI}(x, y) - \log k) \quad (3)$$

When $k = 1$ SPMI is equivalent to positive PMI. $k > 1$ increases the underlying matrix sparsity by keeping only highly associated co-occurrence pairs. $k < 1$ decreases the underlying matrix sparsity by including some unassociated co-occurrence pairs, which are usually excluded due to unreliability of probability estimates (Dagan et al., 1993).

We can apply the same idea to CPMI:

$$\text{SCPMI}_k = \max(0, \text{CPMI}(x, y) - \log 2k) \quad (4)$$

---

[2] SPMI is different from CPMI because $\log \frac{P(x,y)}{P(x)P(y)} - \log k = \log \frac{P(x,y)}{P(x)(P(y)k} \neq \log \left(1 + \frac{P(x,y)}{P(x)P(y)} \right)$.

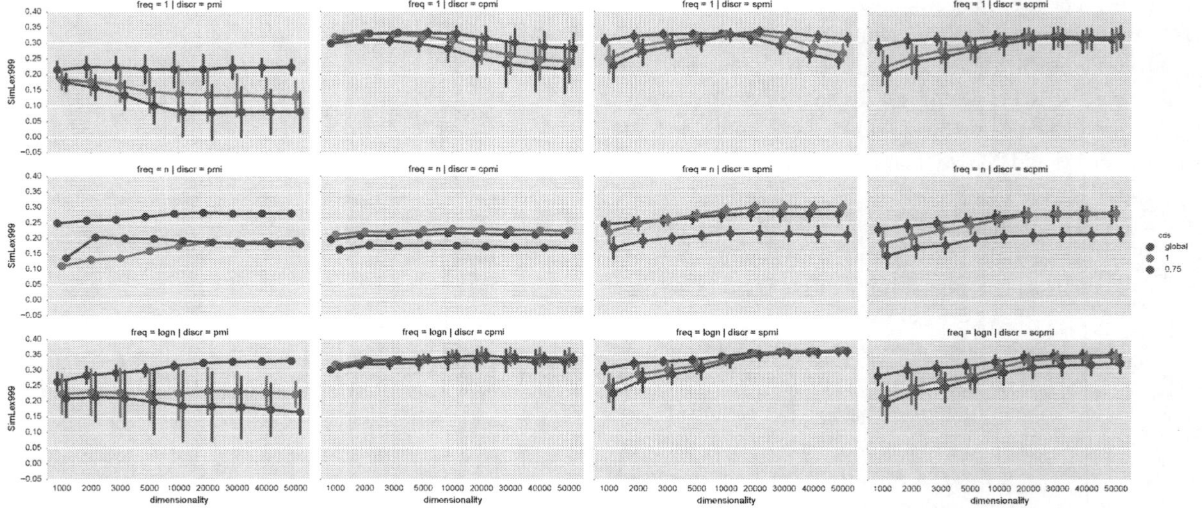

Figure 1: **Effect of PMI variant (`discr`), smoothing (`cds`) and frequency weighting (`freq`) on SimLex-999.** Error bars correspond to a 95% confidence interval as the value is estimated by averaging over all the values of the omitted parameters: `neg` and similarity.

2.3 Frequency weighting (`freq`)

Another issue with PMI is its bias towards rare events (Levy et al., 2015); one way of solving this issue is to weight the value by the co-occurrence frequency (Evert, 2005):

$$\mathrm{LMI}(x, y) = n(x, y)\,\mathrm{PMI}(x, y) \qquad (5)$$

where $n(x, y)$ is the number of times x was seen together with y. For clarity, we refer to n-weighted PMIs as nPMI, nSPMI, etc. When this weighting component is set to 1, it has no effect; we can explicitly label it as 1PMI, 1SPMI, etc.

In addition to the extreme 1 and n weightings, we also experiment with a $\log n$ weighting.

2.4 Context distribution smoothing (`cds`)

Levy et al. (2015) show that performance is affected by smoothing the context distribution $P(x)$:

$$P_\alpha(x) = \frac{n(x)^\alpha}{\sum_c n(c)^\alpha} \qquad (6)$$

We experiment with $\alpha = 1$ (no smoothing) and $\alpha = 0.75$. We call this estimation method *local context probability*; we can also estimate a *global context probability* based on the size of the corpus C:

$$P(x) = \frac{n(x)}{|C|} \qquad (7)$$

2.5 Vector dimensionality (D)

As context words we select the 1K, 2K, 3K, 5K, 10K, 20K, 30K, 40K and 50K most frequent lemmatised nouns, verbs, adjectives and adverbs. All context words are part of speech tagged, but we do not distinguish between refined word types (e.g. intransitive vs. transitive versions of verbs) and do not perform stop word filtering.

3 Experimental setup

Table 1 lists parameters and their values. As the source corpus we use the concatenation of Wackypedia and ukWaC (Baroni et al., 2009) with a symmetric 5-word window (Milajevs et al., 2014); our evaluation metric is the correlation with human judgements as is standard with SimLex (Hill et al., 2014). We derive our parameter selection heuristics by greedily selecting parameters (`cds`, `neg`) that lead to the highest average performance for each combination of frequency weighting, PMI variant and dimensionality D. Figures 1 and 2 show the interaction of `cds` and `neg` with other parameters. We also vary the similarity measure (cosine and correlation (Kiela and Clark, 2014)), but do not report results here due to space limits.[3]

---

[3]The results are available at http://www.eecs.qmul.ac.uk/~dm303/aclsrw2016/

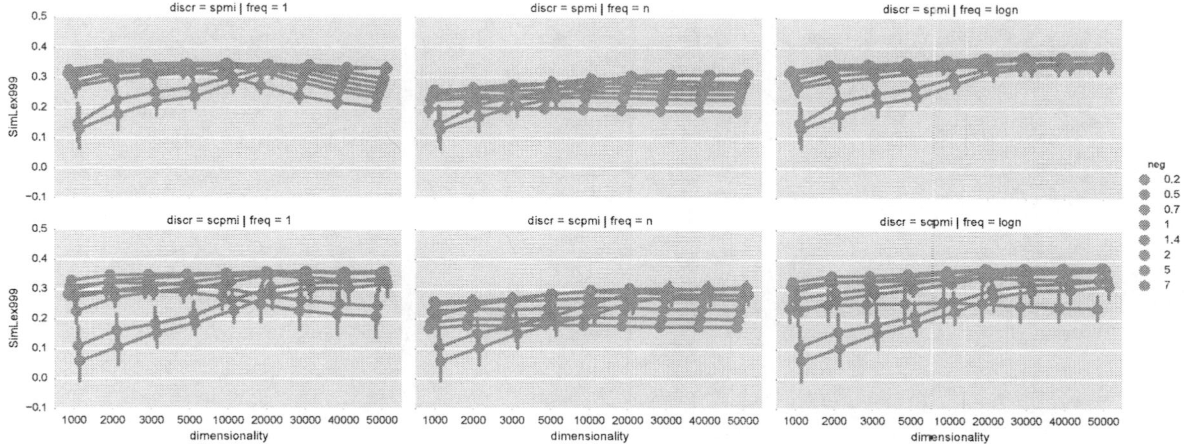

Figure 2: **The behaviour of shifted PMI (SPMI) on SimLex-999.** `discr=spmi`, `freq=1` and `neg=1` corresponds to positive PMI. Error bars correspond to a 95% confidence interval as the value is estimated by averaging over all the values of the omitted parameters: `cds` and similarity.

4 Heuristics

PMI and CPMI PMI should be used with global context probabilities. CPMI generally outperforms PMI, with less sensitivity to parameters; nCPMI and lognCPMI should be used with local context probabilities and 1CPMI should apply context distribution smoothing with $\alpha = 0.75$.

SPMI 10K dimensional 1SPMI is the least sensitive to parameter selection. For models with $D > 20K$, context distribution smoothing should be used with $\alpha = 0.75$; for $D < 20K$, it is beneficial to use global context probabilities. Shifting also depends on the dimensionality: models with $D < 20K$ should set $k = 0.7$, but higher-dimensional models should set $k = 5$. There might be a finer-grained k selection criteria; however, we do not report this to avoid overfitting.

lognSPMI should be used with global context probabilities for models with $D < 20K$. For higher-dimensional spaces, smoothing should be applied with $\alpha = 0.75$, as with 1SPMI. Shifting should be applied with $k = 0.5$ for models with $D < 20K$, and $k = 1.4$ for $D > 20K$. In contrast to 1SPMI, which might require change of k as the dimensionality increases, $k = 1.4$ is a much more robust choice for lognSPMI.

nSPMI gives good results with local context probabilities ($\alpha = 1$). Models with $D < 20K$ should use $k = 1.4$, otherwise $k = 5$ is preferred.

SCPMI With 1SCPMI and $D < 20K$, global context probability should be used, with shifting set to $k = 0.7$. Otherwise, local context probability should be used with $\alpha = 0.75$ and $k = 2$.

With nSCPMI and $D < 20K$, global context probability should be used with $k = 1.4$. Otherwise, local context probability without smoothing and $k = 5$ is suggested.

For lognSCPMI, models with $D < 20K$ should use global context probabilities and $k = 0.7$; otherwise, local context probabilities without smoothing should be preferred with $k = 1.4$.

5 Evaluation of heuristics

We evaluate these heuristics by comparing the performance they give on SimLex-999 against that obtained using the best possible parameter selections (determined via an exhaustive search at each dimensionality setting). We also compare them to the best scores reported by Levy et al. (2015) for their model (PMI and SVD), word2vec-SGNS (Mikolov et al., 2013) and GloVe (Pennington et al., 2014)—see Figure 3a, where only the better-performing SPMI and SCPMI are shown.

For lognPMI and lognCPMI, our heuristics pick the best possible models. For lognSPMI, where performance variance is low, the heuristics do well, giving a performance of no more than 0.01 points below the best configuration. For 1SPMI and nSPMI the difference is higher. With lognSCPMI and 1SCPMI, the heuristics follow

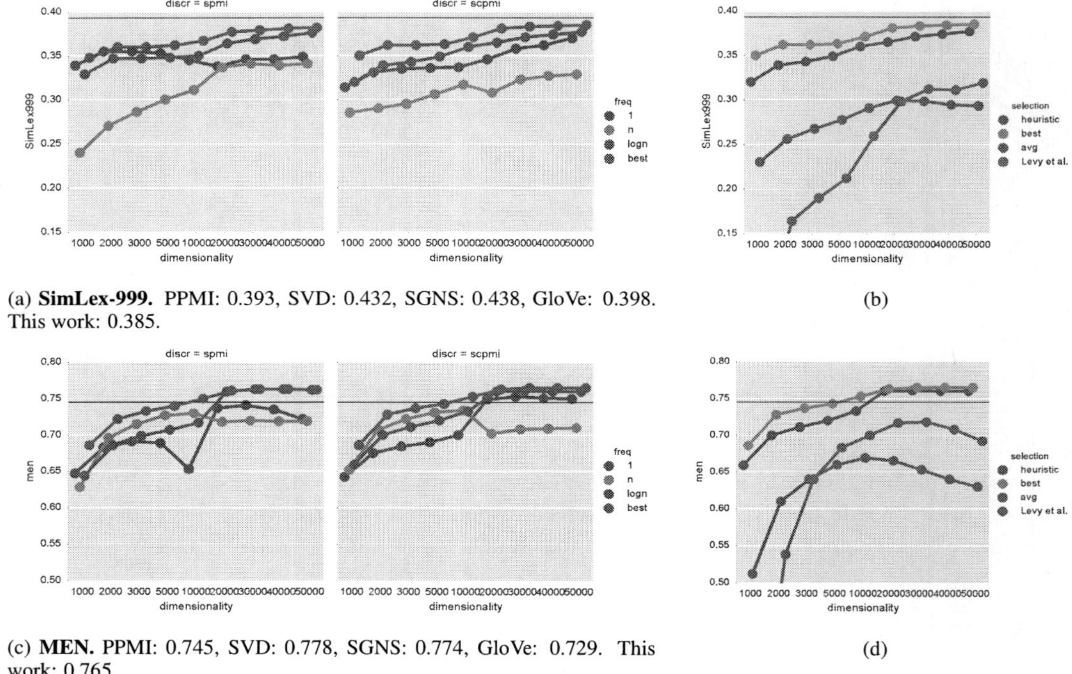

(a) **SimLex-999.** PPMI: 0.393, SVD: 0.432, SGNS: 0.438, GloVe: 0.398.
This work: 0.385.

(b)

(c) **MEN.** PPMI: 0.745, SVD: 0.778, SGNS: 0.774, GloVe: 0.729. This
work: 0.765.

(d)

Figure 3: **Best configurations.** The black lines show the best count models (PPMI) reported by Levy et al. (2015). We also give our best score, SVD, SGNS and GloVe numbers from that study for comparison. On the right, our heuristic in comparison to the best and average results together with the models selected using the recommendations presented in Levy et al. (2015).

the best selection, but with a wider gap than the SPMI models. In general n-weighted models do not perform as well as others.

Overall, $\log n$ weighting should be used with PMI, CPMI and SCPMI. High-dimensional SPMI models show the same behaviour, but if $D < 10K$, no weighting should be applied. SPMI and SCPMI should be preferred over CPMI and PMI. As Figure 3b shows, our heuristics give performance close to the optimum for any dimensionality, with a large improvement over both an average parameter setting and the parameters suggested by Levy et al. (2015) in a high-dimensional setting.[4]

Finally, to see whether the heuristics transfer robustly, we repeat this comparison on the MEN dataset (see Figures 3c, 3d). Again, PMI and CPMI follow the best possible setup, with SPMI and SCPMI showing only a slight drop below ideal performance; and again, the heuristic settings give performance close to the optimum, and significantly higher than average or standard parameters.

6 Conclusion

This paper presents a systematic study of co-occurrence quantification focusing on the selection of parameters presented in Levy et al. (2015). We replicate their recommendation for high-dimensional vector spaces, and show that with appropriate parameter selection it is possible to achieve comparable performance with spaces of dimensionality of 1K to 50K, and propose a set of model selection heuristics that maximizes performance. We foresee the results of the paper are generalisable to other experiments, since model selection was performed on a similarity dataset, and was additionally tested on a relatedness dataset.

In general, model performance depends on vector dimensionality (the best setup with 50K dimensions is better than the best setup with 1K dimensions by 0.03 on SimLex-999). Spaces with a few thousand dimensions benefit from being dense and unsmoothed ($k < 1$, global context probability); while high-dimensional spaces are better sparse and smooth ($k > 1$, $\alpha = 0.75$). However, for unweighted and n-weighted models, these heuristics do not guarantee the best possible result because

---

[4]Our results using Levy et al. (2015)'s parameters differ slightly from theirs due to different window sizes (5 vs 2).

Model	SimLex-999	MEN
PPMI*	0.393	0.745
SVD*	0.432	0.778
SGNS*	0.438	0.774
GloVe*	0.398	0.729
This work	0.385	0.765

Table 2: **Our model in comparison to the previous work.** On the similarity dataset our model is 0.008 points behind a PPMI model, however on the relatedness dataset 0.020 points above. Note the difference in dimensionality, source corpora and window size. SVD, SGNS and GloVe numbers are given for comparison. *Results reported by Levy et al. (2015).

of the high variance of the corresponding scores. Based on this we suggest to use lognSPMI or lognSCPMI with dimensionality of at least 20K to ensure good performance on lexical tasks.

There are several directions for the future work. Our experiments show that models with a few thousand dimensions are competitive with more dimensional models, see Figure 3. Moreover, for these models, unsmoothed probabilities give the best result. It might be the case that due to the large size of the corpus used, the probability estimates for the most frequent words are reliable without smoothing. More experiments need to be done to see whether this holds for smaller corpora.

The similarity datasets are transferred to other languages (Leviant and Reichart, 2015). The future work might investigate whether our results hold for languages other than English.

The qualitative influence of the parameters should be studied in depth with extensive error analysis on how parameter selection changes similarity judgements.

Acknowledgements

We thank Ann Copestake for her valuable comments as part of the ACL SRW mentorship program and the anonymous reviewers for their comments. Support from EPSRC grant EP/J002607/1 is gratefully acknowledged by Dmitrijs Milajevs and Mehrnoosh Sadrzadeh. Matthew Purver is partly supported by ConCreTe: the project ConCreTe acknowledges the financial support of the Future and Emerging Technologies (FET) programme within the Seventh Framework Programme for Research of the European Commission, under FET grant number 611733.

References

Marco Baroni and Roberto Zamparelli. 2010. Nouns are vectors, adjectives are matrices: Representing adjective-noun constructions in semantic space. In *Proceedings of the 2010 Conference on Empirical Methods in Natural Language Processing*, EMNLP '10, pages 1183–1193, Stroudsburg, PA, USA. Association for Computational Linguistics.

Marco Baroni, Silvia Bernardini, Adriano Ferraresi, and Eros Zanchetta. 2009. The wacky wide web: a collection of very large linguistically processed web-crawled corpora. *Language Resources and Evaluation*, 43(3):209–226.

Marco Baroni, Georgiana Dinu, and Germán Kruszewski. 2014. Don't count, predict! a systematic comparison of context-counting vs. context-predicting semantic vectors. In *Proceedings of the 52nd Annual Meeting of the Association for Computational Linguistics (Volume 1: Long Papers)*, pages 238–247, Baltimore, Maryland, June. Association for Computational Linguistics.

Elia Bruni, Nam Khanh Tran, and Marco Baroni. 2014. Multimodal distributional semantics. *J. Artif. Int. Res.*, 49(1):1–47, January.

Kenneth Ward Church and Patrick Hanks. 1990. Word association norms mutual information, and lexicography. *Computational Linguistics*, 16(1):22–29.

Bob Coecke, Mehrnoosh Sadrzadeh, and Stephen Clark. 2010. Mathematical foundations for a compositional distributional model of meaning. *CoRR*, abs/1003.4394.

Ido Dagan, Shaul Marcus, and Shaul Markovitch. 1993. Contextual word similarity and estimation from sparse data. In *Proceedings of the 31st Annual Meeting on Association for Computational Linguistics*, ACL '93, pages 164–171, Stroudsburg, PA, USA. Association for Computational Linguistics.

Georgiana Dinu and Mirella Lapata. 2010. Measuring distributional similarity in context. In *Proceedings of the 2010 Conference on Empirical Methods in Natural Language Processing*, EMNLP '10, pages 1162–1172, Stroudsburg, PA, USA. Association for Computational Linguistics.

Susan T. Dumais. 2004. Latent semantic analysis. *Annual Review of Information Science and Technology*, 38(1):188–230.

Stefan Evert. 2005. *The statistics of word cooccurrences: word pairs and collocations*. Ph.D. thesis, Universitt Stuttgart, Holzgartenstr. 16, 70174 Stuttgart.

Lev Finkelstein, Evgeniy Gabrilovich, Yossi Matias, Ehud Rivlin, Zach Solan, Gadi Wolfman, and Eytan Ruppin. 2002. Placing search in context: The concept revisited. *ACM Trans. Inf. Syst.*, 20(1):116–131, January.

Edward Grefenstette and Mehrnoosh Sadrzadeh. 2011. Experimental support for a categorical compositional distributional model of meaning. In *Proceedings of the Conference on Empirical Methods in Natural Language Processing*, EMNLP '11, pages 1394–1404, Stroudsburg, PA, USA. Association for Computational Linguistics.

Z.S. Harris. 1954. Distributional structure. *Word*.

Felix Hill, Roi Reichart, and Anna Korhonen. 2014. Simlex-999: Evaluating semantic models with (genuine) similarity estimation. *arXiv preprint arXiv:1408.3456*.

Dimitri Kartsaklis and Mehrnoosh Sadrzadeh. 2014. A study of entanglement in a categorical framework of natural language. In *Proceedings of the 11th Workshop on Quantum Physics and Logic (QPL)*, Kyoto, Japan, June.

Douwe Kiela and Stephen Clark. 2014. A systematic study of semantic vector space model parameters. In *Proceedings of the 2nd Workshop on Continuous Vector Space Models and their Compositionality (CVSC)*, pages 21–30, Gothenburg, Sweden, April. Association for Computational Linguistics.

Gabriella Lapesa and Stefan Evert. 2014. A large scale evaluation of distributional semantic models: Parameters, interactions and model selection. *Transactions of the Association for Computational Linguistics*, 2:531–545.

Ira Leviant and Roi Reichart. 2015. Judgment language matters: Multilingual vector space models for judgment language aware lexical semantics. *CoRR*, abs/1508.00106.

Omer Levy and Yoav Goldberg. 2014. Neural word embedding as implicit matrix factorization. In Z. Ghahramani, M. Welling, C. Cortes, N.D. Lawrence, and K.Q. Weinberger, editors, *Advances in Neural Information Processing Systems 27*, pages 2177–2185. Curran Associates, Inc.

Omer Levy, Yoav Goldberg, and Ido Dagan. 2015. Improving distributional similarity with lessons learned from word embeddings. *Transactions of the Association for Computational Linguistics*, 3:211–225.

Stephen McGregor, Kat Agres, Matthew Purver, and Geraint Wiggins. 2015. From distributional semantics to conceptual spaces: A novel computational method for concept creation. *Journal of Artificial General Intelligence*, 6(1):55–86, December.

Tomas Mikolov, Kai Chen, Greg Corrado, and Jeffrey Dean. 2013. Efficient estimation of word representations in vector space. *arXiv preprint arXiv:1301.3781*.

Dmitrijs Milajevs and Sascha Griffiths. 2016. Treating similarity with respect: How to evaluate models of meaning? *CoRR*, abs/1605.04553.

Dmitrijs Milajevs and Matthew Purver. 2014. Investigating the contribution of distributional semantic information for dialogue act classification. In *Proceedings of the 2nd Workshop on Continuous Vector Space Models and their Compositionality (CVSC)*, pages 40–47, Gothenburg, Sweden, April. Association for Computational Linguistics.

Dmitrijs Milajevs, Dimitri Kartsaklis, Mehrnoosh Sadrzadeh, and Matthew Purver. 2014. Evaluating neural word representations in tensor-based compositional settings. In *Proceedings of the 2014 Conference on Empirical Methods in Natural Language Processing (EMNLP)*, pages 708–719, Doha, Qatar, October. Association for Computational Linguistics.

Jeffrey Pennington, Richard Socher, and Christopher Manning. 2014. Glove: Global vectors for word representation. In *Proceedings of the 2014 Conference on Empirical Methods in Natural Language Processing (EMNLP)*, pages 1532–1543, Doha, Qatar, October. Association for Computational Linguistics.

Tamara Polajnar and Stephen Clark. 2014. Improving distributional semantic vectors through context selection and normalisation. In *Proceedings of the 14th Conference of the European Chapter of the Association for Computational Linguistics*, pages 230–238, Gothenburg, Sweden, April. Association for Computational Linguistics.

Herbert Rubenstein and John B. Goodenough. 1965. Contextual correlates of synonymy. *Commun. ACM*, 8(10):627–633, October.

Peter D. Turney and Patrick Pantel. 2010. From frequency to meaning: Vector space models of semantics. *J. Artif. Int. Res.*, 37(1):141–188, January.

Singleton Detection using Word Embeddings and Neural Networks

Hessel Haagsma
University of Groningen
The Netherlands
`hessel.haagsma@rug.nl`

Abstract

Singleton (or non-coreferential) mentions are a problem for coreference resolution systems, and identifying singletons before mentions are linked improves resolution performance. Here, a singleton detection system based on word embeddings and neural networks is presented, which achieves state-of-the-art performance (79.6% accuracy) on the CoNLL-2012 shared task development set. Extrinsic evaluation with the Stanford and Berkeley coreference resolution systems shows significant improvement for the first, but not for the latter. The results show the potential of using neural networks and word embeddings for improving both singleton detection and coreference resolution.

1 Background

Coreference resolution is the task of identifying and linking all expressions in language which refer to the same entity. It is an essential part of both human language understanding and natural language processing. In NLP, coreference resolution is often approached as a two-part problem: finding all referential expressions (a.k.a. 'mentions') in a text, and clustering those mentions that refer to the same entity.

So, in Example (1), the first part consists of finding *My internet*, *It*, and *it*. The second part then consists of clustering *My internet* and *it* together (as indicated by the indices), and not clustering *It* with anything (as indicated by the x).

(1)   [My internet]$_1$ wasn't working properly. [It]$_x$ seems that [it]$_1$ is fixed now, however.

This example also serves to showcase the difficulty of the clustering step, since it is challenging to decide between clustering *My internet* with *it*, clustering *My internet* with *It*, or clustering all three mentions together. However, note that in this sentence *It* is non-referential, i.e. it does not refer to any real world entity. This means that this mention could already be filtered out after the first step, making the clustering a lot easier.

In this paper, we improve mention filtering for coreference resolution by building a system based on word embeddings and neural networks, and evaluate performance both as a stand-alone task and extrinsically with coreference resolution systems.

1.1 Previous Work

Mention filtering is not a new task, and there exists a large body of previous work, ranging from the rule-based non-referential *it* filtering of Paice and Husk (1987) to the machine learning approach to singleton detection by de Marneffe et al. (2015).

Different mention filtering tasks have been tried: filtering out non-referential *it* (Boyd et al., 2005; Bergsma and Yarowsky, 2011), non-anaphoric NPs (Uryupina, 2003), non-antecedent NPs (Uryupina, 2009), discourse-new mentions (Ng and Cardie, 2002), and singletons, i.e. non-coreferential mentions (de Marneffe et al., 2015). All these tasks can be done quite accurately, but since they are only useful as part of an end-to-end coreference resolution system, it is more interesting to look at what is most effective for improving coreference resolution performance.

There is much to gain with improved mention filtering. For example, the authors of one state-of-the-art coreference resolution system estimate that non-referential mentions are the direct cause of 14.8% of their system's error (Lee et al., 2013). The importance of mention detection and filtering

Proceedings of the 54th Annual Meeting of the Association for Computational Linguistics – Student Research Workshop, pages 65–71,
Berlin, Germany, August 7-12, 2016. ©2016 Association for Computational Linguistics

is further exemplified by the fact that several recent systems focus on integrating the processing of mentions and the clustering of mentions into a single model or system (Ma et al., 2014; Peng et al., 2015; Wiseman et al., 2015).

Other lessons regarding mention filtering and coreference resolution performance come from Ng and Cardie (2002) and Byron and Gegg-Harrison (2004). They find that the mentions filtered out by their systems are also the mentions which are least problematic in the clustering phase. As a result, the gain in clustering precision is smaller than expected, and does not compensate for the recall loss. They also find that high precision in mention filtering is more important than high recall.

The state-of-the-art in mention filtering is the system described by de Marneffe et al. (2015), who work on singleton detection. De Marneffe et al. used a logistic regression classifier with both discourse-theoretically inspired semantic features and more superficial features (animacy, NE-type, POS, etc.) to perform singleton detection. They achieve 56% recall and 90% precision on the CoNLL-2012 shared task data, which translates to a coreference resolution performance increase of 0.5-2.0 percentage point in CoNLL F1-score.

1.2 The Current Approach

In this paper, a novel singleton detection system which makes use of word embeddings and neural networks is presented. There are three main motivations for choosing this approach, partly based on lessons drawn from previous work.

The first is that the coreference resolution systems we evaluate with here do not make use of embeddings. Thus, using embeddings as an additional data source can aid in filtering out those singletons which are problematic for the clustering system. Word embeddings are chosen because we expect that the syntactic and semantic information contained in them should help the singleton detection system to generalize over the training data better. For example, knowing that 'snowing' is similar to 'raining' makes it easier to classify 'It' in 'It is snowing' as singleton, when only 'It is raining' occurs in the training data.

Second, previous work indicated that precision in filtering is more important than recall. Therefore, a singleton detection system should not only be able to filter out singletons with high accuracy, but should also be able to vary the precision/recall trade-off. Here, the output is a class probability, which fulfils this requirement.

Third, both Bergsma and Yarowsky (2011) and de Marneffe et al. (2015) find that the context words around the mention are an important feature for mention filtering. Context tokens can easily be included in the current set-up, and by using word embeddings generalization on these context words should be improved.

2 Methods

The singleton detection system presented here consists of two main parts: a recursive autoencoder and a multilayer perceptron. The recursive autoencoder is used to create fixed-length representations for multi-word mentions, based on word embeddings. The multi-layer perceptron is used to perform the actual singleton detection.

2.1 Data

We use the OntoNotes corpus (Weischedel et al., 2011; Weischedel et al., 2013), since it was also used in the CoNLL-2011 and 2012 shared tasks on coreference resolution (Pradhan et al., 2011; Pradhan et al., 2012), and is used by de Marneffe et al. (2015). A downside of the OntoNotes corpus is that singletons are not annotated. As such, an extra mention selection step is necessary to recover the singleton mentions from the data.

We solve this problem by simply taking the mentions as they are selected by the Stanford coreference resolution system (Lee et al., 2013), and use this as the full set of mentions. These are similar to the Berkeley coreference resolution system's mentions (Durrett and Klein, 2013), since they mention they base their mention detection rules on those of Lee et al. This makes them suitable here. In addition, de Marneffe et al. (2015) use the Stanford system's mentions as basis for their singleton detection experiments, so using these mentions aids comparability as well.

2.2 Recursive Autoencoder

A recursive autoencoder (RAE) is applied to the vector representations of mentions, reducing them to a single word-embedding-length sized vector. This is done to compress the variable length mentions to a fixed-size representation, which is required by the multi-layer perceptron.

The RAE used here is similar to the one used by Socher et al. (2011), with the following design choices: a sigmoid activation function is used, training is done using stochastic gradient descent, and the weights are untied. A left-branching binary tree structure is used, since only the final mention representation is of interest. Euclidean distance is used as an error measure, with each vector's error weighted by the number of words it represents.

2.3 Multi-layer Perceptron

The multi-layer perceptron consists of an input layer, one hidden layer, and a binary classification layer. As input, three types of features are used: the mention itself, context words around the mention, and other mentions in the context.

The implementation of the MLP is straightforward. The input order is randomized, to prevent spurious order effects. Stochastic gradient descent is used for training. Experiments with various settings for the parameters governing learning rate, number of training epochs, stopping criteria, hidden layer size, context size and weight regularization are conducted, and their values and optimization are discussed in Section 3.1.

2.4 Integrating Singleton Detection into Coreference Resolution Systems

Two coreference resolution systems are used for the evaluation of singleton detection performance: the Berkeley system (Durrett and Klein, 2013) and the Stanford system (Lee et al., 2013).

The Stanford system is a deterministic rule-based system, in which different rules are applied sequentially. It was the highest scoring coreference resolution system of the CoNLL-2011 shared task. The most natural way of integrating a singleton detection model in this system is by filtering out mentions directly after the mention detection phase.

The Berkeley system, on the other hand, is a learning-based model, which relies on template-based surface-level features. It is currently one of the best-performing coreference resolution systems for English. Because the system is a retrainable learner, the most obvious way to use singleton detection probabilities is as a feature, rather than a filter. For both systems, varying ways of integrating the singleton detection information are presented in Section 3.3.

3 Evaluation & Results

3.1 Preprocessing and Optimization

The recursive autoencoder was trained on the CoNLL-2011 and 2012 training sets, with a learning rate of 0.005. Training was stopped when the lowest validation error was not achieved in the last 25% of epochs. The trained model was then used to generate representations for all mentions in the development and test sets.

Using these mention representations, the parameters of the MLP were optimized on the CoNLL-2012 development set. The stopping criterion was the same as for the RAE, and the learning rate was fixed at 0.001, in order to isolate the influence of other parameters. During optimization, the following default parameter values were used: 50-dimensional embeddings, 150 hidden nodes, 5 context words (both sides), 2 context mentions (both sides), and a 0.5 threshold for classifying a mention as singleton. A competitive baseline was established by tagging each pronoun as coreferential and all other mentions as singleton. We test for significant improvement over the default values using pair-wise approximate randomization tests (Yeh, 2000).

For the hidden layer size, no value from the set $\{50, 100, 300, 600, 800\}$ was significantly better than the default of 150. In order to keep the input/hidden layer proportion fixed, a 5:1 proportion was used during the rest of the optimization and evaluation process.

For the number of context words, the values $\{0, 1, 2, 3, 4, 10, 15, 20\}$ were tested, yielding only small differences. However, the best-performing model, using only 1 context word on either side of the mention, was significantly better than the default of 5 context words.

For the number of context mentions, the default value of 2 turned out to be optimal, as it worked significantly better than most values from the set $\{0, 1, 3, 4, 5, 6\}$.

Of all parameters, the choice for a set of word embeddings was the most influential. Different sets of GloVe embeddings were tested, varying in dimensionality and number of tokens trained on. The default set was 50D/6B, i.e. 50-dimensional embeddings trained on 6 billion tokens of training data. The sets $\{100D/6B, 200D/6B, 300D/6B, 300D/42B, 300D/840B\}$ were evaluated. All out-performed the default set, and the 300D/42B set performed the best.

Test set	Acc.	Singleton Detection		
		P	R	F1
11-dev	76.37	75.72	90.32	82.38
11-test	77.47	77.26	88.42	82.46
12-dev	79.57	79.77	85.83	82.69
12-test	80.08	81.57	83.78	82.66
12-dev-dM15	79.0	81.1	80.8	80.9
12-dev-BL	68.19	66.90	87.21	75.72

Table 1: Singleton detection performance using the best-scoring model. The CoNLL-2012 training set was used as training data. 'dM15' marks the results by de Marneffe et al. (2015) 'BL' marks the baseline performance.

3.2 Singleton Detection Results

The final singleton detection model was evaluated on the CoNLL-2011 development and test set, and the CoNLL-2012 test set, in order to evaluate generalization. Results are reported in Table 1. Generally, performance holds up well across data sets, although the results on the 2011 sets are slightly lower than on the 2012 datasets.

At 76-80% accuracy, the multi-layer perceptron is clearly better than the baseline. Performance is also compared to that of the state-of-the-art, by de Marneffe et al. (2015), who only report scores on the CoNLL-2012 development set. The accuracy of my system is 0.6 percentage points higher.

Because word embeddings are the only source of information used by the system, its performance may be vulnerable to the presence of 'unknown words', i.e. words for which there is no embedding. Looking at the 2012 development set, we see that classification accuracy for mentions containing one or more unknown words is 76.55%, as compared to 79.63% for mentions without unknown words. The difference is smaller when looking at the context: accuracy for mentions with one or more unknown words in their context is 78.73%, whereas it is 79.79% for mentions with fully known contexts.

3.3 Coreference Resolution Results

Table 2 shows the performance of the Stanford system. Multiple variables governing singleton filtering were explored. 'NE' indicates whether named entities were excluded from filtering or not. 'Pairs' indicates whether individual mentions are filtered out, or only links between pairs of

mentions. 'Threshold' indicates the threshold under which mentions are classified singleton. The threshold value of 0.15 is chosen so that the singleton classification has a precision of approximately 90%

We cannot compare directly to the system of de Marneffe et al. (2015), because they used an older, faulty version of the CoNLL-scorer. For the Stanford system, we therefore compare to a precursor of their system, by Recasens et al. (2013), whose singleton detection system is integrated with the Stanford system. For the Berkeley system, this is not possible. In both cases, we also compare to the system without any singleton detection. Differences were tested for significance using a paired-bootstrap re-sampling test (Koehn, 2004) over documents, 10000 times.

The performance of the different filtering methods is as expected. For more widely applicable filters, precision goes up more, but recall also drops more. For more selective filters, the drop in recall is smaller, but so is the gain in precision. The best balance here is yielded by the 'Incl./Yes/0.15'-model, the most restrictive model, except for that it includes named entities in filtering. This model yields a small improvement of 0.7 percentage points over the baseline. This is slightly more than the Recasens et al. (2013) system, and also slightly larger than the 0.5 percentage point gain reported by de Marneffe et al. (2015)

NE	Pairs	Threshold	CoNLL-F1
Incl.	No	0.5	50.41*
Incl.	No	0.15	56.73
Incl.	Yes	0.5	55.46*
Incl.	Yes	0.15	**57.17***
Excl.	No	0.5	53.64*
Excl.	No	0.15	56.71
Excl.	Yes	0.5	55.96*
Excl.	Yes	0.15	56.92*
Recasens et al. (2013)			56.90*
No Singleton Detection			56.44

Table 2: Performance of the Stanford system on the 2012 development set. Significant differences ($p < 0.05$) from the baseline are marked *.

Table 3 shows the performance of the Berkeley system. Here, singleton detection probabilities are incorporated as a feature. Again, there are multiple variations: 'Prob' indicates each mention was assigned its predicted probability as a feature. 'Mentions' indicates each mention was assigned a boolean feature indicating whether it was likely singleton ($P < 0.15$), and a feature indicating whether it was likely coreferential ($P > 0.8$). 'Pairs' indicates the same as 'Mentions', but for pairs of mentions, where both have $P < 0.15$ or $P > 0.8$. 'Both' indicates that both 'Mentions'- and 'Pairs'-features are added.

Here, the performance differences are much smaller, yielding only a non-significant 0.3 percentage point increase over the baseline. All models show an increase in precision, and a drop in recall. In contrast, de Marneffe et al. (2015) report a larger performance increase of almost 2 percentage points for the Berkeley system.

Model	CoNLL-F1
Prob	61.83
Prob + Mentions	61.81
Prob + Pairs	**62.02**
Prob + Both	**62.02**
No Singleton Detection	61.71

Table 3: Performance of the Berkeley system on the 2012 development set. As a baseline system, the system using the 'FINAL' feature set was used. Significant differences ($p < 0.05$) from the baseline are marked *.

4 Discussion

The singleton detection model was optimized with regard to four variables: hidden layer size, number of context tokens, number of context mentions, and set of word embeddings.

For hidden layer size, no clear effect was found. Regarding the set of word embeddings, we found that higher-dimensional embeddings provide better performance, which is in accordance with what Pennington et al. (2014) found. They, and Collobert et al. (2011), also found that embeddings trained on more text performed better on a range of tasks, but we do not see that clearly, here.

As far as the number of context mentions is concerned, the effect is small, and 2 mentions on either side seems an optimal number. Since the closest mentions are likely the most relevant, this makes sense. Also, since the dataset contains both short pronoun mentions and longer NP mentions,

the optimal number is likely a compromise; for pronouns like *it*, one would expect mentions in the left-context to be most important, while this is not the case for NP mentions.

The most counter-intuitive result of parameter optimization is the fact that just 1 context token on either side of the mention proved to be optimal. This contrasts with previous work: de Marneffe et al. (2015) use 2 words around the mention, and semantic information from a larger window, and Bergsma and Yarowsky (2011) use up to 5 words before and 20 words after *it*. Looking at the mention detection literature in general, we see that this pattern holds up: in non-referential *it* detection, larger context windows are used than in works that deal with complete NPs.

Clearly, since large NP mentions already contain more information internally, they require smaller context windows. Likely, the same dynamic is at play here. The OntoNotes dataset contains a majority of NP mentions, and has relatively long mentions, since it only annotates the largest NP of a set of nested head-sharing NPs.

The other main observation to be made on the results is the discrepancy in the effect of singleton information on the Berkeley coreference resolution system in this work and that by de Marneffe et al. (2015). Although singleton detection performance and the performance with the Stanford system are similar, there is almost no performance gain with the Berkeley system here.

Using the Berkeley coreference analyser (Kummerfeld and Klein, 2013), the types of errors made by the resolution systems can be analysed. For the Stanford system, we find the same error type patterns as de Marneffe et al. (2015), which matches well with the similar performance gain. For the Berkeley system, the increases in missing entity and missing mention errors are higher, and we do not find the large decrease in divided entity errors that de Marneffe et al. (2015) found. It is difficult to point out the underlying cause for this, due to the learning-based nature of the Berkeley system. Somehow, there is a qualitative difference between the probabilities produced by the two singleton detection systems.

Regarding the question of how to integrate singleton information in coreference resolution systems, the picture is clear. Both here and in de Marneffe et al. (2015), the best way of using the information is with a high-precision filter, and for pairs of mentions, rather than individual mentions. The only difference is that excluding named entities from filtering was not beneficial here, which might be due to the fact that word embeddings also cover names, which improves handling of them by the singleton detection model.

For future work, several avenues of exploration are available. The first is to split singleton detection according to mention type (similar to Hoste and Daelemans (2005) for coreference resolution). Since the current model covers all types of mentions, it cannot exploit specific properties of these mention types. Training separate systems, for example for pronouns and NPs, might boost performance.

Another improvement lies with the way mentions are represented. Here, a recursive autoencoder was used to generate fixed size representations for variable-length mentions. However, a lot of information is lost in this compression step, and perhaps it is not the best compression method. Alternative neural network architectures, such as recurrent neural networks, convolutional neural networks, and long short-term memories might yield better results.

In addition, an improved treatment of unknown words could boost performance, since their presence hurts classification accuracy. Currently, an average of all embeddings is used to represent unknown words, but more advanced approaches are possible, e.g. by using part-of-speech information.

To further investigate the interaction between singleton detection and coreference resolution, it would be insightful to look into combining the current system with more recent coreference resolution systems (e.g. Wiseman et al., 2016; Clark and Manning, 2015) which perform better than the Stanford and Berkeley systems. On the one hand, singleton detection information could yield larger gains with these systems, as they might be able to exploit the information better. For example, improved clustering algorithms might benefit more from a reduced number of mentions in the search space. On the other hand, improvements in these systems could overlap with the gain from singleton detection information, lowering the added value of a separate singleton detection system.

All in all, it is shown that a word embedding and neural network based singleton detection system can perform as well as a learner based on hand-crafted, linguistic-intuition-based features. With a straightforward neural network architecture, and off-the-shelf word embeddings, neither of which is specifically geared towards this task, state-of-the-art performance can be achieved. As an added benefit, this approach can easily be extended to any other language, if word embeddings are available.

Acknowledgements

I am grateful to Jennifer Spenader for providing inspiration and feedback during all stages of this project, and to the anonymous reviewers for their kind and useful comments.

References

Shane Bergsma and David Yarowsky. 2011. NADA: a robust system for non-referential pronoun detection. In Iris Hendrickx, Sobha Lalitha Devi, António Branco, and Ruslan Mitkov, editors, *Anaphora Processing and Applications*, pages 12–23. Springer, Berlin.

Adriane Boyd, Whitney Gegg-Harrison, and Donna K. Byron. 2005. Identifying non-referential *it*: a machine learning approach incorporating linguistically motivated patterns. In *Proceedings of the ACL Workshop on Feature Engineering for Machine Learning in NLP*, pages 40–47.

Donna K. Byron and Whitney Gegg-Harrison. 2004. Eliminating non-referring noun phrases from coreference resolution. In *Proceedings of DAARC 2004*, pages 21–26.

Kevin Clark and Christopher D. Manning. 2015. Entity-centric coreference resolution with model stacking. In *Proceedings of ACL 2015*, pages 1405–1415.

Ronan Collobert, Jason Weston, Léon Bottou, Michael Karlen, Koray Kavukcuoglu, and Pavel Kuksa. 2011. Natural language processing (almost) from scratch. *Journal of Machine Learning Research*, 12:2493–2537.

Marie-Catherine de Marneffe, Marta Recasens, and Christopher Potts. 2015. Modeling the lifespan of discourse entities with application to coreference resolution. *Journal of Artificial Intelligence Research*, 52:445–475.

Greg Durrett and Dan Klein. 2013. Easy victories and uphill battles in coreference resolution. In *Proceedings of EMNLP 2013*, pages 1971–1982.

Veronique Hoste and Walter Daelemans. 2005. Learning Dutch coreference resolution. In *Proceedings of CLIN 2004*, pages 133–148.

Philipp Koehn. 2004. Statistical significance tests for machine translation evaluation. In *Proceedings of EMNLP 2004*, pages 388–395.

Jonathan K. Kummerfeld and Dan Klein. 2013. Error-driven analysis of challenges in coreference resolution. In *Proceedings of EMNLP 2013*, pages 265–277.

Heeyoung Lee, Angel Chang, Yves Peirsman, Nathanael Chambers, Mihai Surdeanu, and Dan Jurafsky. 2013. Deterministic coreference resolution based on entity-centric, precision-ranked rules. *Computational Linguistics*, 39(4):885–916.

Chao Ma, Janardhan Rao Doppa, J. Walker Orr, Prashanth Mannem, Xiaoli Fern, Tom Dietterich, and Prasad Tadepalli. 2014. Prune-and-Score: Learning for greedy coreference resolution. In *Proceedings of EMNLP 2014*, pages 2115–2126.

Vincent Ng and Claire Cardie. 2002. Identifying anaphoric and non-anaphoric noun phrases to improve coreference resolution. In *Proceedings of COLING 2002*, pages 1–7.

C. D. Paice and G. D. Husk. 1987. Towards the automatic recognition of anaphoric features in English text: the impersonal pronoun "it". *Computer Speech and Language*, 2:109–132.

Haoruo Peng, Kai-Wei Chang, and Dan Roth. 2015. A joint framework for coreference resolution and mention head detection. In *Proceedings of CoNLL 2015*, pages 12–21.

Jeffrey Pennington, Richard Socher, and Christopher D. Manning. 2014. GloVe: Global vectors for word representation. In *Proceedings of EMNLP 2014*, pages 1532–1543.

Sameer Pradhan, Lance Ramshaw, Mitchell Marcus, Martha Palmer, Ralph Weischedel, and Nianwen Xue. 2011. CoNLL-2011 shared task: modeling unrestricted coreference in OntoNotes. In *Proceedings of the Fifteenth Conference on CoNLL*, pages 1–27.

Sameer Pradhan, Alessandro Moschitti, Nianwen Xue, Olga Uryupina, and Yuchen Zhang. 2012. CoNLL-2012 shared task: Modeling multilingual unrestricted coreference in OntoNotes. In *Proceedings of the Joint Conference on EMNLP and CoNLL*, pages 1–40.

Marta Recasens, Marie-Catherine de Marneffe, and Christopher Potts. 2013. The life and death of discourse entities: Identifying singleton mentions. In *Proceedings of NAACL-HLT 2013*, pages 627–633.

Richard Socher, Eric H. Huang, Jeffrey Pennington, Andrew Y. Ng, and Christopher D. Manning. 2011. Dynamic pooling and unfolding recursive autoencoders for paraphrase detection. In *Proceedings of NIPS 2011*, pages 801–809.

Olga Uryupina. 2003. High-precision identification of discourse new and unique noun phrases. In *Proceedings of the ACL 2003 Student Research Workshop*, pages 80–86.

Olga Uryupina. 2009. Detecting anaphoricity and antecedenthood for coreference resolution. *Procesamiento del Lenguaje Natural*, 42:113–120.

Ralph Weischedel, Martha Palmer, Mitchell Marcus, Eduard Hovy, Sameer Pradhan, Lance Ramshaw, Nianwen Xue, Ann Taylor, Jeff Kaufman, Michelle Franchini, Mohammed El-Bachouti, Robert Belvin, and Ann Houston. 2011. OntoNotes Release 4.0. DVD.

Ralph Weischedel, Martha Palmer, Mitchell Marcus, Eduard Hovy, Sameer Pradhan, Lance Ramshaw, Nianwen Xue, Ann Taylor, Jeff Kaufman, Michelle Franchini, Mohammed El-Bachouti, Robert Belvin, and Ann Houston. 2013. OntoNotes Release 5.0. Web Download.

Sam Wiseman, Alexander M. Rush, Stuart M. Shieber, and Jason Weston. 2015. Learning anaphoricity and antecedent ranking features for coreference resolution. In *Proceedings of ACL 2015*, pages 1416–1426.

Sam Wiseman, Alexander M. Rush, and Stuart M. Shieber. 2016. Learning gloabl features for coreference resolution. *arXiv preprint arXiv:1604.03035*.

Alexander Yeh. 2000. More accurate tests for the statistical significance of result differences. In *Proceedings of COLING 2000*, pages 947–953.

A Dataset for Joint Noun–Noun Compound Bracketing and Interpretation

Murhaf Fares
Department of Informatics
University of Oslo
`murhaff@ifi.uio.no`

Abstract

We present a new, sizeable dataset of noun–noun compounds with their syntactic analysis (bracketing) and semantic relations. Derived from several established linguistic resources, such as the Penn Treebank, our dataset enables experimenting with new approaches towards a holistic analysis of noun–noun compounds, such as joint-learning of noun–noun compounds bracketing and interpretation, as well as integrating compound analysis with other tasks such as syntactic parsing.

1 Introduction

Noun–noun compounds are abundant in many languages, and English is no exception. According to Ó Séaghdha (2008), three percent of all words in the British National Corpus (Burnard, 2000, BNC) are part of nominal compounds. Therefore, in addition to being an interesting linguistic phenomenon per se, the analysis of noun–noun compounds is important to other natural language processing (NLP) tasks such as machine translation and information extraction. Indeed, there is already a nontrivial amount of research on noun–noun compounds within the field of computational linguistics (Lauer, 1995; Nakov, 2007; Ó Séaghdha, 2008; Tratz, 2011, inter alios).

As Lauer and Dras (1994) point out, the treatment of noun–noun compounds involves three tasks: identification, bracketing and semantic interpretation. With a few exceptions (Girju et al., 2005; Kim and Baldwin, 2013), most studies on noun–noun compounds focus on one of the aforementioned tasks in isolation, but these tasks are of course not fully independent and therefore might benefit from a joint-learning approach, especially bracketing and semantic interpretation.

Reflecting previous lines of research, most of the existing datasets on noun–noun compounds either include bracketing information or semantic relations, rarely both. In this article we present a fairly large dataset for noun–noun compound bracketing as well as semantic interpretation. Furthermore, most of the available datasets list the compounds out of context. Hence they implicitly assume that the semantics of noun–noun compounds is type-based; meaning that the same compound will always have the same semantic relation. To test this assumption of type-based vs. token-based semantic relations, we incorporate the context of the compounds in our dataset and treat compounds as tokens rather than types. Lastly, to study the effect of noun–noun compound bracketing and interpretation on other NLP tasks, we derive our dataset from well-established resources that annotate noun–noun compounds as part of other linguistic structures, viz. the Wall Street Journal Section of the Penn Treebank (Marcus et al., 1993, PTB), PTB noun phrase annotation by Vadas and Curran (2007), DeepBank (Flickinger et al., 2012), the Prague Czech–English Dependency Treebank 2.0 (Hajič et al., 2012, PCEDT) and NomBank (Meyers et al., 2004). We therefore can quantify the effect of compound bracketing on syntactic parsing using the PTB, for example.

In the following section, we review some of the existing noun compound datasets. In §3, we present the process of constructing a dataset of noun–noun compounds with bracketing information and semantic relations. In §4, we explain how we construct the bracketing of noun–noun compounds from three resources and report 'inter-resource' agreement levels. In §5, we present the semantic relations extracted from two resources and the correlation between the two sets of relations. In §6, we conclude the article and present an outlook for future work.

Proceedings of the 54th Annual Meeting of the Association for Computational Linguistics – Student Research Workshop, pages 72–79,
Berlin, Germany, August 7-12, 2016. ©2016 Association for Computational Linguistics

Dataset	Size	Relations	Bracketing
Nastase & Szpakowicz	600	30	No
Girju et al.	4,500	21	600
Ó Séaghdha & Copestake	1,443	6	No
Kim & Baldwin[1]	2,169	20	No
Tratz & Hovy	17,509	43	No

Table 1: Overview of noun compound datasets. Size: type count

	NNP^h	NNP^0
Compounds	38,917	29,666
Compound types	21,016	14,632

Table 2: Noun–noun compounds in WSJ Corpus

2 Background

The syntax and semantics of noun–noun compounds have been under focus for years, in linguistics and computational linguistics. Levi (1978) presents one of the early and influential studies on noun–noun compounds as a subset of so-called complex nominals. Levi (1978) defines a set of nine "recoverably deletable predicates" which express the "semantic relationship between head nouns and prenominal modifiers" in complex nominals. Finin (1980) presented one of the earliest studies on nominal compounds in computational linguistics, but Lauer (1995) was among the first to study statistical methods for noun compound analysis. Lauer (1995) used the Grolier encyclopedia to estimate word probabilities, and tested his models on a dataset of 244 three-word bracketed compounds and 282 two-word compounds. The compounds were annotated with eight prepositions which Lauer takes to approximate the semantics of noun–noun compounds.

Table 1 shows an overview of some of the existing datasets for nominal compounds. The datasets by Nastase and Szpakowicz (2003) and Girju et al. (2005) are not limited to noun–noun compounds; the former includes compounds with adjectival and adverbial modifiers, and the latter has many noun-preposition-noun constructions. The semantic relations in Ó Séaghdha and Copestake (2007) and Kim and Baldwin (2008) are based on the relations introduced by Levi (1978) and Barker and Szpakowicz (1998), respectively. All of the datasets in Table 1 list the compounds out of context. In addition, the dataset by Girju et al. (2005) includes three-word bracketed compounds, whereas the rest include two-word compounds only. On the other hand, (Girju et al., 2005) is the only dataset in Table 1 that is not publicly available.

3 Framework

This section gives an overview of our method to automatically construct a bracketed and semantically annotated dataset of noun–noun compounds from four different linguistic resources. The construction method consists of three steps that correspond to the tasks defined by Lauer and Dras (1994): identification, bracketing and semantic interpretation.

Firstly, we identify the noun–noun compounds in the PTB WSJ Section using two of the compound identification heuristics introduced by Fares et al. (2015), namely the so-called syntax-based NNP^h heuristic which includes compounds that contain common and proper nouns but excludes the ones headed by proper nouns, and the syntax-based NNP^0 heuristic which excludes all compounds that contain proper nouns, be it in the head position or the modifier position. Table 2 shows the number of compounds and compound types we identified using the NNP^h and NNP^0 heuristics. Note that the number of compounds will vary in the following sections depending on the resources we use.

Secondly, we extract the bracketing of the identified compounds from three resources: PTB noun phrase annotation by Vadas and Curran (2007), DeepBank and PCEDT. Vadas and Curran (2007) manually annotated the internal structure of noun phrases (NPs) in PTB which were originally left unannotated. However, as is the case with other resources, Vadas and Curran (2007) annotation is not completely error-free, as shown by Fares et al. (2015). We therefore crosscheck their bracketing through comparing to those of DeepBank and PCEDT. The latter two, however, do not contain explicit annotation of noun–noun compound bracketing, but we can 'reconstruct' the bracketing based on the dependency relations assigned in both resources, i.e. the logical form meaning representation in DeepBank and the tectogrammatical layer (t-layer) in PCEDT. Based on the bracketing extracted from the three resources, we define the subset of compounds that are bracketed similarly in the three resources. Lastly, we extract the se-

---

[1] In Table 1 we refer to (Kim and Baldwin, 2008), the other dataset by Kim and Baldwin (2013), which includes 1,571 three-word compounds, is not publicly available.

mantic relations of two-word compounds as well as multi-word bracketed compounds from two resources: PCEDT and NomBank.

On a more technical level, we use the so-called phrase-structure layer (*p*-layer) in PCEDT to identify noun–noun compounds, because it includes the NP annotation by Vadas and Curran (2007), which is required to apply the noun–noun compound identification heuristics by Fares et al. (2015). For bracketing, we also use the PCEDT *p*-layer, in addition to the dataset prepared by Oepen et al. (2016) which includes DeepBank and the PCEDT tectogrammatical layer. We opted for the dataset by Oepen et al. (2016) because they converted the tectogrammatical annotation in PCEDT to dependency representation in which the "set of graph nodes is equivalent to the set of surface tokens." For semantic relations, we also use the dataset by Oepen et al. (2016) for PCEDT relations and the original NomBank files for NomBank relations.

Throughout the whole process we store the data in a relational database with a schema that represents the different types of information, and the different resources from which they are derived. As we will show in §4 and §5, this set-up allows us to combine information in different ways and therefore create 'different' datasets.

4   Bracketing

Noun–noun compound bracketing can be defined as the disambiguation of the internal structure of compounds with three nouns or more. For example, we can bracket the compound *noon fashion show* in two ways:

1. Left-bracketing: [[noon fashion] show]
2. Right-bracketing: [noon [fashion show]]

In this example, the right-bracketing interpretation (*a fashion show happening at noon*) is more likely than the left-bracketing one (*a show of noon fashion*). However, the correct bracketing need not always be as obvious, some compounds can be subtler to bracket, e.g. *car radio equipment* (Girju et al., 2005).

4.1   Data & Results

As explained in §3, we first identify noun–noun compounds in the WSJ Corpus, then we extract and map their bracketing from three linguistic resources: PCEDT, DeepBank and noun phrase annotation by Vadas and Curran (2007) (VC-PTB,

henceforth). Even though we can identify 38,917 noun–noun compounds in the full WSJ Corpus (cf. Table 2), the set of compounds that constitutes the basis for bracketing analysis (i.e. the set of compounds that occur in the three resources) is smaller. First, because DeepBank only annotates the first 22 Sections of the WSJ Corpus. Second, because not all the noun sequences identified as compounds in VC-PTB are treated as such in DeepBank and PCEDT. Hence, the number of compounds that occur in the three resources is 26,500. Furthermore, three-quarters (76%) of these compounds consist of two nouns only, meaning that they do not require bracketing, which leaves us a subset of 6,244 multi-word compounds—we will refer to this subset as the bracketing subset.

After mapping the bracketings from the three resources we find that they agree on the bracketing of almost 75% of the compounds in the bracketing subset. Such an agreement level is relatively good compared to previously reported agreement levels on much smaller datasets, e.g. Girju et al. (2005) report a bracketing agreement of 87% on a set of 362 three-word compounds. Inspecting the disagreement among the three resources reveals two things. First, noun–noun compounds which contain proper nouns (NNP) constitute 45% of the compounds that are bracketed differently. Second, 41% of the differently bracketed compounds are actually sub-compounds of larger compounds. For example, the compound *consumer food prices* is left-bracketed in VC-PTB, i.e. *[[consumer food] prices]*, whereas in PCEDT and DeepBank it is right-bracketed. This difference in bracketing leads to two different sub-compounds, namely *consumer food* in VC-PTB and *food prices* in PCEDT and DeepBank.

It is noteworthy that those two observations do not reflect the properties of compounds containing proper nouns or sub-compounds; they only tell us their percentages in the set of differently bracketed compounds. In order to study their properties, we need to look at the number of sub-compounds and compounds containing NNPs in the set of compounds where the three resources agree. As it turns out, 72% of the compounds containing proper nouns and 76% of the sub-compounds are bracketed similarly. Therefore when we exclude them from the bracketing subset we do not see a significant change in bracketing agreement among

	α–β	α–γ	β–γ	α–β–γ
NNP^h	80%	79%	88%	75%
NNP^0	78%	75%	90%	74%
NNP^h w/o sub	82%	82%	86%	75%
NNP^0 w/o sub	81%	77%	90%	74%

Table 3: Bracketing agreement – α: DeepBank; β: PCEDT; γ: VC-PTB; NNP^0: excl. proper nouns; NNP^h: incl. proper nouns; w/o sub: excl. sub-compounds

Compound	Functor	NomBank Arg
Negligence penalty	CAUS	ARG3
Death penalty	RSTR	ARG2
Staff lawyer	RSTR	ARG3
Government lawyer	APP	ARG2

Table 4: Example compounds with semantic relations

the three resources, as shown in the right-most column in Table 3.

We report pairwise bracketing agreement among the three resources in Table 3. We observe higher agreement level between PCEDT and VC-PTB than the other two pairs; we speculate that the annotation of the t-layer in PCEDT might have been influenced by the so-called phrase-structure layer (p-layer) which in turn uses VC-PTB annotation. Further, PCEDT and VC-PTB seem to disagree more on the bracketing of noun–noun compounds containing NNPs; because when proper nouns are excluded (NNP^0), the agreement level between PCEDT and VC-PTB increases, but it decreases for the other two pairs.

As we look closer at the compound instances where at least two of the three resources disagree, we find that some instances are easy to classify as annotation errors. For example, the compound *New York streets* is bracketed as right-branching in VC-PTB, but we can confidently say that this a left-bracketing compound. Not all bracketing disagreements are that easy to resolve though; one example where left- and right-bracketing can be accepted is *European Common Market approach*, which is bracketed as follows in DeepBank (1) and PCEDT and VC-PTB (2):

1. [[European [Common Market]] approach]
2. [European [[Common Market] approach]]

Even though this work does not aim to resolve or correct the bracketing disagreement between the three resources, we will publish a tool that allows resource creators to inspect the bracketing disagreement and possibly correct it.

5   Relations

Now that we have defined the set of compounds whose bracketing is agreed-upon in different resources, we move to adding semantic relations to our dataset. We rely on PCEDT and NomBank to define the semantic relations in our dataset, which includes bracketed compounds from § 4 as well as two-word compounds. However, unlike § 4, our set of noun–noun compounds in this section consists of the compounds that are bracketed similarly in PCEDT and VC-PTB and occur in both resources.[2] This set consists of 26,709 compounds and 14,405 types.

PCEDT assigns syntactico-semantic labels, so-called functors, to all the syntactic dependency relations in the tectogrammatical layer (a deep syntactic structure). Drawing on the valency theory of the Functional Generative Description, PCEDT defines 69 functors for verbs as well as nouns and adjectives (Cinková et al., 2006).[3] NomBank, on the other hand, is about nouns only; it assigns role labels (arguments) to common nouns in the PTB. In general, NomBank distinguishes between predicate arguments and modifiers (adjuncts) which correspond to those defined in PropBank (Kingsbury and Palmer, 2002).[4] We take both types of roles to be part of the semantic relations of noun–noun compounds in our dataset.

Table 4 shows some examples of noun–noun compounds annotated with PCEDT functors and NomBank arguments. The functor CAUS expresses causal relationship; RSTR is an underspecified adnominal functor that is used whenever the semantic requirements for other functors are not met; APP expresses appurtenance. While the PCEDT functors have specific definitions, most of the NomBank arguments have to be interpreted in connection with their predicate or frame. For ex-

---

[2] We do not use the intersection of the three resources as in § 4, because DeepBank does not contribute to the semantic relations of noun–noun compounds and it limits the size of our dataset (cf. § 4). Nonetheless, given our technical set-up we can readily produce the set of compounds that occur in the three resources and are bracketed similarly, and then extract their semantic relations from PCEDT and NomBank.

[3] The full inventory of functors is available on `https://ufal.mff.cuni.cz/pcedt2.0/en/functors.html` (visited on 22/04/2016).

[4] See Table 2 in Meyers (2007, p. 90) for an overview of adjunct roles in NomBank.

ample, ARG3 of the predicate *penalty* in Table 4 describes crime whereas ARG3 of the predicate *lawyer* describes rank. Similarly, ARG2 in *penalty* describes punishment, whereas ARG2 in *lawyer* describes beneficiary or consultant.

5.1 Data & Results

Given 26,709 noun–noun compounds, we construct a dataset with two relations per compound: a PCEDT functor and a NomBank argument. The resulting dataset is relatively large compared to the datasets in Table 1. However, the largest dataset in Table 1, by Tratz and Hovy (2010), is type-based and does not include proper nouns. The size of our dataset becomes 10,596 if we exclude the compounds containing proper nouns and only count the types in our dataset; this is still a relatively large dataset and it has the important advantage of including bracketing information of multi-word compounds, inter alia.

Overall, the compounds in our dataset are annotated with 35 functors and 20 NomBank arguments, but only twelve functors and nine Nom-Bank arguments occur more than 100 times in the dataset. Further, the most frequent NomBank argument (ARG1) accounts for 60% of the data, and the five most frequent arguments account for 95%. We see a similar pattern in the distribution of PCEDT functors, where 49% of the compounds are annotated with RSTR (the least specific adnominal functor in PCEDT). Further, the five most frequent functors account for 89% of the data (cf. Table 5). Such distribution of relations is not unexpected because according to Cinková et al. (2006), the relations that cannot be expressed by "semantically expressive" functors usually receive the functor PAT, which is the second most frequent functor. Furthermore, Kim and Baldwin (2008) report that 42% of the compounds in their dataset are annotated as TOPIC, which appears closely related to ARG1 in NomBank.

In theory, some of the PCEDT functors and NomBank arguments express the same type of relations. We therefore show the 'correlation' between PCEDT functors and NomBank arguments in Table 5. The first half of the table maps PCEDT functors to NomBank arguments, and the second half shows the mapping from Nom-Bank to PCEDT. Due to space limitations, the table only includes a subset of the relations— the most frequent ones. The underlined num-

bers in Table 5 indicate the functors and Nom-Bank arguments that are semantically comparable; for example, the temporal and locative functors (TWHEN, THL, TFRWH and LOC) intuitively correspond to the temporal and locative modifiers in NomBank (ARGM-TMP and ARGM-LOC), and this correspondence is also evident in the figures in Table 5. The same applies to the functor AUTH (authorship) which always maps to the NomBank argument ARG0 (agent). However, not all 'theoretical similarities' are necessarily reflected in practice, e.g. AIM vs. ARGM-PNC in Table 5 (both express purpose). NomBank and PCEDT are two different resources that were created with different annotation guidelines and by different annotators, and therefore we cannot expect perfect correspondence between PCEDT functors and NomBank arguments.

PCEDT often assigns more than one functor to different instances of the same compound. In fact, around 13% of the compound types were annotated with more than one functor in PCEDT, whereas only 1.3% of our compound types are annotated with more than one argument in Nom-Bank. For example, the compound *takeover bid*, which occurs 28 times in our dataset, is annotated with four different functors in PCEDT, including AIM and RSTR, whereas in NomBank it is always annotated as ARGM-PNC. This raises the question whether the semantics of noun–noun compounds varies depending on their context, i.e. token-based vs. type-based relations. Unfortunately we cannot answer this question based on the variation in PCEDT because its documentation clearly states that "[t]he annotators tried to interpret complex noun phrases with semantically expressive functors as much as they could. This annotation is, of course, very inconsistent."[5] Nonetheless, our dataset still opens the door to experimenting with learning PCEDT functors, and eventually determining whether the varied functors are mere inconsistencies or there is more to this than meets the eye.

6 Conclusion & Future Work

In this article we presented a new noun–noun compound dataset constructed from different linguistic resources, which includes bracketing information and semantic relations. In § 4, we explained

---

[5]https://ufal.mff.cuni.cz/pcedt2.0/en/ valency.html (visited on 22/04/2016).

P \ N	ARG1	ARG2	ARG0	ARG3	M-LOC	M-MNR	M-TMP	M-PNC	Count	Freq
RSTR	0.60	0.12	0.08	0.10	0.03	0.03	0.01	0.01	12992	48.64
PAT	0.89	0.05	0.01	0.03	0.01	0.01		0.01	3867	14.48
APP	0.42	0.37	0.17	0.01	0.03	0.00	0.00	0.00	3543	13.27
REG	0.75	0.09	0.07	0.07	0.00	0.01	0.00	0.00	2176	8.15
ACT	0.46	0.03	0.48	0.01	0.01	0.00			1286	4.81
LOC	0.16	0.20	0.09	0.01	0.54				979	3.67
TWHEN	0.12	0.04	0.00		0.01		0.81		367	1.37
AIM	0.65	0.12	0.06	0.08	0.00	0.00		0.05	284	1.06
ID	0.39	0.30	0.27	0.04	0.00				256	0.96
MAT	0.86	0.09	0.01	0.02					136	0.51
NE	0.32	0.46	0.13	0.02	0.06				132	0.49
ORIG	0.20	0.19	0.13	0.37	0.06	0.01		0.01	114	0.43
MANN	0.23	0.07	0.01		0.04	0.65			83	0.31
MEANS	0.45	0.09	0.04	0.12	0.14	0.11			56	0.21
EFF	0.60	0.18	0.11	0.04				0.04	55	0.21
AUTH			1.00						49	0.18
BEN	0.45	0.35	0.03	0.17					40	0.15
THL		0.03		0.03			0.95		38	0.14
	ARG1	ARG2	ARG0	ARG3	M-LOC	M-MNR	M-TMP	M-PNC		
RSTR	0.50	0.40	0.38	0.76	0.37	0.79	0.27	0.66		
PAT	0.22	0.05	0.02	0.06	0.02	0.07		0.13		
APP	0.09	0.34	0.22	0.02	0.09	0.00	0.01	0.01		
REG	0.10	0.05	0.05	0.08	0.01	0.02	0.01	0.07		
ACT	0.04	0.01	0.23	0.00	0.02	0.01				
LOC	0.01	0.05	0.03	0.00	0.47					
TWHEN	0.00	0.00	0.00		0.00		0.58			
AIM	0.01	0.01	0.01	0.01	0.00	0.00		0.09		
ID	0.01	0.02	0.03	0.01	0.00					
MAT	0.01	0.00	0.00	0.00						
NE	0.00	0.02	0.01	0.00	0.01					
ORIG	0.00	0.01	0.01	0.02	0.01	0.00		0.01		
MANN	0.00	0.00	0.00		0.00	0.10				
MEANS	0.00	0.00	0.00	0.00	0.01	0.01				
EFF	0.00	0.00	0.00	0.00				0.01		
AUTH			0.02							
BEN	0.00	0.00	0.00	0.00						
THL		0.00		0.00			0.07			
Count	15811	3779	2701	1767	1131	563	510	149		
Freq	59.20	14.15	10.11	6.62	4.23	2.11	1.91	0.56		

Table 5: Correlation between NomBank arguments and PCEDT functors

the construction of a set of bracketed multi-word noun–noun compounds from the PTB WSJ Corpus, based on the NP annotation by Vadas and Curran (2007), DeepBank and PCEDT. In § 5, we constructed a variant of the set in § 4 whereby each compound is assigned two semantic relations, a PCEDT functor and NomBank argument. Our dataset is the largest data set that includes both compound bracketing and semantic relations, and the second largest dataset in terms of the number of compound types excluding compounds that contain proper nouns.

Our dataset has been derived from different resources that are licensed by the Linguistic Data Consortium (LDC). Therefore, we are investigating the possibility of making our dataset publicly available in consultation with the LDC. Otherwise the dataset will be published through the LDC.

In follow-up work, we will enrich our dataset by mapping the compounds in our dataset to the datasets by Kim and Baldwin (2008) and Tratz and Hovy (2010); all of the compounds in the former and some of the compounds in the latter are extracted from the WSJ Corpus. Further, we will experiment with different classification and ranking approaches to bracketing and semantic interpretation of noun–noun compounds using different combinations of relations. We will also study the use of machine learning models to jointly bracket and interpret noun–noun compounds. Finally, we aim to study noun–noun compound identification, bracketing and interpretation in an integrated setup, by using syntactic parsers to solve the identification and bracketing tasks, and semantic parsers to solve the interpretation task.

Acknowledgments. The author wishes to thank Stephan Oepen and Erik Velldal for their helpful assistance and guidance, as well as Michael Roth and the three anonymous reviewers for thoughtful comments. The creation of the new dataset wouldn't have been possible without the efforts of the resource creators from which the dataset was derived.

References

Ken Barker and Stan Szpakowicz. 1998. Semi-Automatic Recognition of Noun Modifier Relationships. In *Proceedings of the 17th International Conference on Computational Linguistics and the 36th Meeting of the Association for Computational Linguistics*, page 96–102, Montreal, Quebec, Canada.

Lou Burnard. 2000. Reference guide for the British National Corpus version 1.0.

Silvie Cinková, Jan Hajič, Marie Mikulová, Lucie Mladová, Anja Nedolužko, Petr Pajas, Jarmila Panevová, Jiří Semecký, Jana Šindlerová, Josef Toman, Zdeňka Urešová, and Zdeněk Žabokrtský. 2006. Annotation of English on the tectogrammatical level: reference book. Technical report, Charles University, Prague. version 1.0.1.

Murhaf Fares, Stephan Oepen, and Erik Velldal. 2015. Identifying Compounds: On The Role of Syntax. In *International Workshop on Treebanks and Linguistic Theories)*, page 273–283, Warsaw, Poland.

Timothy Wilking Finin. 1980. *The Semantic Interpretation of Compound Nominals*. PhD thesis, University of Illinois at Urbana-Champaign.

Dan Flickinger, Yi Zhang, and Valia Kordoni. 2012. DeepBank. A dynamically annotated treebank of the Wall Street Journal. In *Proceedings of the 11th International Workshop on Treebanks and Linguistic Theories*, page 85–96, Lisbon, Portugal. Edições Colibri.

Roxana Girju, Dan Moldovan, Marta Tatu, and Daniel Antohe. 2005. On the semantics of noun compounds. *Computer Speech & Language*, 19(4):479–496.

Jan Hajič, Eva Hajičová, Jarmila Panevová, Petr Sgall, Ondřej Bojar, Silvie Cinková, Eva Fučíková, Marie Mikulová, Petr Pajas, Jan Popelka, Jiří Semecký, Jana Šindlerová, Jan Štěpánek, Josef Toman, Zdeňka Urešová, and Zdeněk Žabokrtský. 2012. Announcing Prague Czech-English Dependency Treebank 2.0. In *Proceedings of the 8th International Conference on Language Resources and Evaluation*, page 3153–3160, Istanbul, Turkey.

Su Nam Kim and Timothy Baldwin. 2008. Standardised Evaluation of English Noun Compound Interpretation. In *Proceedings of the LREC Workshop: Towards a Shared Task for Multiword Expressions*, page 39–42, Marrakech, Morocco.

Su Nam Kim and Timothy Baldwin. 2013. A lexical semantic approach to interpreting and bracketing English noun compounds. *Natural Language Engineering*, 19(03):385–407.

Paul Kingsbury and Martha Palmer. 2002. From TreeBank to PropBank. In *Proceedings of the 3rd International Conference on Language Resources and Evaluation*, page 1989–1993, Las Palmas, Spain.

Mark Lauer and Mark Dras. 1994. A probabilistic model of compound nouns. In *Proceedings of the 7th Australian Joint Conference on AI*, page 474–481, Armidale, Australia.

Mark Lauer. 1995. *Designing Statistical Language Learners. Experiments on Noun Compounds*. Doctoral dissertation, Macquarie University, Sydney, Australia.

Judith N Levi. 1978. *The syntax and semantics of complex nominals*. Academic Press.

Mitchell Marcus, Beatrice Santorini, and Mary Ann Marcinkiewicz. 1993. Building a large annotated corpora of English. The Penn Treebank. *Computational Linguistics*, 19:313–330.

Adam Meyers, Ruth Reeves, Catherine Macleod, Rachel Szekely, Veronika Zielinska, Brian Young, and Ralph Grishman. 2004. Annotating noun argument structure for NomBank. In *Proceedings of the 4th International Conference on Language Resources and Evaluation*, page 803–806, Lisbon, Portugal.

Adam Meyers. 2007. Annotation guidelines for NomBank-noun argument structure for PropBank. Technical report, New York University.

Preslav Ivanov Nakov. 2007. *Using the Web as an Implicit Training Set: Application to Noun Compound Syntax and Semantics*. Doctoral dissertation, EECS Department, University of California, Berkeley.

Vivi Nastase and Stan Szpakowicz. 2003. Exploring Noun-Modifier Semantic Relations. In *Fifth International Workshop on Computational Semantics*, page 285–301.

Diarmuid Ó Séaghdha and Ann Copestake. 2007. Co-occurrence Contexts for Noun Compound Interpretation. In *Proceedings of the Workshop on A Broader Perspective on Multiword Expressions*, page 57–64, Prague, Czech Republic. Association for Computational Linguistics.

Diarmuid Ó Séaghdha. 2008. Learning compound noun semantics. Technical Report UCAM-CL-TR-735, University of Cambridge, Computer Laboratory, Cambridge, UK.

Stephan Oepen, Marco Kuhlmann, Yusuke Miyao, Daniel Zeman, Silvie Cinková, Dan Flickinger, Jan Hajič, Angelina Ivanova, and Zdeňka Urešová. 2016. Towards Comparability of Linguistic Graph Banks for Semantic Parsing. In *Proceedings of the 10th International Conference on Language Resources and Evaluation (LREC)*, page 3991 – 3995, Portorož, Slovenia. European Language Resources Association.

Stephen Tratz and Eduard Hovy. 2010. A taxonomy, dataset, and classifier for automatic noun compound interpretation. In *Proceedings of the 48th Meeting of the Association for Computational Linguistics*, page 678 – 687, Uppsala, Sweden.

Stephen Tratz. 2011. *Semantically-enriched parsing for natural language understanding*. Doctoral dissertation, University of Southern California.

David Vadas and James Curran. 2007. Adding Noun Phrase Structure to the Penn Treebank. In *Proceedings of the 45th Meeting of the Association for Computational Linguistics*, page 240 – 247, Prague, Czech Republic.

Thesis Proposal:
An Investigation on The Effectiveness of Employing Topic Modeling Techniques to Provide Topic Awareness For Conversational Agents

Omid Moradiannasab
Saarland University
66123 Saarbrcken, Germany
`omidm@coli.uni-saarland.de`

Abstract

The idea behind this proposal is to investigate the possibility of utilizing NLP tools, statistical topic modeling techniques and freely available online resources to propose a system able to provide dialogue contribution suggestions which are relevant to the context, yet out of the main activity of the dialogue (i.e. *off-activity talk*). The aim is to evaluate the effects of a tool that automatically suggests *off-activity talk*s in form of some sentences relevant to the dialogue context. The evaluation is to be done over two test-sets of open domain and closed-domain in a conversational quiz-like setting. The outcome of this work will be a satisfactory point of entry to investigate the hypothesis that adding *automatically generated off-activity talks* feature to a conversational agent can lead to building up engagement of the dialogue partner(s).

1 Introduction

Conversational agents (e.g. virtual characters, chat-bots, etc) are software programs that interact with users employing natural language processing capabilities. The ability to interact with user in natural language enables such automated agents to make task-oriented dialogues with the aim to provide services to human in different fields such as education, entertainment, help desks, etc. *Traditional conversational systems* are designed for specific purposes, such as a banking service or navigating through a website. Dialogue in such systems is limited to *task-bound talks* (also called *activity talks*). These talks have a specific purpose and follow a particular structure. *Traditional conversational systems* are developed to attempt to engage the user in a natural, robust conversation in well-defined domains. However, empirical investigations reveal that the effect of these systems on engagement of the users with the system and their perception of the agent's intelligence is debatable (Dehn and Van Mulken, 2000). *Relational agents*, on the other hand, are defined in literature as "computational artifacts designed to establish and maintain long-term social-emotional relationships with their users" (Bickmore and Picard, 2005).

In order to achieve relational agents, certain amount of user's trust and engagement is required. Various conversational strategies are employed in *relational agents* that comprise models of social dialogues with the aim of raising user's trust. The conversational strategy targeted in this work is *off-activity talk*. An *off-activity talk* is a verbal reaction which is required to be contextually relevant to the content of the previous interaction and preferably includes a provision of some added-information. This verbal reaction can consist of one or more sentences and is extracted from the freely available online resources. The output of this work can be employed as a generator of relevant utterances embedded in an artificial agent (i.e. a virtual character or a robot). The sub-tasks addressed in this work are to analyze the dialogue context, to detect the topic, and to provide a ranked list of appropriate candidate utterances to be employed by the dialogue manager in a conversation system.

With the presented idea as a starting point, advantages or disadvantages of including automatically retrieved OATs in conversation systems can be studied. It is encouraging to investigate the effect of embedding such system on engagement of the users with a conversation system. It is also desirable to investigate whether automatically retrieved OATs can promote users' trust in knowl-

Proceedings of the 54th Annual Meeting of the Association for Computational Linguistics – Student Research Workshop, pages 80–85,
Berlin, Germany, August 7-12, 2016. ©2016 Association for Computational Linguistics

edgeability of the agent and their perception of the agent's intelligence.

2 Background

2.1 Small Talk

As an instance of a conversational strategy employment, *small talk* (also *social talk*) is discussed in literature. It is introduced as a kind of talk which executes conversational strategies. While interleaved between *task-bound talks*, *social talk* indirectly builds trust through the natural progression of a conversation. Bickmore and Cassell (2001) define *small talk* as "any talk in which interpersonal goals are emphasized and task goals are either non-existent or de-emphasized". According to their work, "One strategy for effecting changes to the familiarity dimension of the relationship model is for the speaker to disclose information about him/herself and induce the listener to do the same". Klüwer (2015) defines it as a talk "often perceived as unsophisticated chit-chat in which content exchange is irrelevant and negligible". Following this definition, *small talk* (e.g. about the weather, events and objects around, stories about the environment or the virtual character itself) represents the opposite of *task-bound talk* which aids the execution of a particular task. Thus, the range of topics and contents is definitely much more unrestricted in *small talk* than in *task-bound talk*. *Small talk* is useful to develop the conversation and to avoid pauses. It can be used to ease the situation and to make a user feel more comfortable in a conversation with an agent (Cassell and Bickmore, 2000). It is also introduced as a way of assuring certain amount of *closeness* to the user (e.g. before asking personal questions) (Bickmore and Cassell, 2001). *Small talk* is also helpful to avoid repetitiveness of conversations which is counted in literature as a negative impact factor to the users' motivation in interaction with the agent.

2.2 Off-Activity Talk (OAT)

Similar to *small talk*, *off-activity talk* (also called *non-activity talk*) is another technique to employ conversational strategies. Both *small talk* and *off-activity talk* enrich the task-oriented dialogue via opening the structure of the conversation. However, OAT can be differentiated from *small talk* by the topic and the purpose of the talk. OAT has a specific purpose (e.g. knowledge exchange) and is about a specific topic (see Table 1), while a *small talk* is an independent talk without any functional topic (e.g. talking about the weather). Several studies have found that the purpose of *small talk* is not to negotiate knowledge but to aid in management of social situation. On the other hand, *off-activity talk* is to disclose some information relevant to the dialogue context. Therefore, whenever no divergence from the subject matter of the *task-bound talk* is required, OAT is preferred to *small talk*. Even though OAT is a diversion from the structure of the task-dialogue, it maintains the dialogue topic.

Table 1: Some samples of a suitable OAT

Sub-dialogue(A+B) And Follow-up OAT(C)
A: What is the capital of Chechnya? B: Grozny C: Not long ago, Grozny, the capital of Chechnya, was called the most devastated city on Earth.
A: What is the capital of Chechnya? B: Grozny C: Chechnya Republic is a federal subject of the Russian Federation, part of North Caucasian District.
A: When was the Berlin Wall built? B: in 1961 C: Originally a barbed wire fence, the first concrete sections were built in 1965.
A: When was Elvis Presley's first record recorded? B: on July 5, 1954 C: On July 5 1954, Elvis Presley changed music world forever.
A: How many portions of fruit and vegetables should we try to eat? B: At least five a day C: Healthy diet means 10 portions of fruit and vegetables per day, not five.

OAT was first defined by Kruijff-Korbayova et al. (2014) in resemblance to *small talk*. In their work, the purpose of *activity talk* is knowledge exchange or knowledge probing while *off-activity talk* is used to break out of the fixed structure of task-bound dialogues. They use OAT in form of prerecorded questions around a set of predefined topics (e.g. hobbies, diabetes, eating habits, friends, diary, etc) to encourage the user to talk about those topics in order to elicit information from them. In this study, the focus is on *off-*

activity talk with a similar definition but a different employment. An OAT in the current work is a follow-up added information relevant to the context of the previous interaction with the aim of encouraging users' engagement and possibly promoting their trust in knowledgeability and intelligence of the agent, thus no deliberate direct information elicitation is targeted in this work.

3 Use Case Scenario

The idea of context determination and relevant off-activity talk suggestion for dialogue contribution, in a broad sense, can be used in any task-oriented dialogue setting. However, due to its predominantly verbal character and naturally constrained interaction structure, a conversational quiz-game setting is chosen as a good test bed for the current work. Some examples of dialogues in this setting, in addition to some sample OATs to be uttered by the agent right after this dialogue, are presented in Table 1. In this scenario, the agent asks the user a multiple-choice question from an open domain (A). After the user selects one of the choices (which can be correct or not) (B), the agent should give a verbal reaction (*off-activity talk*) (C). The follow-up needs to be related to the content of the previous interaction. It should be a piece of information on the main subject matter extracted from the available online resources and possibly, but not necessarily, confirm or give the correct answer. It can include a provision of some added information as a follow-up to the previous content.

4 Research Objectives

The goal of this project is to evaluate a tool which takes advantage of the Web as an online resource to seek for relevant sentence(s) to a given dialogue context. A quiz-game setting is used as the test bed for this project. The main benefit of such a tool will be to break out of the fixed structure of task-bound dialogues between an artificial agent and a human user, ideally leading to an increment in users' engagement. *Off-activity talk*s suggested by this tool can be employed in an online or offline mode. In the offline mode, OATs will be used to create (or enrich) a handcrafted knowledge base for a virtual character. However, offline enrichment might not be feasible in open domain scenarios. That is why the author puts the ultimate aim of this work to provide an open-domain solution for real-time OAT suggestion.

In the process of this study, following research questions are to be answered:

1. What are the features of a suitable off-activity talk?

2. Which of the proposed approaches is more effective in providing a high quality sentence selection?

3. How far can one reach by employing topic modeling techniques in the proposed tool?

4. To what extent using online resources can help with breaking out of the fixed structure of the task-bound dialogue?

5. Does providing OATs via sentence selection increase user satisfaction?

6. Does providing OATs via sentence selection boost user's trust in knowledgeability and intelligence of the agent?

7. Does providing OATs via sentence selection increase semantic cohesion of the dialogue?

5 Method

At large, the procedure is as follows. The first step is to identify topic-related *focus terms* of a dialogue. Using these *focus terms*, the second step is to determine the major topic to be followed up in the conversation. The topic labels after this step do not necessarily need to match the terms that occurred within the previous dialogue. In closed-domain solutions, this can be done by mapping the *focus terms* onto a category taxonomy. In such a case, the taxonomy is utilized as a reference point to derive topic labels for a follow-up conversation. On the other hand, for an open-domain problem the task is not as straightforward. The reason to that is the lack of predefined taxonomy. Topic modeling techniques are employed to determine the major topic of the conversation (see 5.1). Identified topic categories are subsequently combined with information retrieval and different linguistic filtering methods to improve candidate content retrieval. In the end, the retrieved content will be ranked based on their relevance to the context and properness for dialogue contribution.

5.1 Topic Modeling

Topic Modeling, as a branch of text mining, is the process of identifying patterns in the text in order to classify words into groups called "topics". A topic is defined as a probability distribution over the terms in the vocabulary. In this process, topics are assigned to documents and terms are assigned to topics each with specific probability distributions. There are different methods to achieve this goal: LDA, HDP, NNMF, etc.

6 Evaluation Strategy

The main goal of the experimental evaluation in this study is to assess the potential of the proposed system in contributing to a dialogue with two distinct partners: a questioner and an answerer. In this quiz-like setting, the output of the system is supposed to be an utterance by a conversational agent which follows the dialogue by elaborating on that and by providing relevant information in an appropriate way for a real-world dialogue contribution.

A dialogue system can be evaluated in various styles. The evaluation approach can be either subjective or objective (Walker et al., 1997). Evaluation metrics can be derived from questionnaires or log files (Paek, 2001). The scale of the metrics can vary from the utterance level to the whole dialogue (Danieli and Gerbino, 1995) (Kamm et al., 1999). The dialogue system can be treated as a "black box" or as a "transparent box" (Hone and Graham, 2000). This variety of styles beside lack of any agreed-upon standards in the research community and incompatibility of evaluation methods make evaluation of dialogue systems a challenge.

6.1 Embedded or Stand-alone Strategy?

An ideal strategy to test a tool, which automatically suggests *off-activity talks* for dialogue contribution, is embedding the developed component in a test-bed application and assessing the change in the usability of that application by carrying out a subjective evaluation of user satisfaction. However, it is not always easy to get access to such platforms and to perform the required embedding scheme. An alternative is to assess this application in a stand-alone scheme. There are some advantages to assessing with a stand-alone scheme instead of an embedded one. As an example, by employing a stand-alone scheme, one can avoid problems which might occur during the interaction with the embedding system. Such problems can influence the usability results while we have no control over them. Therefore, the stand-alone

strategy, in this case, brings the benefit to focus specifically on the quality of the OATs. The author recommends to observe the inputs and outputs of the system and while treating the system as a "black box", to measure the plausibility of the proposed approach. This also means that the measurement scale in the evaluation scheme is at utterance level, in contrast to dialogue level.

6.2 Subjective or Objective Evaluation?

As stated earlier, evaluation of a dialogue system can be done with an objective or subjective approach. In case of objective evaluation, metrics like resources used (e.g. time, turns, user attention, etc) or the number of errors the system makes or inappropriate utterances made by the system can be mentioned. In some cases, a number of specified definitions of task success is used as an objective metric. However, it is not always easy to define task success in an objective way. The subjective measurement of the acceptance of an application or technology belongs to the group of usability evaluation. Usability evaluation focuses on users and their needs. Through usability evaluation, we want to figure out if a system can be used for the specific purpose from the user's point of view, and if it allows the users to achieve their goals, meeting their expectations. The most important criterion for measuring usability is user's satisfaction. The author proposes to assess the usefulness of the suggested OATs from the tool by measuring user satisfaction with regard to a specific factor. That means, the evaluation strategy falls into the category of subjective evaluation.

Information about user satisfaction is usually gathered through interviews and questionnaires in the end of a session of interaction with a dialogue system. In principle, the goal of this work is not to establish a dialogue with the human, but to create a component to be integrated in a dialogue system and provide suggestions to the dialogue manager of such a system. That is why, it is not possible to evaluate user's satisfaction in the end of a dialogue session. Alternatively, we can ask participants to qualify the suggested OATs separately and regardless of any potential preceding or following dialogue. In other words, the experiment is not designed as a dialogue; instead, pairs of inputs and outputs of the system are presented to participants and they are asked to define which output is more satisfactory regarding some well-described aspects.

In contrast to objective evaluation techniques which are fairly well-established, subjective measurements are not as structured and straightforward. A difficulty which arises here is that dialogue systems and their users sometimes have inconsistent attitudes toward a dialogue. As a consequence, extra care needs to be taken to make sure that the participants of the experiments have a correct sense of what is needed to measure in a qualification process. Different factors must be defined with regard to which the quality of an OAT is to be measured. So, It is needed to provide accurate instructions to make sure the participant has comprehended the differences and is able to distinguish between these factors. The author also proposes to use some test questions as a means to make sure that the participants have read and clearly understood the instructions.

6.3 Evaluation Factors

In order to judge the usefulness of an OAT, it is needed to define the aspects of evaluation. The type of application determines the aspects that are important for a usability evaluation. To decide about the main aspect of the evaluation, the author largely relies upon SASSI methodology (Hone and Graham, 2000). SASSI is a methodology for evaluating spoken dialogue systems. They state that the previously reported subjective techniques are unproven. Also, It is argued that their content and structure are, for the most part, arbitrary and the items chosen for a questionnaire or rating scales are based neither on theory nor on well-conducted empirical research. The reasons for choosing a particular structure in the previous studies (e.g. questions, statements or numerical scales) and sub-structure (presentation, number of points on a scale, etc.) are not reported. Therefore, they use factor analysis to determine the main components of users' attitude and also define suitable rating scales for each of these components. Resultant factors after labeling are:

1. response accuracy

2. likability

3. cognitive demand

4. annoyance

5. habitability

6. speed

The first factor (response accuracy) does not fully match this application. The reason is that accuracy or the number of errors refer to the users' expectation of what the system is supposed to do in response to the input utterance. So, a specific goal like acting appropriately should be defined which is not necessarily the case with a free off-activity talk. The third group (Cognitive Demand) refers to the perceived amount of effort needed to interact with a dialogue system and the feelings resulting from this effort. Since in the current case the participant is not actually talking to the system but rating some contributions in a conversation, therefore it is not suitable to ask their opinion about how it will feel to talk to it or how much effort will be needed to say something easily comprehensible to the system. The fifth group (habitability) also refers to whether the user knows what to say to the system at each turn which is not useful as reasoned for the third group. The sixth factor (speed) is also not proper because the participants do not interact in real-time to the system and only rates some logged interactions. So, they do not know how fast the system works.

Among the factors mentioned in SASSI, likability and annoyance are applicable for the current experiment. In addition, questions of some other features are also important to us (e.g. naturalness, repetitiveness, etc). Altogether, the author proposes the items in Table 2. For each appropriateness judgment, this list of statements is disclosed to the participants and they are asked to check those which are true in their subjective opinion.

Table 2: Appropriateness judgment statements

Judgment Statement
This is a natural response.
Talking to a system with such a response is boring.
I would enjoy talking to a system which responds like this.
This talk is repetitive.
Such an utterance by a robot is frustrating.
The system knows how to speak to the human.
The follow-up provides relevant added-information.

References

Timothy Bickmore and Justine Cassell. 2001. Relational agents: a model and implementation of building user trust. In *Proceedings of the SIGCHI conference on Human factors in computing systems*, pages 396–403. ACM.

Timothy W Bickmore and Rosalind W Picard. 2005. Establishing and maintaining long-term human-computer relationships. *ACM Transactions on Computer-Human Interaction (TOCHI)*, 12(2):293–327.

Justine Cassell and Timothy Bickmore. 2000. External manifestations of trustworthiness in the interface. *Communications of the ACM*, 43(12):50–56.

Morena Danieli and Elisabetta Gerbino. 1995. Metrics for evaluating dialogue strategies in a spoken language system. In *Proceedings of the 1995 AAAI spring symposium on Empirical Methods in Discourse Interpretation and Generation*, volume 16, pages 34–39.

Doris M Dehn and Susanne Van Mulken. 2000. The impact of animated interface agents: a review of empirical research. *International journal of human-computer studies*, 52(1):1–22.

Kate S Hone and Robert Graham. 2000. Towards a tool for the subjective assessment of speech system interfaces (sassi). *Natural Language Engineering*, 6(3&4):287–303.

Candace Kamm, Marilyn A Walker, and Diane Litman. 1999. Evaluating spoken language systems. In *Proc. of AVIOS*. Citeseer.

Tina Klüwer. 2015. Social talk capabilities for dialogue systems.

Ivana Kruijff-Korbayova, Elettra Oleari, Ilaria Baroni, Bernd Kiefer, Mattia Coti Zelati, Clara Pozzi, and Alberto Sanna. 2014. Effects of off-activity talk in human-robot interaction with diabetic children. In *Robot and Human Interactive Communication, 2014 RO-MAN: The 23rd IEEE International Symposium on*, pages 649–654. IEEE.

Tim Paek. 2001. Empirical methods for evaluating dialog systems. In *Proceedings of the workshop on Evaluation for Language and Dialogue Systems-Volume 9*, page 2. Association for Computational Linguistics.

Marilyn A Walker, Diane J Litman, Candace A Kamm, and Alicia Abella. 1997. Paradise: A framework for evaluating spoken dialogue agents. In *Proceedings of the eighth conference on European chapter of the Association for Computational Linguistics*, pages 271–280. Association for Computational Linguistics.

Improving Dependency Parsing Using Sentence Clause Charts

Vincent Kríž and Barbora Hladká
Charles University
Faculty of Mathematics and Physics
Institute of Formal and Applied Linguistics
{kriz, hladka}@ufal.mff.cuni.cz

Abstract

We propose a method for improving the dependency parsing of complex sentences. This method assumes segmentation of input sentences into clauses and does not require to re-train a parser of one's choice. We represent a sentence clause structure using clause charts that provide a layer of embedding for each clause in the sentence. Then we formulate a parsing strategy as a two-stage process where (i) coordinated and subordinated clauses of the sentence are parsed separately with respect to the sentence clause chart and (ii) their dependency trees become subtrees of the final tree of the sentence. The object language is Czech and the parser used is a maximum spanning tree parser trained on the Prague Dependency Treebank. We have achieved an average 0.97% improvement in the unlabeled attachment score. Although the method has been designed for the dependency parsing of Czech, it is useful for other parsing techniques and languages.

1 Introduction

Syntactic parsing is an integral part of a complex text processing pipeline whose quality impacts the overall performance of the text processing system.

For illustration, we share our experience with a system focused on extracting semantic relations from unstructured texts. Namely, we have developed the RExtractor system,[1] which processes texts by linguistically-aware tools and extracts entities and relations using queries over dependency trees. The language used for testing RExtractor was Czech and the legal domain was chosen

to be explored in detail (Kríž et al., 2014; Kríž and Hladká, 2015). We evaluated RExtractor on the Czech Legal Text Treebank (CLTT) enriched with manually annotated entities and their relations (Kríž et al., 2016). Because of the lack of any Czech gold legal-domain treebank, we used a parser trained on newspaper texts to parse CLTT. The RExtractor system achieved precision of 80.6% and recall of 63.2% and we identified three sources of errors: (i) incorrect dependency tree (59.7%), (ii) missing or incorrectly formulated extraction query (38.3%), (iii) missing or incorrectly recognized entity (2.1%).

One can see that the errors are caused mainly by the insufficient quality of dependency parsing. The main reason why it happens is that newspaper texts differ from legal texts in several language phenomena influenced by the high frequency of very long sentences in legal texts. Figure 1 provides evidence of difficulty with dependency parsing long sentences – as the sentence length increases, the unlabeled attachment score decreases. The numbers are provided for two Czech dependency treebanks, namely the Prague Dependency Treebank with the development and evaluation test subsets[2] (PDT, dtest, etest, resp.) and the Czech Academic Corpus (CAC)[3], see Bejček et al. (2013) and Hladká et al. (2008), resp.

This paper describes our method how to use information about a sentence clause structure in full-scale dependency parsing. Section 2 lists a number of previous approaches to improve dependency parsing including selected works on parsing Czech. The data and tools used in our experiments are summarized in Section 3. We represent sentence clause structures using clause charts defined and quantitatively studied in Section 4. In

---

[1]The system is available on-line at
http://quest.ms.mff.cuni.cz:14280/

[2]https://ufal.mff.cuni.cz/pdt3.0
[3]https://ufal.mff.cuni.cz/cac

Proceedings of the 54th Annual Meeting of the Association for Computational Linguistics – Student Research Workshop, pages 86–92,
Berlin, Germany, August 7-12, 2016. ©2016 Association for Computational Linguistics

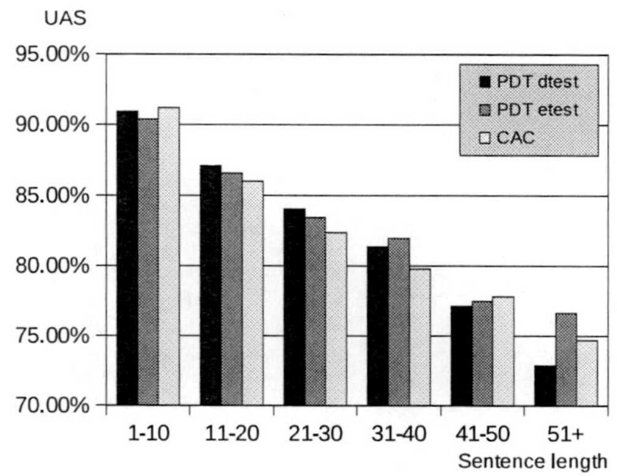

Figure 1: The longer the sentence the lower the unlabeled attachment score. The figures come from experiments run on the Prague Dependency Treebank and the Czech Academic Corpus.

Section 5, we propose an original strategy to parse pairs of coordinated and subordinated clauses and apply it on the data. Section 6 outlines our future plans towards better parsing long sentences.

2   Related Work

Several approaches which deal with the idea of dividing the parsing process into several parts were presented. The idea of cascaded parsing exploits a cascade of specialized parsers instead of having one very complex general parser (Abney, 1996; Ciravegna and Lavelli, 1999). The identification of chunks, syntactically related non-overlapping groups of words (Tjong Kim Sang and Buchholz, 2000), was used mainly in shallow parsing strategies (Federici et al., 1996). Clausal parsing was designed to parse Hindi texts (Husain et al., 2011).

However, there is no work on exploiting chunks for full-scale parsing. A very interesting approach dividing the parsing process into several parts has been introduced in the XDG theory (Debusmann et al., 2005). Most recent approaches to dependency parsing focus almost exclusively on improving full-scale parsing algorithms using mostly neural networks (Pei et al., 2015; Weiss et al., 2015; Zhu et al., 2015).

We address the issue of parsing sentences that are already segmented into clauses. The ideas and concepts of segmentation of Czech sentences are presented by Kuboň (2001), Kuboň et al. (2007), and Lopatková and Holan (2009). They present the concept of segments and show that it is possi-

ble to draw the segmentation charts which reflect the mutual position of segments in complex sentences without applying syntactic parsing of the whole sentence first. The method is based on the identification of separators (segment boundaries) and their classification.

Lopatková et al. (2012) show how clauses forming complex sentences can be identified based on the sentence segment annotation. In addition, they present the project aiming at building a collection of Czech sentences enriched with manually annotated clauses and their relationships. Krůza and Kuboň (2014) use this collection to develop an automatic procedure for recognizing clauses and their mutual relationship. Another automatic procedure for clause identification over dependency trees is introduced by Bejček et al. (2013) achieved F-measure 97.51% and was used for the clause annotation of the Prague Dependency Treebank.

3   Data and Tools

We experimented with two manually annotated dependency treebanks, namely the Prague Dependency Treebank 3.0 (PDT 3.0) and the Czech Academic Corpus 2.0 (CAC 2.0). Both corpora are enriched with the clause annotation done automatically using the procedure presented by Bejček et al. (2013).

Our goal is to beat the MST dependency parser (McDonald et al., 2005) trained on the PDT 3.0 train set. Table 1 presents basic characteristics of the two treebanks and the MST parser performance on them.

Treebank	Split	Sent.	Tokens	UAS
PDT 3.0	train	29,768	518,648	93.41
	dtest	4,042	70,974	84.50
	etest	4,672	80,923	84.32
CAC 2.0	–	24,709	493,306	82.68

Table 1: Part of the treebank (*Split*), the number of sentences (*Sent.*), the number of tokens (*Tokens*) and the unlabeled attachment score (*UAS*) of MST.

4   Clause Charts

A *clause chart* is defined to visualize relationships between clauses within the sentence and captures the layer of embedding of each individual clause. It is an $m \times n$ table where n is the number of clauses in the sentence and m is the number of layers. A cell (i, j) stands for relationship between the j-th clause and the i-th layer of embedding. Its value is initialized to the value of 0 corresponding to no relationship.

We defined four rules for changing the cell value from 0 to 1, i.e., for assigning a layer of embedding to each clause in the sentence: (1) All main clauses belong to the basic layer 0. (2) The clauses that depend on the clauses at the k-th layer belong to the $(k+1)$-th layer. (3) The coordinated clauses and the clauses in apposition belong to the same layer. (4) The clauses in parentheses belong to the $(k+1)$-th layer with respect to the k-th layer of their adjacent clauses.

Our definition is analogous to a segmentation chart defined by Lopatková and Holan (2009). However, we handle the following situations differently: (1) subordinating conjunctions at the beginning of each clause are considered as boundaries and are excluded from the clause; (2) clauses split into two parts by an embedded subordinated clause are considered as two different clauses.

4.1 Generating Clause Charts

We designed a simple procedure that generates a clause chart from a dependency tree with the clause annotation. Particularly, it generates a clause tree first and then a clause chart.

We assume a dependency tree where each non-boundary node has a special attribute bearing the identification of the clause it belongs to. The nodes with the same clause number belong to the same clause and thus generating a clause chart is uniquely determined by the clause identification. A layer of embedding of the clause is defined as its depth in a sentence clause tree where its nodes contain tokens with the same clause identification.

Figure 2 displays both the clause tree and the clause chart of the sample sentence presented in (Kuboň et al., 2007):

> **While** *failure is usually an orphan,*
> *the success tends to have many fathers,*
> *claiming eagerly **that** particularly they*
> *were present at its conception.*

This sentence consists of four clauses delimited by the boundaries printed in bold, namely *while*, *that*, and two commas. In general, clause boundaries are either a single token or a sequence of tokens. Clause boundaries are not components of the clause tree. They are displayed there for

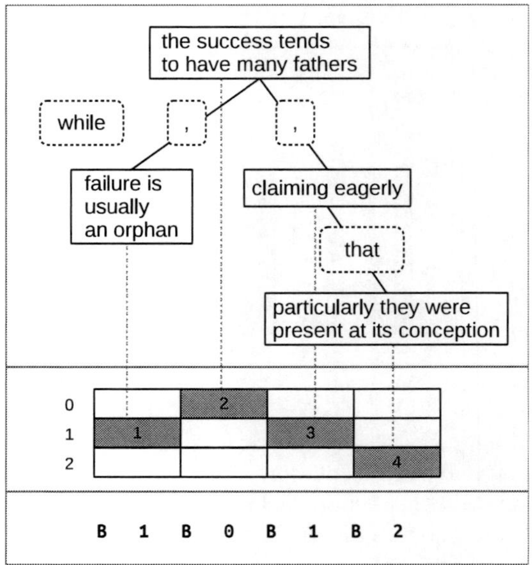

Figure 2: Clause tree (above), clause chart and its linear representation (below).

understanding a linear representation of a clause chart, see B1B0B1B2 where B stands for a clause boundary and the numbers are the layers of clause embedding.

4.2 Exploring Clause Charts

We explored PDT 3.0 and CAC 2.0 to study different types of clause charts. Table 2 provides statistics for the five most frequent clause charts that occur in the treebanks. For example, 14.4% of the sentences in PDT 3.0 and CAC 2.0 contain a main clause and a subordinated clause described with the 0B1 pattern. Moreover, we measure the MST parser performance on the sentences having the given clause charts. For example, MST achieved UAS of 92.9% on the 0B1B0 sentences in the PDT training data set.

The texts in the treebanks come from newspapers. Thus there is no surprise that the most frequent sentences in the treebanks are simple one clause sentences (0). They present more than half of the data. The second most frequent sentence structure consists of one main clause and one subordinated clause (0B1). It is quite surprising that the parser processes these sentences better than the one clause sentences. Even more, we observe decrease in the parser performance on coordination of two main clauses (i.e., on the 0B0 sentence).

For curiosity's sake, the most complex sentence

in the treebanks consists of 36 clauses and the `OB1B2B3B4B5B6` clause chart is a chart with the highest number of layers of embedding.

	O	OB1	OB0	OB1B0	OB1B2
Rel. freq.	50.1	14.5	8.0	3.6	2.5
PDT train	93.6	95.8	92.9	92.9	95.9
PDT dtest	85.7	88.2	82.3	81.7	90.0
PDT etest	85.4	88.0	83.4	82.0	88.1
CAC 2.0	84.1	85.7	81.0	79.7	87.3

Table 2: Relative frequency of the five most frequent clause charts in PDT 3.0 and CAC 2.0 (*Rel. freq.*) and the unlabeled attachment score of MST evaluated on the particular subsets PDT train, PDT dtest, PDT etest, CAC 2.0.

5 Methods and Experiments

We present a method for improving dependency parsing of long sentences. In particular, we formulate an algorithm for parsing the two most frequent clause structures, namely coordinated clauses `OB0` and governing and dependent clauses `OB1`. The other types of clause structures are processed as usual using full-scale parsing. The experiments exploit an existing dependency parser trained on complete sentences, namely the MST parser – see Section 3 for details.

5.1 Parsing Coordinated Clauses

Given the clause chart representation, we can recognize coordinated clauses in sentences in a straightforward way. Thus, we consider neighboring coordinated clauses $C_1, C_2, \ldots, C_n$ on the same layer ($n > 1$) and we propose the following parsing strategy that we call *clause chart parsing* (CCP):

1. Using MST parse $C_1, C_2, \ldots, C_n$ individually to get dependency trees $T_1, T_2, \ldots, T_n$ with the $r_1, r_2, \ldots, r_n$ root nodes, respectively.

2. Create a sequence $S = r_1 \, B_{1,2} \, r_2 \, B_{2,3} \ldots r_n$ where $B_{i,i+1}$ is a boundary between C_i and C_{i+1}.

3. Using MST parse the sequence S to get a dependency tree T_S.

4. Build a final dependency tree so that the trees $T_1, \ldots, T_n$ become subtree of T_S.

For illustration, we assume the sentence *John loves Mary and Linda hates Peter*. The sentence consists of two coordinated clauses $C_1 = \{John loves Mary\}$, $C_2 = \{Linda hates Peter\}$ and one clause boundary $B_{1,2} = \{and\}$. Therefore, the clause chart of the sentence is `OB0`. In Step 1, C_1 and C_2 are parsed to get T_1 and T_2 with the root nodes $r_1 = loves$ and $r_2 = hates$, resp. In Step 2, the sequence $S = loves$ *and* $hates$ is created. In Step 3, S is parsed to get T_S and, finally, in Step 4, T_1 and T_2 become subtrees of T_S.

We evaluated the proposed parsing strategy only on the sentences having the `OB0` clause chart, i.e., on the subsets of the treebank datasets. Table 3 presents the unlabeled attachment score achieved for

- full-scale parsing, i.e., parsing complete sentences using MST (*FS*)

- parsing individual clauses instead of parsing complete sentences, i.e., MST performance is measured on individual clauses (*Clauses*)

- full-scale parsing using the *CCP* strategy

We observe that parsing performance measured on complete sentences is the highest when parsing individual clauses. Using the CCP method we achieved an average 1.36% improvement in UAS.

Data	Sent.	FS	Clauses	CCP
PDT dtest	319	82.28	86.87	84.80
PDT etest	352	83.43	87.16	84.67
CAC 2.0	2,272	80.96	84.69	82.34

Table 3: Parsing evaluation on the `OB0` sentences of three different parsing strategies: full-scale parsing (*FS*) using MST, parsing individual clauses (*Clauses*), and full-scale parsing using CCP (*CCP*).

5.2 Parsing governing and dependent clauses

Table 4 presents the unlabeled attachment score achieved for full-scale parsing and parsing individual clauses.

We observe almost no improvement when parsing individual clauses. Also, we observe that the parser performance on the `OB1` sentences is significantly higher than the parser performance on the

Data	Sent.	FS	Clauses
PDT dtest	604	88.24	88.23
PDT etest	704	87.98	88.64
CAC 2.0	3,669	85.68	85.76

Table 4: Parsing evaluation on the OB1 sentences.

whole datasets, compare the *FS* column in Table 4 and the *UAS* column in Table 1.

Given this observation, we proposed the following strategy for parsing subordinated clauses and we updated the *CCP* method as follows:

1. Find the longest sequence of neighboring subordinated clauses C_1, C_2, ..., C_n so that $layer(C_{i+1}) = layer(C_i) + 1$ where $layer$ stands for a layer of embedding in a clause chart.

2. Create a sequence $S = C_1 B_{1,2} C_2 B_{2,3} \ldots C_n$ where $B_{i,i+1}$ is a boundary between C_i and C_{i+1}.

3. Using MST parse sequence S to get a dependency tree T_S.

Using the CCP strategy for parsing the OB0 and OB1 sentences, we can parse the OB1B0 sentences so that we apply the CCP strategy for subordinated clauses first and subsequently for coordinated clauses. Table 5 presents the comparison of full-scale parsing and CCP.

Data	Sent.	FS	CCP
PDT dtest	166	81.72	82.98
PDT etest	160	81.98	84.22
CAC 2.0	885	79.68	80.84

Table 5: Parsing evaluation on the OB1B0 sentences.

5.3 CCP as Full-scale Parsing

We have learned from the experiments that

1. it is efficient to parse coordinated clauses individually and connect their trees subsequently;

2. it is effective to parse a sequence of governing and dependent clauses at once.

Therefore we proposed and evaluated a final algorithm for dependency parsing that exploits sentence clause charts and a given dependency parser. The algorithm works in iterations. In each iteration, at least one layer of embedding in the clause chart is eliminated using the CCP strategy for OB0 and OB1 clauses.

Table 6 and Table 7 present the final comparison of full-scale parsing and the CCP strategy. The figures in Table 6 exclude simple sentences (one-clause sentences) from evaluation. We achieved an average 0.97% improvement in UAS when parsing all the sentences in the treebanks.

Data	Sent.	FS	CCP
PDT dtest	2,044	83.93	84.72
PDT etest	2,339	83.84	84.64
CAC 2.0	12,756	81.99	83.42

Table 6: Parsing evaluation on the sentences containing at least two clauses.

Data	Sent.	FS	CCP
PDT dtest	4,042	84.50	85.03
PDT etest	4,672	84.32	84.87
CAC 2.0	24,709	82.68	83.64

Table 7: Final comparison of full-scale parsing and CCP.

6 Future Work

Our motivation to address the task of parsing of long sentences arises from a project of extracting entities and relations from legal texts. We plan to apply the CCP strategy on the Czech Legal Text Treebank that contains significantly large number of long sentences than PDT 3.0. Consequently, we will do an eccentric evaluation of the RExtractor system to see whether better parsing results influence the extraction.

A sentence clause structure used in our experiments was generated automatically. However, the used procedure requires gold standard dependency trees on the input. We plan to develop an automatic procedure for obtaining the clause charts. This procedure will not require gold standard dependency trees on the input. Some experiments have been already done by Krůza and Kuboň (2009). In addition, we see several different approaches which could be implemented and evaluated.

In the presented experiments, we used the parser trained on complete sentences. However, the CCP strategy parses individual clauses in some situations. We believe that training a new model especially for clauses will bring a significant improvement. Another model could be trained for parsing sequences defined in Step 3 of proposed algorithm from Section 5.1.

Our parsing strategy is formulated to be language independent. The English part of the Czech-English Prague Dependency Treebank contains the entire Penn Treebank that is enhanced with segmentation of sentences into clauses.[4] We plan to apply the CCP strategy on this dataset.

7 Conclusion

In our pilot experiments, we showed that sentence clause charts improve dependency parsing of long sentences. We proposed a method that assumes segmentation of input sentences into clauses. Having such annotation at hand, we represent sentence clause structure using a clause chart that provides a layer of embedding for each clause in the sentence.

Our parsing strategy does not need to re-train a parser of one's choice. Instead of that, we separately parse coordinated and subordinated clauses with respect to the sentence clause chart and then connect their dependency trees.

The object language of our experiments is Czech and the parser used is a maximum spanning tree parser trained on the Prague Dependency Treebank. We achieved an average 0.97% improvement in the unlabeled attachment score.

Acknowledgments

We gratefully acknowledge support from the SVV project No. SVV 260 333 and from the LINDAT/CLARIN Research Infrastructure project of the Ministry of Education, Youth and Sports of the Czech Republic No. LM2015071. This work has also been using language resources developed and distributed by the LINDAT/CLARIN project. We thank three anonymous reviewers for their useful comments and remarks and we truly appreciate suggestions provided by Kemal Oflazer.

---

[4]`http://ufal.mff.cuni.cz/pcedt2.0/en/`

References

Steven Abney. 1996. Partial Parsing via Finite-State Cascades. *Natural Language Engineering*, 2(04):337–344.

Eduard Bejček, Eva Hajičová, Jan Hajič, Pavlína Jínová, Václava Kettnerová, Veronika Kolářová, Marie Mikulová, Jiří Mírovský, Anna Nedoluzhko, Jarmila Panevová, Lucie Poláková, Magda Ševčíková, Jan Štěpánek, and Šárka Zikánová. 2013. Prague Dependency Treebank 3.0. `http://ufal.mff.cuni.cz/pdt3.0`.

Fabio Ciravegna and Alberto Lavelli. 1999. Full Text Parsing Using Cascades of Rules: An Information Extraction Perspective. In *Proceedings of the Ninth Conference on European Chapter of the Association for Computational Linguistics*, EACL '99, pages 102–109, Stroudsburg, PA, USA. Association for Computational Linguistics.

Ralph Debusmann, Denys Duchier, and Andreas Rossberg. 2005. Modular Grammar Design with Typed Parametric Principles. *Proceedings of FG-MOL 2005*.

Stefano Federici, Simonetta Montemagni, and Vito Pirrelli. 1996. Shallow Parsing and Text Chunking: a View on Underspecification in Syntax. *Cognitive Science Research Paper - University of Sussex CSRP*, pages 35–44.

Barbora Vidová Hladká, Jan Hajič, Jiří Hana, Jaroslava Hlaváčová, Jiří Mírovský, and Jan Raab. 2008. The Czech Academic Corpus 2.0 Guide. *The Prague Bulletin of Mathematical Linguistics*, (89):41–96.

Samar Husain, Phani Gadde, Joakim Nivre, and Rajeev Sangal. 2011. Clausal parsing helps data-driven dependency parsing: Experiments with Hindi. In *PProceedings of the 5th International Joint Conference on Natural Language Processing*, page 1279–1287, Chiang Mai, Thailand.

Vincent Kríž and Barbora Hladká. 2015. RExtractor: a Robust Information Extractor. In Matt Gerber, Catherine Havasi, and Finley Lacatusu, editors, *Proceedings of the 2015 Conference of the North American Chapter of the Association for Computational Linguistics: Demonstrations*, pages 21–25, Denver, CO, USA. Association for Computational Linguistics.

Vincent Kríž, Barbora Hladká, Martin Nečaský, and Tomáš Knap. 2014. Data Extraction Using NLP Techniques and Its Transformation to Linked Data. In *Human-Inspired Computing and Its Applications - 13th Mexican International Conference on Artificial Intelligence, MICAI 2014, Tuxtla Gutiérrez, Mexico, November 16-22, 2014. Proceedings, Part I*, pages 113–124.

Oldřich Krůza and Vladislav Kuboň. 2009. Automatic Extraction of Clause Relationships from a

Treebank. In Alexander Gelbukh, editor, *Computational Linguistics and Intelligent Text Processing. 10th International Conference, CICLing 2009, Mexico City, Mexico, March 1-7, 2009, Proceedings*, volume 5449 of *Lecture Notes in Computer Science*, pages 195–206, Berlin / Heidelberg. Springer.

Oldřich Krůza and Vladislav Kuboň. 2014. Automatic Recognition of Clauses. *International Journal of Computational Linguistics and Applications*, 5(1):125–138.

Vincent Kríž, Barbora Hladká, and Zdeňka Urešová. 2016. Czech Legal Text Treebank 1.0. In Nicoletta Calzolari (Conference Chair), Khalid Choukri, Thierry Declerck, Marko Grobelnik, Bente Maegaard, Joseph Mariani, Asuncion Moreno, Jan Odijk, and Stelios Piperidis, editors, *Proceedings of the Tenth International Conference on Language Resources and Evaluation (LREC 2016)*, Paris, France, may. European Language Resources Association (ELRA).

Vladislav Kuboň, Markéta Lopatková, Martin Plátek, and Patrice Pognan. 2007. A Linguistically-Based Segmentation of Complex Sentences. In David Wilson and Geoffrey Sutcliffe, editors, *Proceedings of FLAIRS 2007 (20th International Florida Artificial Intelligence Research Society Conference)*, pages 368–373, Key West, FL, USA. AAAI Press.

Vladislav Kuboň. 2001. *Problems of Robust Parsing of Czech*. Ph.D. thesis, Faculty of Mathematics and Physics, Charles University in Prague, Prague, Czech Republic.

Markéta Lopatková and Tomáš Holan. 2009. Segmentation Charts for Czech – Relations among Segments in Complex Sentences. In Adrian Dediu, Armand Ionescu, and Carlos Martín-Vide, editors, *Language and Automata Theory and Applications. Third International Conference, LATA 2009, Tarragona, Spain, April 2-8, 2009. Proceedings*, volume 5457 of *Lecture Notes in Computer Science*, pages 542–553, Berlin / Heidelberg. Universitat Rovira i Virgili, Springer.

Markéta Lopatková, Petr Homola, and Natalia Klyueva. 2012. Annotation of Sentence Structure: Capturing the Relationship between Clauses in Czech Sentences. *Language Resources and Evaluation*, 46(1):25–36.

Ryan McDonald, Fernando Pereira, Kiril Ribarov, and Jan Hajič. 2005. Non-Projective Dependency Parsing using Spanning Tree Algorithms. In *Proceedings of Human Language Technology Conference and Conference on Empirical Methods in Natural Language Processing*, pages 523–530, Vancouver, BC, Canada. Association for Computational Linguistics.

Wenzhe Pei, Tao Ge, and Baobao Chang. 2015. An Effective Neural Network Model for Graph-based Dependency Parsing. In *Proceedings of the 53rd Annual Meeting of the Association for Computational Linguistics and the 7th International Joint Conference on Natural Language Processing (Volume 1: Long Papers)*, pages 313–322, Beijing, China, July. Association for Computational Linguistics.

Erik F. Tjong Kim Sang and Sabine Buchholz. 2000. Introduction to the CoNLL-2000 Shared Task: Chunking. In *Proceedings of the 2nd Workshop on Learning Language in Logic and the 4th Conference on Computational Natural Language Learning - Volume 7*, CoNLL'00, pages 127–132, Stroudsburg, PA, USA. Association for Computational Linguistics.

David Weiss, Chris Alberti, Michael Collins, and Slav Petrov. 2015. Structured Training for Neural Network Transition-Based Parsing. In *Proceedings of the 53rd Annual Meeting of the Association for Computational Linguistics and the 7th International Joint Conference on Natural Language Processing (Volume 1: Long Papers)*, pages 323–333, Beijing, China, July. Association for Computational Linguistics.

Chenxi Zhu, Xipeng Qiu, Xinchi Chen, and Xuanjing Huang. 2015. A Re-ranking Model for Dependency Parser with Recursive Convolutional Neural Network. In *Proceedings of the 53rd Annual Meeting of the Association for Computational Linguistics and the 7th International Joint Conference on Natural Language Processing (Volume 1: Long Papers)*, pages 1159–1168, Beijing, China, July. Association for Computational Linguistics.

Graph- and surface-level sentence chunking

Ewa Muszyńska
Computer Laboratory
University of Cambridge
`emm68@cam.ac.uk`

Abstract

The computing cost of many NLP tasks increases faster than linearly with the length of the representation of a sentence. For parsing the representation is tokens, while for operations on syntax and semantics it will be more complex. In this paper we propose a new task of *sentence chunking*: splitting sentence representations into coherent substructures. Its aim is to make further processing of long sentences more tractable. We investigate this idea experimentally using the Dependency Minimal Recursion Semantics (DMRS) representation.

1 Introduction

Long sentences pose a challenge in many Natural Language Processing (NLP) tasks, such as parsing or translation. We propose chunking as a way of making such sentences more tractable before further processing. Chunking a sentence means cutting a complex sentence into grammatical constituents that can be processed independently and then recombined without loss of information. Such an operation can be defined both on the surface string of a sentence and on its semantic representation, and is applicable to a wide range of tasks.

Some approaches to parsing have space and time requirements which are much worse than linear in sentence length. This can lead to practical difficulties in processing. For example, the ACE processor[1] running the English Resource Grammar (ERG) (Copestake and Flickinger, 2000) requires roughly 530 MB of RAM to parse Sentence 1. In fact, longer and more complicated sen-

---

[1] Woodley Packard's Answer Constraint Engine, `http://sweaglesw.org/linguistics/ace/`

tences can cause the parser to time out or run out of memory before a solution is found.

(1) Marcellina has hired Bartolo as her counsel, since Figaro had once promised to marry her if he should default on a loan she had made to him, and she intends to enforce that promise.

Chunking would make processing of long sentences more tractable. For example, we aim to split sentences like Sentence 1 into chunks 2a–d.

(2) a. Marcellina has hired Bartolo as her counsel.

b. Figaro had once promised to marry her.

c. He should default on a loan she made to him.

d. She intends to enforce that promise.

Each of these shorter sentences can be parsed with less than 20 MB, requiring in total less than a fifth of RAM needed to parse the full sentence.

What exactly constitutes a valid chunk has to be considered in the context of the task which we want to simplify by chunking. In this sense a potentially useful analogy could be made to the use of factoids in summarisation (Teufel and Van Halteren, 2004; Nenkova et al., 2007). However, we can make some general assumptions about the nature of 'good' chunks. They have to be semantically and grammatically self-contained parts of the larger sentence.

Sentence chunking resembles clause splitting as defined by the CoNLL-2001 shared task (Tjong et al., 2001). Each of the chunks a–d is a finite clause, although each consists of multiple smaller clauses. This points to a crucial difference between sentence chunking and clause splitting which justifies treating them as separate tasks.

Proceedings of the 54th Annual Meeting of the Association for Computational Linguistics – Student Research Workshop, pages 93–99,
Berlin, Germany, August 7-12, 2016. ©2016 Association for Computational Linguistics

We define chunking in terms of its purpose as a pre-processing step and because of that it is more restrictive. Not every clause boundary is a chunk boundary. A key aspect of sentence chunking is deciding where to place a chunk border so that the resulting chunks can be processed and recombined without loss of information.

Another difference between sentence chunking and clause splitting is the domain of the task. Clause splitting is performed on the surface string of a sentence, while we can define chunking not only on the surface representation but also on more complex ones, such a graph-based semantic representation.

There are two reasons why chunking a semantic representation is a good idea:

1. Many operations on graphs have worse than linear complexity, some types of graph matching are NP-complete. Chunking semantic representations can make their manipulation more tractable (Section 1.1).

2. Such a form of chunking, apart from being useful in its own right, can also help chunking surface sentences (Section 1.2).

1.1 Chunking semantic representations

In this paper we describe an approach to sentence chunking based on Dependency Minimal Recursion Semantics (DMRS) graphs (Copestake, 2009). We chunk a sentence by dividing its semantic representation into subgraphs corresponding to logical chunks. The link structure of a DMRS graph reveals appropriate chunk boundaries. Since we envision chunking to be one of the steps in a processing pipeline, we prioritize precision over coverage to minimize error propagation. The goal is to chunk fewer sentences but correctly rather than more but with low precision.

Sentence chunking understood as graph chunking of a semantic representation can be directly useful for applications that already use the representation. Although we use the DMRS, chunking could be just as well adapted for other semantic representations, for example AMR (Abstract Meaning Representation) (Banarescu et al., 2013). Part of our reason to choose the DMRS framework was the fact that the DMRS format is readily interchangeable with Minimal Recursion Semantics (MRS). Thanks to this relationship our system is compatible with any applications stemming from the DELPH-IN initiative[2].

Horvat et al. (2015) introduce a statistical approach to realization, in which they treat realization like a translation problem. As part of their approach, they extract grammatical rules based on DMRS subgraphs. Since operations on subgraphs are computationally expensive, chunking the sentence before the algorithm is applied could reduce the complexity of the task.

Another task which could benefit from chunking is treebanking. LinGO Redwoods 2 (Oepen et al., 2004) is an initiative aimed at designing and developing a treebank which supports the HPSG grammar. The treebank relies on discriminants to differentiate and choose between possible parses. Chunking could be used to preferentially select parses which contain subtrees corresponding to well-formed chunk subgraphs.

1.2 Towards string chunking

The DMRS-based rule approach cannot be itself used to improve parsing because it requires a full parse to find the chunks in the first place. However, development of the surface chunking machine learning algorithm can extend applicability of chunking to parsing and other tasks for which a deep parse is unavailable.

The alignment between the semantic and surface representations of a sentence allows us to cut the sentence string into surface chunks. We intend to use the rule-based approach to create training data for a minimally supervised machine learning algorithm.

Following Rei (2013, pp. 11-12) we use the term 'minimally supervised' to mean a system trained using "domain-specific resources, other than annotated training data, which could be produced by a domain-expert in a relatively short time". In our case the resource is a small set of manually coded rules developed through examination of data.

The ultimate goal of our work is the creation of a reliable tool which performs chunking of sentence strings without relying on semantic representation and deep parsing. The applicability of chunking would then extend to tasks which cannot rely on deep parsing, such as statistical machine translation or parsing itself.

The next sections give more details on the

<hr>

[2]Deep Linguistic Processing with HPSG, www.delph-in.net

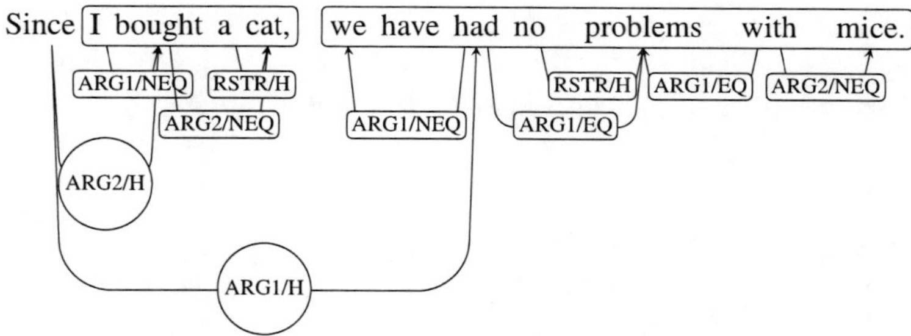

Figure 1: A DMRS graph of a sentence *Since I bought a cat, we have had no problems with mice*. The two chunks are marked, while *since* is separated as a functional chunk and chunking trigger. The links with circular labels are crucial for chunking.

DELPH-IN framework, DMRS and our approach to rule-based chunking. We present our preliminary results in Section 4 and outline our current investigation focus and future research directions in Sections 5. Chunking is a new task, however it is related to several existing ones as discussed in Section 6.

2 DELPH-IN framework and DMRS

The rule-based chunking system we developed is based on the English Resource Grammar (ERG) (Flickinger, 2000), a broad-coverage, symbolic grammar of English. It was developed as part of DELPH-IN initiative and LinGO[3] project. The ERG uses Minimal Recursion Semantics (MRS) (Copestake et al., 2005) as its semantic representation. The MRS format can be transformed into a more readable Dependency Minimal Recursion Semantics (DMRS) graph (Copestake, 2009), which represents its dependency structure. The nodes correspond to predicates; edges, referred to as links, represent relations between them. An example of a DMRS graph is shown in Figure 1.

DMRS graphs can be manipulated using two existing Python libraries. The `pyDelphin`[4] is a more general MRS-dedicated library. It allows conversions between MRS and DMRS representations but internally performs operations on MRS objects. The `pydmrs` library[5] (Copestake et al., 2016) is dedicated solely to DMRS manipulations. The work described in Section 4 used `pyDelphin`.

The ERG is a bidirectional grammar which supports both parsing and generation. There exist several processors, which parse sentences into MRSs and generate surface forms from MRS representations using chart generation. In our experiments we use ACE[6] to obtain MRSs and to generate from them, so that parsing and generation themselves are performed using already existing DELPH-IN tools. The chunking algorithm operates on graphs – we use the `pyDelphin` and `pydmrs` libraries for MRS-DMRS conversion and for manipulating DMRS objects.

3 DMRS-based chunking

In our research so far we have restricted valid chunks to finite clauses. A sentence is chunked correctly if all the chunks are either full finite clauses with a subject-verb structure or functional trigger chunks, such as *since* or *and*. A chunk can consist of multiple clauses if it is needed to ensure that all chunks are satisfactory.

The finite clause restriction was introduced because well-formedness of finite clauses can be easily checked and they can be more readily processed independently and recombined than other types of clauses.

We developed the chunking rules through examination of data and finding structural patterns in DMRS graphs. Currently chunking is based on three grammatical constructions: clausal coordination (3), suboordinating conjunctions (4ab) and clausal complements (5).

(3)   The cat chased a toy and the dog slept under the table.

[3]Linguistic Grammars Online, `lingo.stanford.edu`

[4]`https://github.com/delph-in/pydelphin`
[5]`https://github.com/delph-in/pydmrs`

[6]Woodley Packard's Answer Constraint Engine, `http://sweaglesw.org/linguistics/ace/`

(4) a. The cat chased a toy because it was
         bored.

     b. Since the dog slept, Kim didn't offer it
         a snack.

(5) Kim thought that they should talk.

Extending the coverage of the technique to other
structures is one of future directions of investigation.

We discover potential chunking points by spot-
ting trigger nodes. Those are the nodes which
correspond to coordinating and subordinating conjunctions, and to verbs with clausal complements.
In the example from Figure 1 *since* is a trigger.

After a trigger is found, we check whether the
clauses associated with it are finite. We can do
that by following links outgoing from the trigger node which lead to heads of the clauses. We
marked these links in the figure with circular labels. In symmetric constructions, such as coordination, chunks are separated unambiguously by a
conjunction. In other cases, such as the one in the
example, we can find the chunk border by detecting a gap in the graph's link structure. No links
outgoing from either of the main chunks span the
gap between *cat* and *we* in Figure 1.

4 Preliminary results

So far we evaluated the system using a parsing and
regeneration procedure, leveraging bidirectional-
ity of the ERG. The surface of each sentence was
chunked into substrings based on its semantic representation. Each of the resulting surface chunks
was then parsed using the ACE. Next we fed the
top parse for each chunk as input to the ACE generator, which produced the surface matching the
semantic representation of the chunk. Finally, we
recombined the surfaces generated in this fashion
and compared the results with the original sentence.

The parsing and regeneration is a way of check-
ing whether any information loss was caused by
chunking. We do not attempt to improve parsing, only to evaluate how well the chunks meet
the criteria of well-formedness and applicability
we posit. At the same time this form of evaluation assesses the semantic representation chunking only indirectly, focusing on the quality of produced surface chunks. This is desirable in for creating a good quality dataset for the minimally supervised machine learning algorithm discussed in
Section 1.2.

As our dataset, we used the 1212 release of the
WikiWoods corpus (Flickinger et al., 2010) which
is a snapshot of Wikipedia from July 2008. The
entire corpus contains 44,031,336 entries, from
which we selected only long sentences, viz. sentences with more than 40 nodes in their DMRS
graph. Additionally we filtered out some non-
sentential entries.

We compared the results obtained using the
DMRS-based system with a simple string-based
heuristic baseline, similar to one of the techniques
used currently in statistical machine translation
community[7]. The baseline attempts to chunk 67%
of long sentences it encounters, compared with
25% attempted by the DMRS-based approach. As
a result, the absolute number of sentences the
baseline chunks correctly is greater but low precision makes the heuristic approach highly unreliable. Any application which used it would require
a lot of human supervision. The DMRS-based
procedure correctly chunks 42.0% of sentences in
which it finds chunking opportunities, while baseline correctly chunks only 19.6% of sentences.

The evaluation method with which we obtained
these results was harsh. It required all non-
functional chunks to be finite clauses. If even one
of many chunks was not a finite clause, we counted
the entire sentence as chunked incorrectly. Some
errors occurred in the final step of the evaluation:
generation from chunk's surface string. We required a high similarity between the reconstructed
sentence and the original. For example, according
to the ERG lexicon, *St* and *Street* have the same
semantic representation and the generator can't
choose between them. If a generated string contained *Baker Street* when the original used *Baker
St*, the difference would be penalised even though
the two are equivalent. More than one mistake of
this kind in a sentence would be enough to reject
the result as incorrect.

A significant percentage of errors stems from
the dataset itself. Sentences and parses in the
WikiWoods dataset were not checked by humans.
In fact, not all Wikiwoods entries are grammatical
sentences and many of them could not be easily
filtered out. Bearing that in mind we briefly repeated the experiment with a smaller WeScience
corpus[8] (Ytrestøl et al., 2009). Like WikiWoods,

---

[7]Cambridge SMT system: Source sentence chopping, `http://ucam-smt.github.io/tutorial/
basictrans.html#chopping`
[8]`http://moin.delph-in.net/WeScience`

Algorithm (Dataset)	Precision	Correct	Incorrect	Attempted
DMRS-based (WikiWoods)	42.0%	3036	4195	24.9%
Baseline (WikiWoods)	19.6%	3783	15526	66.6%
DMRS-based (WeScience)	62.7%	106	63	22.7%
Baseline (WeScience)	14.2%	60	362	56.7%

Table 1: Performance of the DMRS-based chunking algorithm and the baseline on the WikiWoods and WeScience datasets. Precision is the percentage of attempted sentences which were chunked correctly, while Correct and Incorrect columns give absolute numbers of correctly and incorrectly chunked sentences. Attempted column is the percentage of sentences for which a chunking opportunity was found and attempted.

it originates from Wikipedia but has been checked by human annotators.

Indeed, the chunking procedure performs much better on the human-checked dataset: 62.7% correct chunkings as compared with 42% for Wiki-Woods (Table 1), indicating the algorithm's sensitivity to parsing errors.

The error analysis of the WeScience experiment reveals that over 25% of the errors made by the rules-based system can be explained by the presence of grammatical structures which the rules did not account for. Increasing the coverage of structures used for chunking should decrease the number of errors of this origin. Another common source of errors were adverbs and prepositional phrases left behind after chunking sentences beginning with *However, when...* or *For example, if...*. We address this issue in the newer version of the system.

For comparison, the string heuristics baseline makes chunking decisions based solely on the presence of trigger words, such as *and*, without the knowledge of what clauses are involved. The position of good chunking boundaries is often determined by dependencies between distant parts of the surface, which are difficult to capture with string-based rules, but are clearly reflected in the DMRS link structure. This results in the baseline yielding unsatisfactory chunks like those underlined in Sentence 6.

(6) The dog barked *and* chased the cat.

5   Current work and future research

Currently we are preparing a different evaluation technique which will directly compare DMRS representations of chunks and the original sentence, eliminating the generation step responsible for many errors. In the new evaluation chunk graphs are matched against the full graph using the `pyDmrs` matching module (Copestake et al., 2016) which scores the degree of the match on a continuous scale.

We are also cooperating with the authors of the statistical approach to realisation (Horvat et al., 2015) on incorporating chunking into their graph manipulations. We hope to use their system for extrinsic evaluation.

Sentences which would most benefit from chunking are also, not accidentally, sentences with which parsers struggle most. Chunking often fails because the parse on which we base it is incorrect. In the future we would like to experiment with considering a number of parses instead of just the top one. This would enable us to mix chunking into the correct parse selection procedure.

One of the investigation directions is extending the catalogue of grammatical structures on which we base the chunks. Some syntactical structures we consider as extensions are relative clauses, verb phrase coordinations, gerund-based adjuncts, parentheticals and appositions. Their inclusion would increase the coverage and quality of chunks, crucial for our purposes.

The treatment of clausal complements needs improvement as well. Some clauses are obligatory syntactic elements and their removal changes how the main clause is parsed. We do not address this issue in the current early version of the system but the lexicalist nature of the ERG offers a solution. The information about whether a clausal complement is obligatory for a given verb is contained in the grammar's lexicon and can be leveraged to improve chunking decisions. We aim to include this mechanism in a later version of the algorithm.

DMRS graphs store information about the alignment between nodes and surface fragments. This information allows us to chunk surfaces of sentences based on the results of graph chunking.

As discussed in Section 1.2, we intend to create a training dataset for a machine learning algorithm which would perform surface chunking. Since, as the WeScience experiment showed, our rule-based approach is sensitive to errors in original parses of full sentences, we might base our training corpus on the RedWoods treebank, which is larger than WeScience but still human-checked.

6   Related work

We define sentence chunking as a new task. As discussed in Introduction, it bears similarity to clause splitting but because of its definition in terms of functionality, it has to be considered separately.

The most important similarity between chunking and clause splitting is how the two problems can be defined for the purpose of machine learning. Clause splitting was the CoNLL-2001 shared task (Tjong et al., 2001) and the results of that research can guide the development of a machine learning system for chunking. Another task which can provide insights into how to design a suitable machine learning system is Sentence Boundary Disambiguation (SBD) task (Walker et al., 2001).

Other research related to chunking was conducted in the context of text simplification. Sentence chunking is a natural step in a simplification process, among other rewrite operations such as paraphrase extraction, but the two tasks have different goals. While sentence simplification modifies sentences, replacing lexical items and rearranging order of information, sentence chunking aims to preserve as much of the original sentence as possible.

Chandrasekar et al. (1996) suggested using dependency structures for simplifying sentences. The authors gave an example of simplifying relative clauses that is similar to chunking but outside of the current scope of our experiments. This research represented early work on automatic syntactic simplification and was succeeded by Siddharthan (2010) who performs simplification by defining transformation rules over type dependency structures. Siddharthan's approach mixes lexical and syntactical transformations and cannot be directly compared with chunking.

Another example of work on simplification is a paper by Woodsend and Lapata (2011). The authors call sentence chunking sentence splitting and approach it from the perspective of tree-based Quasi-synchronous Grammar (QG). Their algorithm learns possible chunking points by aligning the original sentence with two shorter target sentences. Unlike the method we propose, the QG approach requires a manually created dataset consisting of original and target sentences from which the rules can be inferred. Unfortunately, it is impossible to compare the performance of our sentence chunking and the authors' sentence splitting. The QG splitting algorithm is an integral part of the text simplification system and the paper describing it does not give any numbers regarding the performance of individual parts of the system.

7   Conclusions

We defined sentence chunking in terms of its usefulness for other tasks. Its aim is to produce chunks which can be processed and recombined without loss of information. The procedure can be defined for both the surface of a sentence and for its semantic representation.

In our experiments we perform chunking using rules based on the DMRS graphs of sentences. Our work is an early attempt at the task so we focus on easier cases, aiming to gradually increase coverage. Since chunking is intended as a preprocessing step for other tasks, the reliability and precision are more important than chunking as many sentences as possible. Bearing this in mind, we are satisfied to report that according to preliminary experiments, our chunking procedure attempted 25% of all sentences in the dataset and it chunked 42% of these correctly. For comparison, a baseline using heuristics attempted to chunk 67% of sentences, but only 19.6% of these sentences were chunked correctly.

The DMRS-based graph chunking can be used to improve existing systems such as the statistical realization algorithm (Horvat et al., 2015) or to guide the selection of parses for LinGO RedWoods 2 treebank (Oepen et al., 2004).

The surface chunking machine learning tool will extend the applicability of chunking even further. Eliminating the immediate reliance on the parse could allow chunking to replace the string heuristics for machine translation and to influence parsing itself, reducing the difficulty of the task.

References

Laura Banarescu, Claire Bonial, Shu Cai, Madalina Georgescu, Kira Griffitt, Ulf Hermjakob, Kevin Knight, Philipp Koehn, Martha Palmer, and Nathan Schneider. 2013. Abstract Meaning Representation for sembanking. In *Proceedings of the 7th Linguistic Annotation Workshop and Interoperability with Discourse*, pages 178–186.

R. Chandrasekar, Christine Doran, and B. Srinivas. 1996. Motivations and methods for text simplification. In *Proceedings of the Sixteenth International Conference on Computational Linguistics (COLING '96*, pages 1041–1044.

Ann Copestake and Dan Flickinger. 2000. An open source grammar development environment and broad-coverage English grammar using HPSG. In *Proceedings of LREC 2000*, pages 591–600.

Ann Copestake, Dan Flickinger, Carl Pollard, and Ivan A. Sag. 2005. Minimal recursion semantics: An introduction. *Research on Language and Computation*, 3(2):281–332.

Ann Copestake, Guy Emerson, Michael Wayne Goodman, Matic Horvat, Alexander Kuhnle, and Ewa Muszyńska. 2016. Resources for building applications with Dependency Minimal Recursion Semantics. In *Proceedings of the Tenth Language Resources and Evaluation Conference (LREC '16)*. In press.

Ann Copestake. 2009. Slacker semantics: Why superficiality, dependency and avoidance of commitment can be the right way to go. In *Proceedings of the 12th Conference of the European Chapter of the ACL (EACL 2009)*, pages 1–9, Athens, Greece, March. Association for Computational Linguistics.

Dan Flickinger, Stephan Oepen, and Gisle Ytrestøl. 2010. WikiWoods: syntacto-semantic annotation for English Wikipedia. In Nicoletta Calzolari (Conference Chair), Khalid Choukri, Bente Maegaard, Joseph Mariani, Jan Odijk, Stelios Piperidis, Mike Rosner, and Daniel Tapias, editors, *Proceedings of the Seventh International Conference on Language Resources and Evaluation (LREC'10)*, Valletta, Malta, may. European Language Resources Association (ELRA).

Dan Flickinger. 2000. On building a more efficient grammar by exploiting types. *Natural Language Engineering*, 6(1):15–28.

Matic Horvat, Ann Copestake, and William Byrne. 2015. Hierarchical Statistical Semantic Realization for Minimal Recursion Semantics. In *Proceedings of the International Conference on Computational Semantics (IWCS 2015)*.

Ani Nenkova, Rebecca Passonneau, and Kathleen McKeown. 2007. The pyramid method: Incorporating human content selection variation in summarization evaluation. *ACM Trans. Speech Lang. Process.*, 4(2), May.

Stephan Oepen, Dan Flickinger, Kristina Toutanova, and ChristopherD. Manning. 2004. LinGO Redwoods. *Research on Language and Computation*, 2(4):575–596.

Marek Rei. 2013. Minimally supervised dependency-based methods for natural language processing. Technical Report 840, Computer Laboratory, University of Cambridge. PhD thesis.

Advaith Siddharthan. 2010. Complex lexico-syntactic reformulation of sentences using typed dependency representations. In *Proceedings of the 6th International Natural Language Generation Conference*, INLG '10, pages 125–133, Stroudsburg, PA, USA. Association for Computational Linguistics.

Cambridge SMT system: source sentence chopping. `http://ucam-smt.github.io/tutorial/basictrans.html#chopping`. Accessed: 2016-04-26.

Simone Teufel and Hans Van Halteren. 2004. Evaluating information content by factoid analysis: Human annotation and stability. In *Proceedings of Conference on Empirical Methods on Natural Language Processing (EMNLP)*, pages 419–426.

Erik F. Tjong, Kim Sang, and Hervé Déjean. 2001. Introduction to the CoNLL-2001 shared task: Clause identification. In *Proceedings of the 2001 Workshop on Computational Natural Language Learning - Volume 7*, ConLL '01, Stroudsburg, PA, USA. Association for Computational Linguistics.

Daniel J. Walker, David E. Clements, Maki Darwin, and Jan W. Amtrup. 2001. Sentence boundary detection: A comparison of paradigms for improving MT quality. In *roceedings of MT Summit VIII: Santiago de Compostela*, pages 18–22.

Kristian Woodsend and Mirella Lapata. 2011. Learning to simplify sentences with quasi-synchronous grammar and integer programming. In *Proceedings of the Conference on Empirical Methods in Natural Language Processing*, EMNLP '11, pages 409–420, Stroudsburg, PA, USA. Association for Computational Linguistics.

Gisle Ytrestøl, Dan Flickinger, and Stephan Oepen. 2009. Extracting and annotating Wikipedia subdomains - towards a new eScience community resource. In *Proceedings of the Seventh International Workshop on Treebanks and Linguistic Theories (TLT 7)*, pages 185–197, Groningen, The Netherlands.

From Extractive to Abstractive Summarization: A Journey

Parth Mehta
Information Retrieval and Language Processing Lab
Dhirubhai Ambani Institute of Information and Communication Technology
Gandhinagar, India
parth_me@daiict.ac.in

Abstract

The availability of large document-summary corpora have opened up new possibilities for using statistical text generation techniques for abstractive summarization. Progress in Extractive text summarization has become stagnant for a while now and in this work we compare the two possible alternates to it. We present an argument in favor of abstractive summarization compared to an ensemble of extractive techniques. Further we explore the possibility of using statistical machine translation as a generative text summarization technique and present possible research questions in this direction. We also report our initial findings and future direction of research.

1   Motivation for proposed research

Extractive techniques of text summarization have long been the primary focus of research compared to abstractive techniques. But recent reports tend to suggest that advances in extractive text summarization have slowed down in the past few years (Nenkova and McKeown, 2012). Only marginal improvements are being reported over previous techniques, and more often than not these seem to be a result of variation in the parameters used during evaluation using ROUGE, and some times due to other factors like a better redundancy removal module (generally used after the sentences are ranked according to their importance) rather than the actual algorithm. Overall it seems that the current state of the art techniques for extractive summarization have more or less achieved their peak performance and only some small improvements can be further achieved. In such a scenario there seem to be two possible directions of fur-

ther research. One approach that could be used is making an ensemble of these techniques which might prove to be better than the individual methods. The other option is to focus on abstractive techniques instead.

A large number of extractive summarization techniques have been developed in the past decade especially after the advent of conferences like *Document Understanding Conference (DUC)*[1] and *Text Analysis Conference (TAC)*[2]. But very few inquiries have been made as to how these differ from each other and what are the salient features on some which are absent in others. (Hong et al., 2014) is first such attempt to compare summaries beyond merely comparing the ROUGE(Lin, 2004) scores. They show that many systems, although having a similar ROUGE score indeed have very different content and have little overlap among themselves. This difference, at least theoretically, opens up a possibility of combining these summaries at various levels, like fusing rank lists(Wang and Li, 2012), choosing the best combination of sentences from several summaries(Hong et al., 2015) or using learning-to-rank techniques to generate rank lists of sentences and then choosing the top-k sentences as a summary, to get a better result. In the next section we report our initial experiments and show that a meaningful ensemble of these techniques can help in improving the coverage of existing techniques. But such a scenario is not always guaranteed, as shown in the next section, and given that such fusion techniques do have a upper bound to the extent to which they can improve the summarization performance as shown by (Hong et al., 2015), an ensemble approach would be of limited interest.

Keeping this in mind we plan to focus on

---

[1] `duc.nist.gov`
[2] `www.nist.gov/tac`

Proceedings of the 54th Annual Meeting of the Association for Computational Linguistics – Student Research Workshop, pages 100–106,
Berlin, Germany, August 7-12, 2016. ©2016 Association for Computational Linguistics

both approaches for abstractive text summarization, those that depend on initial extractive summary and those that do not (text generation approach). Also availability of large document-summary corpora, as we discuss in section 3, has opened up new possibilities for applying statistical text generation approaches to summarization. In the next section we present a brief overview of the initial experiments that we have performed with an ensemble of extractive techniques. In section 3 we then propose further research directions using the generative approach towards text summarization. In the final section we present some preliminary results of summarizing documents using a machine translation system.

2 Fusion of Summarization systems

In this section we report some of our experiments with fusion techniques for combining extractive summarization systems. For the first experiment we consider five basic techniques mentioned in (Hong et al., 2014) for the simple reason that they are tested extensively and are simple yet effective. These systems include LexRank, the much popular graph based summarization technique(Erkan and Radev, 2004), and Greedy-KL(Haghighi and Vanderwende, 2009), which iteratively chooses the sentence that has least KL-divergence compared to the remaining document. Other systems are FreqSum, a word frequency based system, and TsSum, which uses topic signatures computed by comparing the documents to a background corpus. A Centroid based technique finds the sentences most similar to the document based on cosine similarity. We also combine the rank lists from these systems using the Borda count[3] and Reciprocal Rank Methods.

System	Rouge-1	Avg-Rank
Centroid	0.3641	1.94
FreqSum	0.3531	1.48
Greedy-KL	**0.3798**	2.2
LexRank	0.3595	1.72
TsSum	0.3587	1.88
BC	0.3621	**2.5**
RR	0.3633	2.46

Table 1: Effect of Fusion

We evaluated the techniques based on ROUGE-

[3]https://en.wikipedia.org/wiki/Borda_count

1, ROUGE-2 and ROUGE-4 Recall (Lin, 2004) using the parameters mentioned in (Hong et al., 2014). We report only ROUGE-1 results due to space constraints. We also computed Average-Rank for each system. Average-Rank indicates the average number of systems that the given system outperformed. The higher the average-rank the more consistent a given system. When systems are ranked based on ROUGE-1 metric, both Borda and Reciprocal Rank perform better than four of the five systems but couldn't beat the Greedy-KL method. Both combination techniques outperformed all five methods when systems are ranked based on ROUGE-2 and ROUGE-4. Even in case where Borda and Reciprocal Rank did outperform all the other systems, the increase in ROUGE scores were negligible. These results are contrary to what has been reported previously (Wang and Li, 2012) as neither of the fusion techniques performed significantly better than the candidate systems. The only noticeable improvement in all cases was in the Average-Rank. The combined systems were more consistent than the individual systems. These results indicate that Fusion can at least help us in improving the consistency of the meta-system.

One clear trend we observed was that not all combinations performed poorly, and summaries from certain techniques when fused together performed well (on both ROUGE score and consistency). To further investigate this issue we conducted another experiment where we try to make an informed fusion of various extractive techniques.

Due to space constraints we report results only on two families of summarization techniques: one is a graph based iterative method as suggested in (Erkan and Radev, 2004) and (Mihalcea and Tarau, 2004) and the other is the 'Greedy approach' where we greedily add a sentence that is most similar to the entire document, remove the sentence from the document and repeat the process until we have the desired number of sentences. We then chose three commonly used sentence similarity measures: Cosine similarity, Word overlap and KL-Divergence. Several other similar approaches are possible, for example TsSum and FreqSum are related in the sense that each method rates a sentence based on the average number of important words in it, the difference being in the way in which importance of the word is computed.

We perform this experiment in a very constrained manner and leave it to the future experimenting with other such possible combinations.

	Graph	Greedy	Borda
Cosine	0.3473	0.3313	0.3370
Word Overlap	0.3139	0.3229	0.3039
KLD	0.3248	0.3429	0.3121
Borda	**0.3638**	**0.3515**	-

Table 2: Effect of 'Informed' Fusion

We generate summaries using all the possible 6 combinations of two approaches and three sentence similarity metrics. We then combine the summaries resulting from a particular sentence similarity metric or from a particular sentence ranking algorithm. The results in table 2 show that techniques that have a similar ranking algorithm but use different sentence similarity metrics, when combined produce an aggregate summary whose coverage is much better than the original summary. The aggregate summaries from the systems that have different ranking algorithm but the same sentence similarity measure do not beat the best performing system. Figures in bold indicate the maximum score for that particular approach. We have tested this for several other ranking algorithms like centroid based and LSA based and sentence similarity measures. The hypothesis holds in most cases. We consider this experiment to be indicative of a future direction of research and do not consider it in any way to be conclusive. But it definitely indicates the difficulties that might be encountered when attempting to fuse summaries from different sources compared to the limited improvement in the coverage (ROUGE scores). This combined with availability of a larger training set of document-summary pairs, which enables us to use several text generation approaches, is our principle motivation behind the proposed research.

3   Abstractive Summarization

Abstractive Summarization covers techniques which can generate summaries by rewriting the content in a given text, rather than simply extracting important sentences from it. But most of the current abstractive summarization techniques still use sentence extraction as a first step for abstract generation. In most cases, extractive summaries reach their limitation primarily because only a part of every sentence selected is informative and the other part is redundant. Abstractive techniques try to tackle this issue by either dropping the redundant part altogether or fusing two similar sentences in such a way as to maximize the information content and minimize the sentence lengths. We discuss some experiments we plan to do in this direction. An alternative to this technique is what is known as the *Generative approach* for text summarization. These techniques extract concepts (instead of sentences or phrases) from the given text and generate new sentences using those concepts and the relationships between them. We propose a novel approach of using statistical machine translation for document summarization. We discuss the possibilities of exploiting Statistical machine translation techniques, which in themselves are generative techniques and have a sound mathematical formulation, for translating a text in *Document Language* to *Summary Language*. In this section we highlight the research questions we are trying to address and issues that we might face in doing so. We also mention another approach we would like to explore which uses topic modeling for generating summaries.

3.1   Sentence Fusion

Most abstractive summarization techniques rely on sentence fusion to remove redundancy and create a new concise sentence. Graph based techniques similar to (Ganesan et al., 2010) and (Banerjee et al., 2015) have become very popular recently. These techniques rely on extractive summarization to get important sentences, cluster lexically similar sentences together, create a word graph from this cluster and try to generate a new meaningful sentence by selecting a best suited path from this word graph. Several factors like the linguistic quality of the sentence, informativeness, length of the sentence are considered when selecting an appropriate path form the word graph.

Informativeness of the selected path can be defined in several ways, and the choice defines how good my summary would be (at least when using ROUGE as a evaluation measure). In one of our experiments we changed the informativeness criteria from TextRank scores of words as used in the original approach in (Banerjee et al., 2015) to Log-Likelihood ratio of the words compared to a large background corpus as suggested in (Lin and Hovy, 2000). We observed that changing measure of informativeness produces a dramatic change in the quality of the summaries. We would like to continue working in this direction.

3.2 Summarization as a SMT problem

The idea is to model the text summarization problem as a Statistical Machine Translation (SMT) problem of translating text written in a *Document Language* to that in a *Summary Language*. Machine translation techniques have well defined and well accepted generative models which have been researched extensively over more than two decades. At least on the surface, the idea of modeling a text summarization problem as that of translation between two pairs of texts might enable us to leverage this progress in the field of SMT and extend it to abstractive text summarization, albeit with several modifications. We expect this area to be our primary research focus. While a similar approach has been used in the case of Question Answering (Zhang et al., 2014), to the best of our knowledge it has not yet been used for Document Summarization.

While the idea seems very intuitive and appealing, there are several roadblocks to it. The first and perhaps the biggest issue has been the lack of availability of a large training corpus. Traditionally SMT systems have depended on large volumes of parallel texts that are used to learn the phrase level alignment between sentences from two languages and the probability with which a particular phrase in the source language might be translated to another in the target language. The Text Summarization community on the other hand has relied on more linguistic approaches or statistical approaches which use limited amount of training data. Most of the evaluation benchmark datasets generated by conferences like DUC or TAC are limited to less than a hundred Document-Summary pairs and the focus has mainly been on short summaries of very few sentences. This makes the available data too small (especially when considering the number of sentences).

We hope to solve this problem partially using the *Supreme Court Judgments* dataset released by the organizers of *Information Access in Legal Domain Track*[4] at *FIRE 2014*. The dataset has 1500 Judgments with a corresponding summary known as a headnote, manually written by legal experts. The organizers released another dataset of additional 10,000 judgment-headnote pairs from the *Supreme court of India* spread over four decades, that are noisy and need to be curated. The average judgment length is 150 sentences while a headnote is 30 sentence long on an average. Using this we can create a parallel corpus of approximately 45,000 sentences using the clean data, and an additional 300,000 sentences after curating the entire dataset. This is comparable to the size of standard datasets used for training SMT systems.

Given this data is only semi-parallel and aligned at document level and not at sentence level, the next issue is extracting pairs of source sentence and target sentence. The exception being that both the source sentence and target sentence can actually be several sentences instead of a single sentence, the possibility being higher in case of the source than the target. This might seem to be a classic example of the problem of extracting parallel sentences from a comparable corpus. But there are several important differences, the biggest one being that it is almost guaranteed that several sentences from the text written in *Document Language* will map to a single sentence in the *Summary Language*. This itself makes this task more challenging compared to the already daunting task of finding parallel sentences in a comparable corpora. Another notable difference is that unlike in case of SMT, the headnotes (or the *Summary Language*) are influenced a lot by the stylistic quality of its author. The nature of headnotes seems to vary to a large extent over the period of four decades, and we are in the process of trying to figure out how this affects the sentence alignment as well as the overall translation process. The other major difference can actually be used as leverage to improve the quality of sentence level alignment. The headnotes tend to follow a general format, in the sense that there are certain points about the Court judgment that should always occur in the headnote and certain phrases or certain types of sentences are always bound to be excluded. How to leverage this information is one of the research questions we plan to address in the proposed work.

Another issue that we plan to address in particular is how to handle the mismatch between lengths of a sentence (i.e. multiple sentences considered to be a single sentence) in the *Document Language* when compared to the *Summary Language*. Currently two different languages do vary in the average sentence lengths, for example Ger-

---

[4] http://www.isical.ac.in/~fire/2014/legal.html

man sentences are in general longer than English. But in our case the ratio of sentence lengths would be almost 3:1 with the *Document Language* being much longer than their *Summary Language* counterparts. While most current translation models do have a provision for a penalty on sentence lengths which can make the target sentence longer or shorter, the real challenge lies in finding phrase level alignments when either the source sentence or the target sentence is too long compared to the other. This leads to a large number of phrases having no alignment at all which is not a common phenomenon in cases of SMT.

In effect we propose to address the following research questions:

- Exploring the major challenges that one might face when modeling Summarization as a Machine translation problem ?
- How to create a sentence aligned parallel corpus from a given document and its handwritten summary ?
- How to handle the disparity in lengths of sentence of *Document Language* and *Summary Language* ?
- How to reduce the sparsity in training data created due to the stylistic differences present within the Documents and Summaries ?

3.3 Topic model based sentence generation

The graph based approaches of sentence fusion mentioned above assumes availability of a number of similar sentences from which a word graph can be formed. It might not always be easy to get such similar sentences, especially in case of single document summarization. We wish to explore the possibility of using topic modeling to extract informative phrases and entities and then use standard sentence generation techniques to generate representative sentences.

4 Preliminary experiment

We would like to conclude by reporting results of a very preliminary experiment wherein we used simple cosine similarity to align sentences between the original Judgments and the manually generated headnotes (summaries). For a small training set of 1000 document-summary pairs, we compute the cosine similarity of each sentence in the judgment to each sentence in the corresponding headnote. Sentences in the judgment which do not have a cosine similarity of at least 0.5 with any sentence in the headnote are considered to have no alignment at all. The remaining sentences are aligned to a single best matching sentence in the headnote. Hence each sentence in the judgment is aligned to exactly one or zero sentences in the headnote, while each sentence in the headnote can have a many to one mapping. All the judgment sentences aligned to the same headnote sentence are combined to form a single sentence, thus forming a parallel corpus between *Judgment Language* and *Headnote Language*. Further we used the Moses[5] machine translation toolkit to generate a translation model with the source language as the *judgment (or the document Language)* and the target language as the *headnote (or summary language)*. Since we have not yet used the entire training data, the results in the current experiment were not very impressive. But there are certain examples worth reporting, where good results were indeed obtained.

4.1 Example Translation

Original: There can **in my opinion** be no escape from the conclusion that section 12 of the Act by which **a most important protection or** safeguard conferred on the subject by the Constitution has been taken away is not **a valid provision** since it **contravenes** the very provision in the Constitution under which the Parliament derived its competence to enact it.

Translation: There can be no escape from the conclusion that section 12 of the Act by which safeguard conferred on the subject by the Constitution has been taken away is not valid since it contravened the very provision in the Constitution under which the Parliament derived its competence to enact it.

The highlighted parts in the original sentence are the ones that have been changed in the corresponding translation. We can attribute the exclusion of *'in my opinion'* solely to the language model of the Summary Language. Since the summaries are in third person while many statements in the original judgment would be in first person, such a phrase which is common in the Judgment will never occur in the headnote. Similarly the headnotes are usually written in past tense and that might account for changing *'contravenes'* to *'contravened'*. We are not sure what the reasons might be behind the other changes. We plan to do an

---

exhaustive error analysis on the results of this experiment, which will provide further insights and ideas. We have reported some more examples in the appendix section.

Although not all translations are linguistically correct and many of them don't make much sense, we believe that by using a larger training corpus (which we are currently curating) and a better technique for creating a sentence aligned corpus the results can be significantly improved. Also currently the target sentences are not much shorter than their source, and we need to further work on that issue. Overall the idea of using SMT for document summarization seems to be promising and worth pursuing.

References

Siddhartha Banerjee, Prasenjit Mitra, and Kazunari Sugiyama. 2015. Multi-document abstractive summarization using ilp based multi-sentence compression. In *24th International Joint Conference on Artificial Intelligence (IJCAI)*.

Günes Erkan and Dragomir R Radev. 2004. Lexrank: Graph-based lexical centrality as salience in text summarization. *Journal of Artificial Intelligence Research*, pages 457–479.

Kavita Ganesan, ChengXiang Zhai, and Jiawei Han. 2010. Opinosis: a graph-based approach to abstractive summarization of highly redundant opinions. In *Proceedings of the 23rd international conference on computational linguistics*, pages 340–348. Association for Computational Linguistics.

Aria Haghighi and Lucy Vanderwende. 2009. Exploring content models for multi-document summarization. In *Proceedings of Human Language Technologies: The 2009 Annual Conference of the North American Chapter of the Association for Computational Linguistics*, pages 362–370. Association for Computational Linguistics.

Kai Hong, John M Conroy, Benoit Favre, Alex Kulesza, Hui Lin, and Ani Nenkova. 2014. A repository of state of the art and competitive baseline summaries for generic news summarization. In *LREC*.

Kai Hong, Mitchell Marcus, and Ani Nenkova. 2015. System combination for multi-document summarization. In *Proceedings of the 2015 Conference on Empirical Methods in Natural Language Processing*, pages 107–117. Association for Computational Linguistics.

Chin-Yew Lin and Eduard Hovy. 2000. The automated acquisition of topic signatures for text summarization. In *Proceedings of the 18th conference on Computational linguistics-Volume 1*, pages 495–501. Association for Computational Linguistics.

Chin-Yew Lin. 2004. Rouge: A package for automatic evaluation of summaries. In *Text summarization branches out: Proceedings of the ACL-04 workshop*, volume 8.

Rada Mihalcea and Paul Tarau. 2004. Textrank: Bringing order into texts. In *Proceedings of the Conference on Empirical Methods in Natural Language Processing*. Association for Computational Linguistics.

Ani Nenkova and Kathleen McKeown. 2012. A survey of text summarization techniques. In *Mining Text Data*, pages 43–76. Springer.

Dingding Wang and Tao Li. 2012. Weighted consensus multi-document summarization. *Information Processing & Management*, 48(3):513–523.

Kai Zhang, Wei Wu, Haocheng Wu, Zhoujun Li, and Ming Zhou. 2014. Question retrieval with high quality answers in community question answering. In *Proceedings of the 23rd ACM International Conference on Conference on Information and Knowledge Management*, pages 371–380. ACM.

A Additional Examples

- The underlined parts in the original sentence are the ones that are correctly omitted in the target sentence. The striked out part in the original sentences are wrongly missing in the translation, affecting the comprehensibility of the sentence.
- The striked out parts in the Translation are the ones that are misplaced in the sentence. Boldfaced parts in the Translation are the ones newly introduced.
- The boldfaced parts in the Expected Translations are the corrections that are made compared to the actual translation.

Original:

The Act provides for levy of **two kinds of taxes called** the general tax and the special tax by the two charging sections 5 and 10 respectively. ~~Seervai attempted to make out~~ that the provisions of the charging sections 5 and 10 fixing Rs. 30000 and Rs. 5000 as the minimum taxable turnover for general tax and special tax respectively were found discriminatory and void under article 14 read with article 13 of the Constitution and he gave us several tables of figures showing how the imposition of the tax actually works **out in practice in hypothetical cases**.

Translation:

The Act provides for the levy of the general tax and special tax by the two charging sections 5 and 10 respectively. that the provisions of the charging sections 5 and 10 fixing Rs. 30000 and Rs. 5000 as the minimum taxable turnover for general tax and special tax respectively are discriminatory and void under ~~art~~ of the Constitution and he gave the several tables of figures showing how the imposition of the tax actually works.

Expected Tranlsation:

The Act provides for the levy of the general tax and special tax by the two charging sections 5 and 10 respectively. **Seervai attempted to make out** that the provisions of the charging sections 5 and 10 fixing Rs. 30000 and Rs. 5000 as the minimum taxable turnover for general tax and special tax respectively are discriminatory and void under **article 14 read with article 13** of the Constitution and he gave the several tables of figures showing how the imposition of the tax actually works.

Original:

The **learned trial** magistrate **believed the prosecution evidence rejected the pleas raised by the defence convicted** the appellants of the charge framed and sentenced them to undergo simple imprisonment for two months each. ~~The appellate court~~ confirmed the conviction of the appellants but reduced their sentence from simple imprisonment for two months to a fine of Rs. 50 or in default simple imprisonment for one month each.

Translation:

The Magistrate **found** the appellants of the charge framed and sentenced them to undergo simple imprisonment for two months ~~guilty~~. confirmed the conviction of the appellants but reduced their sentence from simple imprisonment for two months to a fine of Rs. 50 or in default simple imprisonment for one month each.

Expected Tranlsation:

The Magistrate found the appellants **guilty** of the charge framed and sentenced them to undergo simple imprisonment for two months. **The appellate court** confirmed the conviction of the appellants but reduced their sentence from simple imprisonment for two months to a fine of Rs. 50 or in default simple imprisonment for one month each.

Putting Sarcasm Detection into Context:
The Effects of Class Imbalance and Manual Labelling on Supervised Machine Classification of Twitter Conversations

Gavin Abercrombie and Dirk Hovy
Center for Language Technology
University of Copenhagen, Denmark
Njalsgade 140, DK-2300 Copenhagen S
`jst662@alumni.ku.dk, dirk.hovy@hum.ku.dk`

Abstract

Sarcasm can radically alter or invert a phrase's meaning. Sarcasm detection can therefore help improve natural language processing (NLP) tasks. The majority of prior research has modeled sarcasm detection as classification, with two important limitations: 1. Balanced datasets, when sarcasm is actually rather rare. 2. Using Twitter users' self-declarations in the form of hashtags to label data, when sarcasm can take many forms. To address these issues, we create an unbalanced corpus of manually annotated Twitter conversations. We compare human and machine ability to recognize sarcasm on this data under varying amounts of context. Our results indicate that both class imbalance and labelling method affect performance, and should both be considered when designing automatic sarcasm detection systems. We conclude that for progress to be made in real-world sarcasm detection, we will require a new class labelling scheme that is able to access the 'common ground' held between conversational parties.

1 Introduction

Sarcasm, or verbal irony, is prevalent both in spoken and written communication, and can radically alter or invert a phrase's meaning. Automatic sarcasm detection can therefore help improve natural language processing (NLP) tasks, such as sentiment analysis, where failure to take ironic intent into account has been recognised as a major cause of errors.

However, automatic sarcasm detection is a nontrivial problem, and research into this subject is in its infancy. The majority of prior research has treated sarcasm detection as a classification task, with two important limitations: 1. It focuses on balanced datasets, when sarcasm is actually rather rare. 2. In order to obtain labelled data for supervised learning, many studies relied on Twitter users' supposed self-declarations of sarcasm in the form of hashtags such as `#sarcasm`, but sarcasm can take many forms.

Although reporting impressive results for sarcasm detection, even state-of-the-art systems fail to address the above issues. Research suggesting that verbal irony occurs in less than a fifth of conversations (Gibbs, 2000) implies that, rather than using balanced datasets, a more realistic approach may be to view sarcasm recognition as a problem of anomaly detection, in which positive examples are scarce. While convenient, obtaining labelled data from hashtags has been found to introduce both noise, in the form of incorrectly labelled examples, and bias to the datasets used – analysis suggests that only certain forms of sarcasm are likely to be tagged in this way (Davidov et al., 2010), and predominantly by certain types of Twitter users (Bamman and Smith, 2015).

To address these issues, we create a novel corpus of manually annotated Twitter conversations and, using the feature classes of Bamman and Smith (2015), perform sarcasm classification experiments on both balanced and unbalanced datasets. We also compare model performance to a dataset of conversations automatically retrieved using hashtags.

Our contributions In this paper, we present a novel corpus of manually annotated two-part Twitter conversations for use in supervised classification of sarcastic and non-sarcastic text. We compare human vs. machine learning classification performance under varying amounts of contextual information, and evaluate machine perfor-

Proceedings of the 54th Annual Meeting of the Association for Computational Linguistics – Student Research Workshop, pages 107–113,
Berlin, Germany, August 7-12, 2016. ©2016 Association for Computational Linguistics

mance on balanced and unbalanced, and manually labelled and automatically retrieved datasets.

2 Data

Most prior research into sarcasm detection has been conducted on Twitter. To make comparisons with other research, and because use of sarcasm seems to be prevalent on Twitter, we too make use of Twitter data for this study.

However, the collection of data using explicit markers of sarcasm (hashtags) has been shown to introduce bias to the datasets used in prior research (Davidov et al., 2010; González-Ibánez et al., 2011; Maynard and Greenwood, 2014; Bamman and Smith, 2015). We therefore create a novel hand-annotated corpus of contextualised sarcastic and non-sarcastic Twitter conversations. For comparison, we also create an automatically collected dataset using hashtags.

Corpus creation The data set is taken from a Twitter corpus of 64 million tweets gathered in 2013. Matching tweet reply IDs to the status IDs of other tweets, and filtering by language, produces 650,212 two-line English Twitter 'conversations.' We manually annotate these, finding 448 positive examples, to which we add 1,792 negatively labelled examples in which sarcasm was found not to be present. The resulting corpus contains 2,240 conversations in total. A second corpus, which is automatically retrieved using hashtags, is created, producing 448 Twitter conversation where the second tweet contains #sarcasm, and 1,792 without this feature. Following previous work, we remove usernames and web addresses. For the second corpus, we also remove the term #sarcasm. We collect up to 3,200 historical tweets written by each user ID in the datasets.

Annotation We annotated the conversations manually with full access to the text of the conversations and user profile information and tweet history of the users. Following prior work (Kreuz and Caucci, 2007), and because people have been found to conflate many forms of verbal irony under the term *sarcasm* (Gibbs, 1986), positive labels were not assigned according to any fixed criteria or definition, but according to our intuitive understanding of whether or not examples contained verbal irony[1]

3 Human performance baseline study

This study was undertaken with the participation of 60 native English speaking volunteers. We randomly selected 300 Twitter conversations from the corpus and assigned them each one of five conditions: *tweet only* – the text of the reply tweet from the conversation, *tweet + author* – including access to the Twitter profile of the author, *tweet + audience* – including the profile of the writer of the original tweet in the conversation, *tweet + environment* – the texts of both tweets, and *tweet + author + audience + environment* – access to all the above information. Each participant rated 10 conversations.

Procedure We asked two participants to rate the reply tweet of each conversation as either *sarcastic* or *non-sarcastic*. Again, following Kreuz and Caucci (2007), raters were not provided with a definition of sarcasm, but were asked to judge the tweets based on their intuitive understanding of the term.

Inter-rater agreement We use inter-rater agreement measures to assess both the difficulty of the sarcasm recognition task under different conditions and the reliability of the participants. We report both raw percentage agreement and – as in previous work on sarcasm annotation (Swanson et al., 2014) – Krippendorffs α, which takes into account expected chance disagreement.

Contrary to expectations, annotators are *not* more likely to agree if given access to more information. Agreement is highest for the *tweet only* condition (% = 70.49, α = 0.35). Krippendorffs α scores for *tweet + audience* (0.08) and *tweet + original + author + audience* (0.18) are very low, while *tweet + audience* produces a negative score (-0.10) which indicates that agreement is below chance levels.

Rater reliability Agreement scores are generally low. Only two pairs obtain 'good' agreement scores.[2] The majority (20 pairs) receive a score between 0.0 and 0.67, while eight of the pairs achieve negative scores, indicating less than chance expected agreement. Two possible explanations for low rater agreement are (1) that sarcasm recognition is a difficult task for humans (Kreuz and Caucci, 2007; González-Ibánez et al.,

---

[1]This was also necessary because prior sarcasm detection studies relied on self-annotation of sarcasm by Twitter users applying their own judgements of sarcastic meaning e.g., Davidov et al. (2010) 2010, González-Ibánez et al. (2011).

[2]Krippendorff (2012) considers 0.67 to be lowest acceptable agreement score.

2011), especially without access to the surrounding context (Filatova, 2012; Wallace et al., 2014), and (2) that people undertaking such tasks remotely online are often guilty of 'spamming,' or providing careless or random responses (Hovy et al., 2013).

To mitigate the effects of unreliable raters and get an upper bound for human performance, we use two measures: (1) discard the results of the worst performing rater in each pair (in terms of F1) and use the vote of the higher scoring raters. (2) identify the least trustworthy raters and downweight their votes using scores from an item-response model, MACE (Hovy et al., 2013).

The first requires access to the original annotated labels, the latter can be done with or without access to the gold standard. We compare both F1 and Area Under the Curve (AUC) scores of both raters in each pair, the better performing rater only, and the MACE most competent rater in each pair over all conditions.

For both measures, MACE competent rater scores (F1: 0.547; AUC: 0.731) are marginally higher than the mean of both raters (F1: 0.523; AUC: 0.729), while the best rater scores (F1: 0.641; AUC: 0.817) are highest of all, as might be expected.

3.1 Machine classification experiments

To compare human to machine performance, we fit binary classification models on both balanced and unbalanced splits of the two datasets.

Experimental setup We evaluate performance using a standard logistic regression model with ℓ_2 regularization, evaluated via five-fold cross-validation.

Features For the five conditions, we use the following feature classes, as named and described by Bamman and Smith (2015):

Tweet features: Unigrams, bigrams, Brown cluster unigrams, Brown cluster bigrams, part-of-speech features, pronunciation features, and intensifier features.

Author features: Author historical salient terms, profile information, profile unigrams.

Audience features: Audience historical salient terms, profile unigrams, profile information, and historical communication features.

Environment features: Pairwise Brown features and unigram features of audience tweets.

Normalisation We convert all features to binary or numeric values and normalize them to the range between zero and one.

Procedure Following Bamman and Smith (2015), we evaluate classification performance on the above feature sets in the following combinations: *tweet features* only, *tweet + author features*, *tweet + audience features*, *tweet + environment features*, and *tweet + author + audience + environment*.

4 Results

Accuracy is commonly reported in classification tasks, but unsuitable for unbalanced datasets (López et al., 2013), so we report two other metrics frequently used with uneven class distributions: F1 score, and Area Under the ROC Curve (AUC), which reflects the relationship between the true positive rate (TPR) and false positive rate (FPR). Unlike accuracy, these measures penalize predicting only the majority class. AUC is considered to be more resistant to the skew of unbalanced data than F1 (Fawcett, 2004).

Comparison with baselines Figure 1 compares random performance, human raters,[3] and the classifier's AUC scores. The scores of both the human raters and the machine classifier surpass random performance in all conditions, with the classifier attaining the lowest score of 0.615 on *tweet + author features*. Machine classification is not, however, able to match human performance. But there are parallels between human and machine performance: the classifier achieves its highest score using *tweet + environment* features (human: 0.802; machine: 0.630). Interestingly, both humans and the classifier appear to suffer from an 'information saturation' effect, obtaining lowest scores when trained on a combination of all the possible features.

Machine classification performance across conditions We have two data-related factors that affect performance, namely (1) label prevalence (i.e., balanced vs. unbalanced splits), and (2) the labelling scheme (manual vs. automatically induced from #sarcasm). Figure 2 shows the effects on F1 and AUC for each combination of these two factors under all five conditions.

---

[3]Using the MACE most competent rater scores, which we judge to be the fairest comparison.

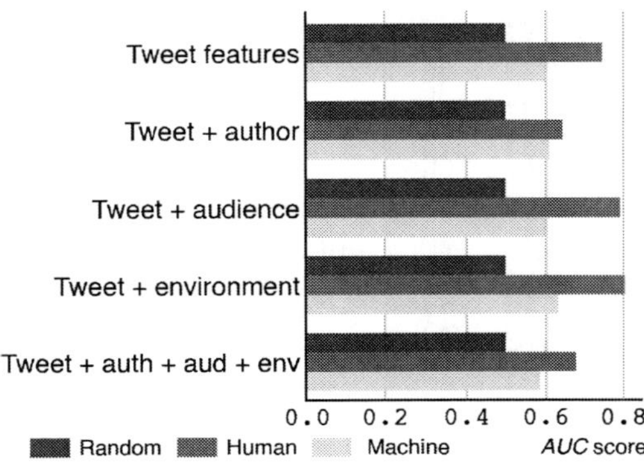

Figure 1: AUC scores of random performance, the *most competent* human raters, and machine classification on an unbalanced split of the manually annotated data.

Class label balance

AUC scores are largely unaffected by change in label balance. We see broadly similar results on both balanced and unbalanced data splits across all the feature classes on both corpora. The small changes in performance that do occur can be attributed to the increase in size of the unbalanced datasets, which have more negative training examples compared to the balanced sets.

However, for both corpora, and across all feature classes, F1 scores suffer large drops on the unbalanced data compared to results on the balanced datasets. These results indicate that F1, known to be biased to the negative class and to ignore the effect of *true negatives* (Powers, 2015), may not be a suitable metric for this task, as it is very sensitive to the changes in class balance of the datasets. Nevertheless, even when measured with AUC score, in the majority of feature configurations classifier performance drops on the unbalanced datasets. Results therefore suggest that class balance (and dataset size) should be taken into account when designing sarcasm detection systems.

Labelling scheme

Overall, higher scores are achieved with the automatically collected corpus. All feature combinations obtain higher F1 and AUC scores on this data using the balanced split, as do *tweet + auth* and *tweet + aud* on the unbalanced data. This points to greater homogeneity in the data in the automatically collected corpus. This may be because it is often certain types of users, such as those who do not know their audience personally, who feel the need to label their sarcastic statements with hash-

tags (Bamman and Smith, 2015). Manually annotated data includes instances of sarcasm which the author has not deemed necessary to explicitly label as sarcastic. This may lead to greater variation in the features of the positive examples in the manually annotated data, and hence lower classification scores.

The only feature category in which F1 and AUC scores for the manually annotated data are higher than those for the automatically collected data are on the unbalanced split for *tweet features* (F1: +0.012, AUC: +0.08) and *tweet + env* (F1: +0.037, AUC: +0.015), while *tweet + auth + aud + env* produces a higher F1 score (+0.275), but a slightly lower AUC score (-0.023). These figures point to the fact that for the manually annotated data, performance is best when linguistic features from both tweets in the conversations are included. Indeed, on both balanced and unbalanced data splits of the manually annotated data, better results are generally produced using these textual features than using features related to the writers of those texts. It would therefore seem that the annotation process has introduced some biases to the data. This process, in which sarcasm, or the ambiguous possibility of sarcasm, is first recognised in the dialogues and then confirmed by scrutiny of users Twitter pages, heavily favours textual features. Twitter conversations automatically selected using hashtags on the other hand, are likely to be highly ambiguous once those hashtags are removed and, as discussed above, more likely to be predictable from information in the conversational participants' profile metadata than from linguistic features.

5   Related Work

Research in both cognitive psychology (Utsumi, 2000; Gibbs and Colston, 2007) and NLP (Filatova, 2012) has suggested that it may not be possible to produce an overarching definition of sarcasm. Kreuz (1996) noted that use of sarcasm often depends on the 'common ground' people share. Work on human sarcasm recognition (Kreuz and Caucci, 2007) and automatic sarcasm detection (Bamman and Smith, 2015) has relied on people's intuitive understanding of the term 'sarcasm' for rating and data labelling purposes.

Following the insights of Kreuz and Caucci (2007), Carvalho et al. (2009), González-Ibánez et al. (2011) and Tsur et al. (2010), among others, used textual cues for automatic sarcasm detection.

110

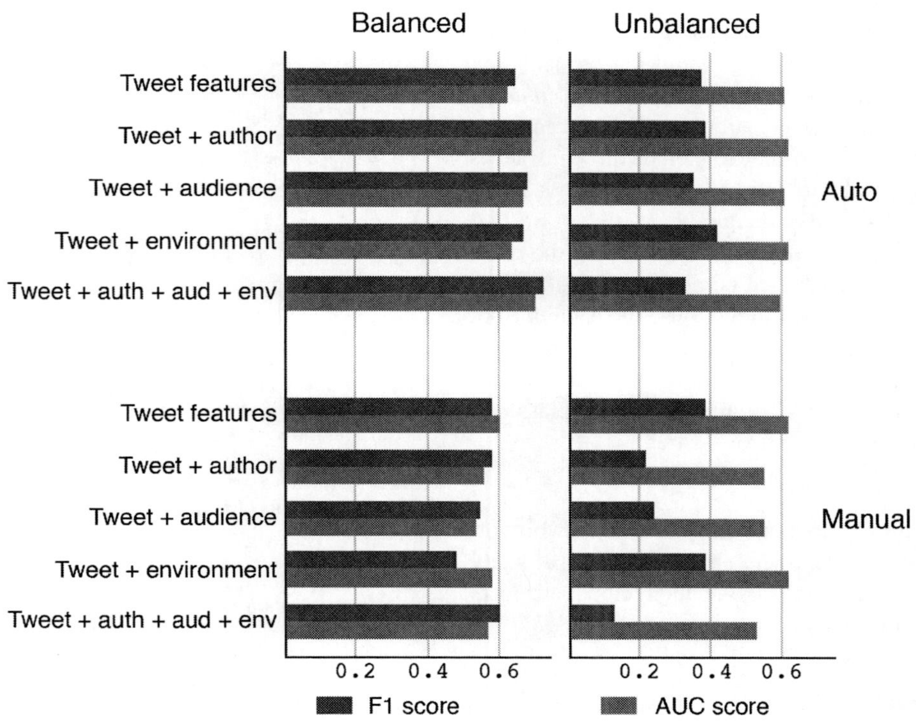

Figure 2: Effects of labeling method (top vs. bottom row) and label prevalance (left vs. right column) on F1 and AUC scores.

Addressing the wider context in which tweets are written, Rajadesingan et al. (2015) mapped information from the posting history of Twitter users to research on why, when, and how sarcasm tends to be used. They also tested their model on both balanced and unbalanced datasets. Bamman and Smith (2015) showed that a variety of contextual features can improve classification performance over use of textual features alone. However, like González-Ibánez et al. (2011) and Maynard and Greenwood (2014), they concluded that the use of hashtags for data labelling introduced biases to their dataset.

6 Conclusions

We evaluated the performance of human raters and a machine learning algorithm on sarcasm detection under different information conditions. We find that humans generally benefit from context more than machines, but that machine performance is even more affected by the labeling scheme (automatically induced vs. hand-annotated) and the prevalence of the target class. Our results indicate that sarcasm detection is far from solved, and that any results on the task need to be viewed in the light of the two factors outlined here.

In automatic sarcasm detection, use of unbalanced datasets led to large drops in F1 scores, due to this metric not taking into account true negatives. As the ratio of TNs is necessarily large for effective sarcasm detection on data in which positive examples are rare, AUC seems a more appropriate performance metric.

Although more robust to class imbalance, AUC scores also varied between the balanced and unbalanced datasets. This indicates that label class balance and dataset size should be taken into account when designing sarcasm detection systems.

Previous work suggests that the automatic selection of positive examples using user-written hashtags biases the data towards (1) particularly ambiguous forms of sarcasm, and (2) 'celebrity' Twitter users who are anxious not to be misunderstood. Our labelling method avoids these pitfalls, as well as eliminating noise in the form of tweets that use sarcastic hashtags but are not in fact ironic. However, in using the labels of an outside observer to the conversations, we may be introducing other forms of bias. It seems that a gold standard sarcasm corpus would require labelling by the annotators who are party to the *'common ground'* shared by the participants in the conversations. It would also need to include those instances that they would *not* normally publicly mark as being sarcastic with hashtags.

Future work will focus on improving the quality and size of labelled corpora available for this task. It will also explore the use of features from the wider conversational context beyond the two-sentence dialogues examined here, and investigate the effects of data labelling method and class balance on media other than Twitter.

Acknowledgements

We would like to thank the participants who volunteered their time and effort to make this study possible. We also thank the anonymous reviewers for their invaluable comments.

References

David Bamman and Noah A Smith. 2015. Contextualized sarcasm detection on twitter. In *Ninth International AAAI Conference on Web and Social Media*.

Paula Carvalho, Luís Sarmento, Mário J Silva, and Eugénio De Oliveira. 2009. Clues for detecting irony in user-generated contents: oh...!! it's so easy;-). In *Proceedings of the 1st international CIKM workshop on Topic-sentiment analysis for mass opinion*, pages 53–56. ACM.

Dmitry Davidov, Oren Tsur, and Ari Rappoport. 2010. Semi-supervised recognition of sarcastic sentences in twitter and amazon. In *Proceedings of the Fourteenth Conference on Computational Natural Language Learning*, pages 107–116. Association for Computational Linguistics.

Tom Fawcett. 2004. Roc graphs: Notes and practical considerations for researchers. *Machine learning*, 31(1):1–38.

Elena Filatova. 2012. Irony and sarcasm: Corpus generation and analysis using crowdsourcing. In *LREC*, pages 392–398.

Raymond Gibbs and Herbert Colston. 2007. The future of irony studies. *Irony in Language and Thought*, pages 339–360.

Raymond W Gibbs. 1986. On the psycholinguistics of sarcasm. *Journal of Experimental Psychology: General*, 115(1):3.

Raymond W Gibbs. 2000. Irony in talk among friends. *Metaphor and symbol*, 15(1-2):5–27.

Roberto González-Ibáñez, Smaranda Muresan, and Nina Wacholder. 2011. Identifying sarcasm in twitter: a closer look. In *Proceedings of the 49th Annual Meeting of the Association for Computational Linguistics: Human Language Technologies: short papers-Volume 2*, pages 581–586. Association for Computational Linguistics.

Dirk Hovy, Taylor Berg-Kirkpatrick, Ashish Vaswani, and Eduard H Hovy. 2013. Learning whom to trust with mace. In *HLT-NAACL*, pages 1120–1130.

Roger J Kreuz and Gina M Caucci. 2007. Lexical influences on the perception of sarcasm. In *Proceedings of the Workshop on computational approaches to Figurative Language*, pages 1–4. Association for Computational Linguistics.

Roger J Kreuz. 1996. The use of verbal irony: Cues and constraints. *Metaphor: Implications and applications*, pages 23–38.

Klaus Krippendorff. 2012. *Content analysis: An introduction to its methodology*. Sage.

Victoria López, Alberto Fernández, Salvador García, Vasile Palade, and Francisco Herrera. 2013. An insight into classification with imbalanced data: Empirical results and current trends on using data intrinsic characteristics. *Information Sciences*, 250:113–141.

Diana Maynard and Mark A Greenwood. 2014. Who cares about sarcastic tweets? investigating the impact of sarcasm on sentiment analysis. In *Proceedings of LREC*.

D. M. W. Powers. 2015. What the F-measure doesn't measure: Features, Flaws, Fallacies and Fixes. *ArXiv e-prints*, March.

Ashwin Rajadesingan, Reza Zafarani, and Huan Liu. 2015. Sarcasm detection on twitter: A behavioral modeling approach. In *Proceedings of the Eighth ACM International Conference on Web Search and Data Mining*, pages 97–106. ACM.

Reid Swanson, Stephanie M Lukin, Luke Eisenberg, Thomas Corcoran, and Marilyn A Walker. 2014. Getting reliable annotations for sarcasm in online dialogues. In *LREC*, pages 4250–4257.

Oren Tsur, Dmitry Davidov, and Ari Rappoport. 2010. Icwsm-a great catchy name: Semi-supervised recognition of sarcastic sentences in online product reviews. In *ICWSM*.

Akira Utsumi. 2000. Verbal irony as implicit display of ironic environment: Distinguishing ironic utterances from nonirony. *Journal of Pragmatics*, 32(12):1777–1806.

Byron C Wallace, Laura Kertz Do Kook Choe, and Eugene Charniak. 2014. Humans require context to infer ironic intent (so computers probably do, too).

In *Proceedings of the Annual Meeting of the Association for Computational Linguistics (ACL)*, pages 512–516.

Unsupervised Authorial Clustering Based on Syntactic Structure

Alon Daks and **Aidan Clark**
Computer Science Division
University of California, Berkeley
Berkeley, CA 94720
{alon.daks, aidanbclark}@berkeley.edu

Abstract

This paper proposes a new unsupervised technique for clustering a collection of documents written by distinct individuals into authorial components. We highlight the importance of utilizing syntactic structure to cluster documents by author, and demonstrate experimental results that show the method we outline performs on par with state-of-the-art techniques. Additionally, we argue that this feature set outperforms previous methods in cases where authors consciously emulate each other's style or are otherwise rhetorically similar.

1 Introduction

Unsupervised authorial clustering is the process of partitioning n documents written by k distinct authors into k groups of documents segmented by authorship. Nothing is assumed about each document except that it was written by a single author. Koppel et al. (2011) formulated this problem in a paper focused on clustering five books from the Hebrew Bible. They also consider a 'multi-author document' version of the problem: decomposing sentences from a single composite document generated by merging randomly sampled chunks of text from k authors. Akiva and Koppel (2013) followed that work with an expanded method, and Aldebei et al. (2015) have since presented an improved technique in the 'multi-author document' context by exploiting posterior probabilities of a Naive-Bayesian Model. We consider only the case of clustering n documents written by k authors because we believe that, in most cases of authorial decomposition, there is some minimum size of text (a 'document'), for which it can be reliably asserted that only a single author is present. Furthermore, this formulation precludes results dependent

on a random document generation procedure.

In this paper, we argue that the biblical clustering done by Koppel et al. (2011) and by Aldebei et al. (2015) do not represent a grouping around true authorship within the Bible, but rather around common topics or shared style. We demonstrate a general technique that can accurately discern multiple authors contained within the Books of Ezekiel and Jeremiah. Prior work assumes that each prophetic book reflects a single source, and does not consider the consensus among modern biblical scholars that the books of Ezekiel and Jeremiah were written by multiple individuals.

To cluster documents by true authorship, we propose that considering part-of-speech (POS) n-grams as features most distinctly identifies an individual writer. The use of syntactic structure in authorial research has been studied before. Baayen et al. (1996) introduced syntactic information measures for authorship attribution and Stamatatos (2009) argued that POS information could reflect a more reliable authorial fingerprint than lexical information. Both Zheng et al. (2006) and Layton et al. (2013) propose that syntactic feature sets are reliable predictors for authorial attribution, and Tschuggnall and Specht (2014) demonstrates, with modest success, authorial decomposition using pq-grams extracted from sentences' syntax trees. We found that by combining the feature set of POS n-grams with a clustering approach similar to the one presented by Akiva (2013), our method of decomposition attains higher accuracy than Tschuggnall's method, which also considers grammatical style. Additionally, in cases where authors are rhetorically similar, our framework outperforms techniques outlined by Akiva (2013) and Aldebei (2015), which both rely on word occurrences as features.

This paper is organized as follows: section 2 outlines our proposed framework, section 3 clari-

Proceedings of the 54th Annual Meeting of the Association for Computational Linguistics – Student Research Workshop, pages 114–118,
Berlin, Germany, August 7-12, 2016. ©2016 Association for Computational Linguistics

fies our method in detail through an example, section 4 contains results, section 5 tests an explanation of our results, and section 6 concludes our findings and discusses future work.

2   Our Framework

Given n documents written by k distinct authors, where it is assumed that each document is written entirely by one of the k authors, our method proceeds in the following way:

First, represent each document as a frequency vector reflecting all n-grams occurring in the 'POS-translated' document.

Second, cluster documents into k groups using an unsupervised clustering algorithm.

Third, determine 'core elements', documents that most strongly represent authorship attributes of their respective clusters.

Fourth, use 'core elements' to train a supervised classifier in order to improve accuracies of documents that were not central to any cluster.

A key improvement our framework presents over prior techniques is in step one, where we represent documents in terms of POS n-grams. Specifically, each document, x_i, is transformed into a 'POS-translated' version, x'_i, such that every word or punctuation symbol from the original document is replaced with its respective POS or punctuation token in the translated version. Consider the following sentences from a *New York Times* (NYT) column written by Paul Krugman: "Last week the Federal Reserve chose not to raise interest rates. It was the right decision." In the 'POS-translated' version these sentences appear as "JJ NN DT NNP NNP NN RB TO VB NN NNS PERIOD PRP VBD DT JJ NN PERIOD".[1] We use a POS tagger from the Natural Language Toolkit to translate English documents (Bird et al., 2009) and use hand annotations for the Hebrew Bible. Our framework will work with any text for which POS-annotations are obtainable. The requirement that k is a fixed parameter is a limitation of the set of unsupervised clustering algorithms available in step two.

3   Clarifying Details with NYT Columns

We shall describe a clustering of *New York Times* columns to clarify our framework. The NYT cor-

---

[1] A list of POS tags and explanations:
`http://www.ling.upenn.edu/courses/`
`Fall_2003/ling001/penn_treebank_pos.html`

Authors	1st	2nd	3rd
TF-PK	4 - 4	5 - 5	3 - 4
TF-GC	**3 - 5**	3 - 4	4 - 4
TF-MD	5 - 5	3 - 4	**3 - 5**
GC-PK	4 - 4	**3 - 5**	3 - 4
MD-PK	**3 - 5**	3 - 4	4 - 4
GC-MD	**3 - 5**	3 - 4	4 - 4

Table 1: The top three ranges for n-grams by F1 accuracy for each two-way split of NYT columnists. Here, TF = Thomas Friedman, GC = Gail Collins, MD = Maureen Dowd, PK = Paul Krugman.

pus is used both because the author of each document is known with certainty and because it is a canonical dataset that has served as a benchmark for both Akiva and Koppel (2013) and Aldebei et al. (2015). The corpus is comprised of texts from four columnists: Gail Collins (274 documents), Maureen Dowd (298 documents), Thomas Friedman (279 documents), and Paul Krugman (331 documents). Each document is approximately the same length and the columnists discuss a variety of topics. Here we consider the binary ($k = 2$) case of clustering the set of 629 Dowd and Krugman documents into two groups.

In step one, the documents are converted into their 'POS-translated' form as previously outlined. Each document is represented as a frequency vector that reflects all 3, 4, and 5-grams that appear in the 'POS-translated' corpus. This range of n-grams was determined through validation of different values for n across several datasets. Results of this validation for the two way split over NYT columnists is displayed in Table 1. These results are consistent when validating against other datasets. Using 3, 4, and 5-grams, the resulting design matrix has dimension 629 by 302,395. We re-weight every element in the design matrix according to its term frequency–inverse document frequency.

In step two, we apply spectral clustering to the design matrix to partition the documents into two clusters. This is implemented with the Shi and Malik (2000) algorithm, which solves a convex relaxation of the normalized cuts problem on the affinity graph (Pedregosa et al., 2011). Edge-weights of the affinity graph are computed using a linear kernel. In the case of clustering several ($k > 2$) authors, we apply the Yu and Shi (2003) algorithm to perform multiclass spectral clustering.

In step three, we calculate the centroid of each cluster produced by step two. For each document

Columnist	Cluster I	Cluster II
Dowd	**294**	4
Krugman	3	**328**

Table 2: Results when clustering 629 documents written by Maureen Dowd and Paul Krugman into two clusters.

x'_i, we determine θ_i, the angle between that document and the centroid of its cluster, and call a document a 'core element' if θ_i is within 2 standard deviations of the average of θ_i in x'_i's cluster.

In step four, 'core elements' are used to train a 500 tree random forest where at each split the standard heuristic of $\sqrt{p}$ features are considered (here $p = 302,395$). Finally, we reclassify all 629 documents according to this random forest to produce our final class labels, summarized in Table 2. The final accuracy of the Dowd-Krugman clustering, measured as an F1-score, is 98.8%.

4   Results

All accuracy scores given in the rest of this paper are calculated using the F1-score. Because our technique contains stochastic elements, results reflect an average of 20 runs.

4.1   NYT Columns

When clustering over all six binary-pairs of NYT columnists, our framework achieves an average accuracy of 94.5%, ranging from 90.0% to 98.8%. Aldebei et al. (2015) addresses the slightly different problem of decomposing artificially merged NYT documents, and acknowledging the distinction between the two problems, our results are comparable to their accuracies which range from 93.3% to 96.1%.

4.2   *Sanditon*: An Uncompleted Novel

Another canonical authorship test is that of the novel *Sanditon*, a text left incomplete at the death of its author, Jane Austen, and finished some years later by an anonymous person known as "Another Lady." She closely emulated Austen's style and added 19 chapters to Austen's original 11. Researchers have long examined this text and most recently Moon et al. (2006) analyzed *Sanditon* using supervised techniques in the context of authorship attribution. Much progress has been made in the field since then, but examining *Sanditon* has fallen out of style. Our framework clusters Austen's chapters from Another Lady's with 93.8% accuracy, only mislabeling two documents.

4.3   Obama-McCain & Ezekiel-Jeremiah

In order to confirm our framework is accurate over a variety of documents, we considered campaign speeches from the 2008 presidential election. Collecting 27 speeches from President Obama and 20 from Senator McCain, we expected our technique to excel in this context. We found instead that our method performed exceptionally poorly, clustering these speeches with only 74.2% accuracy. Indeed, we were further surprised to discover that by adjusting our framework to be similar to that presented in Akiva and Koppel (2013) and Aldebei et al. (2015) – by replacing POS n-grams with ordinary word occurrences in step one – our framework performed very well, clustering at 95.3%.

Similarly, our framework performed poorly on the Books of Ezekiel and Jeremiah from the Hebrew Bible. Using the English-translated King James Version, and considering each chapter as an individual document, our framework clusters the 48 chapters of Ezekiel and the 52 chapters of Jeremiah at 54.7%. Aldebei et al. (2015) reports 98.0% on this dataset, and when considering the original English text instead of the POS-translated text, our framework achieves 99.0%. The simultaneous success of word features and failure of POS features on these two datasets seemed to completely contradict our previous results.

We propose two explanations. First, perhaps too much syntactic structure is lost during translation. This could certainly be a factor, but does not explain the Obama-McCain results. The second explanation comes from the wide consensus among biblical scholars that there was no single 'Ezekiel' or 'Jeremiah' entirely responsible for each book. Instead, the books are composites from a number of authors, sometimes written over the span of hundreds of years (McKane, 1986; Zimmerli, 1979; Mowinckel, 1914). Koppel et al. (2011) acknowledges this shortcoming in their original paper, and suggest that in this authorial interpretation their clustering is one of style, not authorship. We hypothesize that in both failed cases, accuracy is low because our assumption that only two authors were represented among the documents is incorrect. This theory holds for the Obama-McCain dataset, because Obama had up to three primary speechwriters during the '08 election and McCain likely had a similar number (Parker, 2008). Perhaps emulating syntactic patterns is more difficult than emulating word choice. If so, using word fea-

Author	Cluster I	Cluster II
Ezekiel 1	**37**	2
Ezekiel 2	1	**8**

Table 3: Results when clustering the Hebrew text of the Book of Ezekiel split over the two authors.

Author	Cluster I	Cluster II
Jeremiah 1	**21**	2
Jeremiah 2	0	**14**

Table 4: Results when clustering the Hebrew text of the Book of Jeremiah split over the two primary authors.

Author	C I	C II	C III	C IV
Ezekiel 1	**32**	2	5	0
Ezekiel 2	1	**8**	0	0
Jeremiah 1	0	0	**21**	2
Jeremiah 2	0	0	0	**14**

Table 5: Results when clustering Ezekiel 1 and 2 and Jeremiah 1 and 2 simultaneously with $k = 4$.

tures, a model can discern Obama's rhetoric from that of McCain. However, since the syntax of more than two individuals is present in the text, POS features cannot accurately cluster the documents into two groups. Our goal is for POS features to cluster more accurately than word features when the true authorship of the documents is correctly considered.

5 Testing Our Theory

We first attempt to cluster the Ezekiel and Jeremiah texts in the original Hebrew in order to test if too much syntactic structure is lost during translation. For the Hebrew text, we use hand-tagged POS information because a reliable automatic tagger was not available (van Peursen et al., 2015; Roorda, 2015). Clustering Ezekiel and Jeremiah using Hebrew POS features obtains 62.5% accuracy. This is an improvement over the English text, but still performs far worse than lexical feature sets.

We next attempt to cluster the Ezekiel and Jeremiah texts according to the authorial strata within each book that is widely agreed upon by biblical scholars, in order to test if incorrect authorial assumptions were causing the decrease in accuracy. Unfortunately, there is no public breakdown of Obama and McCain speeches by speechwriter, so testing our hypothesis is limited here to the biblical dataset.

We therefore cluster the Book of Ezekiel assuming there are two nested authors, which according to modern scholarship are Ezekiel 1 (chapters 1–39) and Ezekiel 2 (chapters 40–48) (Zimmerli, 1979). Summarized in Table 3, according to this division our framework clusters the Ezekiel chapters with 93.6% accuracy, mislabeling only three documents. We also consider the Book of Jeremiah, which is composed of two primary authors with four secondary authors. In clus-

tering a corpus containing Jeremiah 1 (23 non-contiguous chapters) and Jeremiah 2 (14 non-contiguous chapters) (McKane, 1986), our framework divides the 37 chapters into two groups with 94.5% accuracy, mislabeling only two documents. These results are summarized in Table 4. When considering the 4-way split between Ezekiel 1, Ezekiel 2, Jeremiah 1 and Jeremiah 2, our method achieves 87.5% accuracy as summarized in Table 5.

When comparing these results with those obtained by looking at word frequencies in the original Hebrew texts partitioned into the four correct authors, we find that our approach performs significantly better. With word frequencies as features, our framework clusters Ezekiel 1 from Ezekiel 2 with only 76.3% accuracy, Jeremiah 1 from Jeremiah 2 with only 74.9% accuracy, and crucially, clusters the four-way between both Ezekiels and both Jeremiahs with only 47.9% accuracy. While lexical features outperform syntactic features when considering incorrect authorship, syntactic features substantially outperform lexical features when considering the true authorial divisions of Ezekiel and Jeremiah.

6 Conclusion and Future Work

We have demonstrated a new framework for authorial clustering that not only clusters canonical datasets with state-of-the-art accuracy, but also discerns nested authorship within the Hebrew Bible more accurately than prior work. While we believe it is possible for an author to emulate another author's word choice, it is much more difficult to emulate unconscious syntactic structure. These syntactic patterns, rather than lexical frequencies, may therefore be key to understanding authorial fingerprints. Finding testing data for this problem is difficult, since documents for which authorship is misconstrued or obfuscated but for which true authorship is known with certainty are rare. However, when clustering texts for which authorship is not known, one would wish to have a framework which most accurately discerns authorship, rather than rhetorical similarity. We believe that our framework, and syntactic feature sets in particular, clusters documents based on authorship more accurately than prior work. While we have shown that POS feature sets can succeed independently, future work should examine augmenting syntactic and lexical feature sets in order to utilize the benefits of each.

Finally, authorial clustering performs poorly when the number of true and expected authors within a corpus do not match. An important next step is to automatically identify the number of authors contained within a set of documents. We believe that a more reliable method of generating 'core elements' is essential, and should not be reliant on a predetermined number of authors.

Acknowledgments

We thank Laurent El Ghaoui, Professor of EECS and IEOR, UC Berkeley, and Ronald Hendel, Norma and Sam Dabby Professor of Hebrew Bible and Jewish Studies, UC Berkeley, for comments that greatly improved the paper.

References

Navot Akiva and Moshe Koppel. 2013. A generic unsupervised method for decomposing multi-author documents. *Journal of the American Society for Information Science and Technology*, pages 2256–2264.

Khaled Aldebei, Xiangjian He, and Jie Yang. 2015. Unsupervised decomposition of a multi-author document based on naive-bayesian model. *Proceedings of the 53rd Annual Meeting of the Association for Computational Linguistics and the 7th International Joint Conference on Natural Language Processing (Short Papers)*, pages 501–505.

Harald Baayen, Hans Van Halteren, and Fiona Tweedie. 1996. Outside the cave of shadows: Using syntactic annotation to enhance authorship attribution. *Literary and Linguistic Computing*, 11:121–131.

Steven Bird, Ewan Klein, and Edward Loper. 2009. *Natural Language Processing with Python*. O'Reilly Media.

Moshe Koppel, Navot Akiva, Idan Dershowitz, and Nachum Dershowitz. 2011. Unsupervised decomposition of a document into authorial components. *Proceedings of the 49th Annual Meeting of the Association for Computational Linguistics*, pages 1356–1364.

Robert Layton, Paul Watters, and Richard Dazeley. 2013. Automated unsupervised authorship analysis using evidence accumulation clustering. *Natural Language Engineering*.

William McKane. 1986. *A Critical and Exegetical Commentary on Jeremiah*. Edinburgh, Edinburgh, UK.

Todd K. Moon, Peg Howland, and Jacob H Gunther. 2006. Document author classification using generalized discriminant analysis. *Proc. Workshop on Text Mining, SIAM Int'l Conf. on Data Mining*.

Sigmund Mowinckel. 1914. *Zur Komposition des Buches Jeremia*. Kristiania.

Ashley Parker. 2008. What would obama say? *New York Times*, January 20.

F. Pedregosa, G. Varoquaux, A. Gramfort, V. Michel, B. Thirion, O. Grisel, M. Blondel, P. Prettenhofer, R. Weiss, V. Dubourg, J. Vanderplas, A. Passos, D. Cournapeau, M. Brucher, M. Perrot, and E. Duchesnay. 2011. Scikit-learn: Machine learning in Python. *Journal of Machine Learning Research*, 12:2825–2830.

Dirk Roorda. 2015. Laf-fabric software. https://github.com/ETCBC/laf-fabric. GitHub repository.

Jianbo Shi and Jitendra Malik. 2000. Normalized cuts and image segmentation. *IEE Transactions On Pattern Analysis And Machine Intelligence*, 22:888–905.

Efstathios Stamatatos. 2009. A survey of modern authorship attribution methods. *Journal of the American Society for Information Science and Technology*, 60:538–556.

Michael Tschuggnall and Gunther Specht. 2014. Enhancing authorship attribution by utilizing syntax tree profiles. *Proceedings of the 14th Conference of the European Chapter of the Association for Computational Linguistics*, pages 195–199.

W.T. van Peursen, M. Sc. C. Sikkel, and D. Roorda. 2015. Hebrew text database etcbc4b. http://dx.doi.org/10.17026/dans-z6y-skyh. DANS.

Stella X. Yu and Jianbo Shi. 2003. Multiclass spectral clustering. *Proceedings of the Ninth IEEE International Conference on Computer Vision*, 1:313–319.

Rong Zheng, Jiexun Li, Hsinchun Chen, and Zan Huang. 2006. A framework for authorship identification of online messages: Writing-style features and classification techniques. *J. Am. Soc. Inf. Sci. Technol.*, 57(3):378–393, February.

Walther Zimmerli. 1979. *Ezekiel 1-2: A Commentary on the Book of the Prophet Ezekiel*. Fortress Press of Philadelphia, Philadelphia, US.

Suggestion Mining from Opinionated Text

Sapna Negi

Insight Centre for Data Analytics

National University of Ireland, Galway

`sapna.negi@insight-centre.org`

Abstract

In addition to the positive and negative sentiments expressed by speakers, opinions on the web also convey suggestions. Such text comprise of advice, recommendations and tips on a variety of points of interest. We propose that suggestions can be extracted from the available opinionated text and put to several use cases. The problem has been identified only recently as a viable task, and there is a lot of scope for research in the direction of problem definition, datasets, and methods. From an abstract view, standard algorithms for tasks like sentence classification and keyphrase extraction appear to be usable for suggestion mining. However, initial experiments reveal that there is a need for new methods, or variations in the existing ones for addressing the problem specific challenges. We present a research proposal which divides the problem into three main research questions; we walk through them, presenting our analysis, results, and future directions.

1 Introduction

Online text is becoming an increasingly popular source to acquire public opinions towards entities like persons, products, services, brands, events, social debates etc. State of the art opinion mining systems primarily utilise this plethora of opinions to provide summary of positive and negative sentiments towards entities or topics. We stress that opinions also encompass suggestions, tips, and advice, which are often explicitly sought by stakeholders. We collaboratively refer to this kind of information as suggestions. Suggestions about a variety of topics of interest may be found on opin-

ion platforms like reviews, blogs, social media, and discussion forums. These suggestions, once detected and extracted, could be exploited in numerous ways. In the case of commercial entities, suggestions present among the reviews can convey ideas for improvements to the brand owners, or tips and advice to customers.

Suggestion extraction can also be employed for the summarisation of dedicated suggestion forums[1]. People often provide the context in such posts, which gets repetitive over a large number of posts. Suggestion mining methods can identify the exact textual unit in the post where a suggestion is conveyed.

Table 1 provides examples of suggestions found in opinion mining datasets. In our previous work (Negi and Buitelaar, 2015b), we showed that suggestions do not always possess a particular sentiment polarity. Thus the detection of suggestions in the text goes beyond the scope of sentiment polarity detection, while complements its use cases at the same time.

In the recent past, suggestions have gained the attention of the research community. However, most of the related work so far performs a binary classification of sentences into *suggestions* or *non-suggestions*, where suggestions are defined as the sentences which propose improvements in a reviewed entity (Brun and Hagege, 2013; Ramanand et al., 2010; Dong et al., 2013). These studies annotated datasets accordingly and developed systems for the detection of only these type of suggestions; and performed an in-domain evaluation of the classifier models on these datasets.

We emphasise that in addition to the classification tasks performed earlier, there are a lot more aspects associated with the problem, including a well-formed and consistent problem defini-

---

[1] https://feedly.uservoice.com/forums/192636-suggestions/category/64071-mobile

Proceedings of the 54th Annual Meeting of the Association for Computational Linguistics – Student Research Workshop, pages 119–125,
Berlin, Germany, August 7-12, 2016. ©2016 Association for Computational Linguistics

tion. We divide the study of suggestion mining into three guiding aspects or research questions:
1) Definition of suggestions in the context of suggestion mining, 2) Their automatic detection from opinionated text, and 3) Their representation and summarisation.

A comprehensive research on suggestion mining demands the problem specific adaptation and integration of common NLP tasks, like text classification, keyphrase extraction, sequence labelling, text similarity etc. Last but not least, recent progress in the adaptation of deep learning based methods for NLP tasks opens up various possibilities to employ them for suggestion mining.

2 Research Problem

A broad statement of our research problem would be, *mining expressions of suggestions from opinionated text*. There are several aspects of the problem which can lead to a number of research questions. We identify three broad research questions which are the guiding map for our PhD research.

- Research Question 1 (RQ1): How do we define suggestions in suggestion mining?

- Research Question 2 (RQ2): How do we detect suggestions in a given text ?

- Research Question 3 (RQ3): How can suggestions be represented and summarised ?

The following sections will give a more detailed description of these aspects, including the preliminary results, challenges, and future directions.

3 Research Methodology

In this section we address each of the research questions, our findings so far, and the future directions.

3.1 RQ1: Suggestion Definition

The first sense of *suggestion* as listed in the oxford dictionary is, *an idea or plan put forward for consideration*, and the listed synonyms are *proposal, proposition, recommendation, advice, counsel, hint, tip, clue* etc. This definition, however needs to be defined on a more fine grained level, in order to perform manual and automatic labelling of a text as an expression of suggestion.

There have been variations in the definition of suggestions targeted by the related works, which renders the system performances from some of the works incomparable to the others. We identify three parameters which can lead us to a well-formed task definition of *suggestions* for suggestion mining task: What is the unit of a suggestion, who is the intended receiver, and whether the suggestion is expressed explicitly or not.

Unit: Currently, we consider sentence as a unit of suggestion, which is in-line with related works. However, it was observed that some sentences tend to be very long, where suggestion markers are present in only one of the constituent clauses. For example: *When we booked the room the description on the website said it came with a separate seating area, despite raising the issue with reception we were basically told this was not so , I guess someone needs to amend the website.* In this sentence, although the full sentence provides context, the suggestion is identifiable from the last clause. It is common to witness such non-uniform choice of punctuation in online content. Considering this, we intend to build classification models which can identify the exact clause/phrase where a suggestion is expressed, despite of individual instances being sentences.

Receiver: Different applications of suggestion mining may target different kinds of suggestions, which can differ on the basis of intended receiver. For example, in domains like online reviews, there are two types of intended receivers, brand owners, and fellow customers. Therefore, suggestions need to be defined on the basis of the intended receivers.

How is a suggestion expressed: The first round of suggestion labelling performed by us resulted in a very low inter-annotator agreement, i.e. a kappa score of 0.4 - 0.5. It was observed that given a layman definition of suggestions, humans do not distinguish between explicit and implicit forms of suggestions, since they can inherently infer suggestions from their implicit forms. Figure 1 illustrates the two forms. Specifically, in the case of domains like reviews, annotators mostly disagreed on whether the implicit ones are suggestions or not. We define an explicit suggestion as the text which directly proposes, recommends, or advices an action or an entity; whereas the implicit ones provide the information

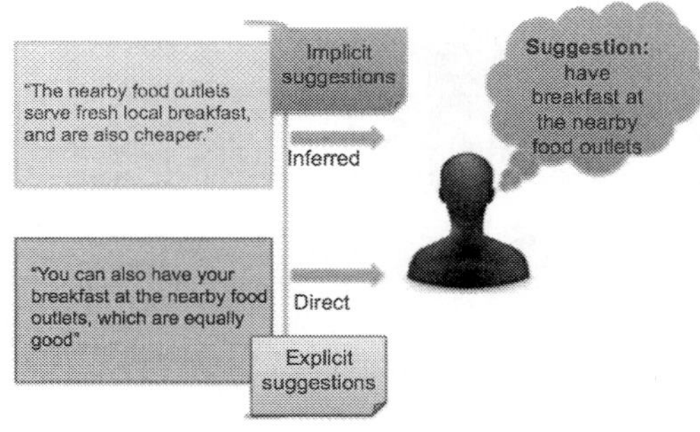

Figure 1: Implicit and explicit forms of suggestions

from which the suggested action or entity can be inferred. In remainder of the paper, we refer to explicit suggestions as *suggestions*.

We observe that certain linguistic properties consistently mark suggestions across different datasets (Table 1). One such phenomenon is imperative and subjunctive mood (Negi and Buitelaar, 2015a; Negi and Buitelaar, 2015b). The presence of these properties makes it more likely, but does not guarantee a text to be a suggestion. Another linguistic property is *speech act* (Searle, 1969). Speech act is a well studied area of computational linguistics, and several typologies for speech acts exist in literature, some of which consider suggestions as a speech act (Zhang et al., 2011).

3.2 RQ2: Suggestion Detection

The problem of suggestion detection in a big dataset of opinions can be defined as a sentence classification problem: Given a set S of sentences $\{s_1, s_2, s_3, ..., s_n\}$, predict a label l_i for each sentence in S, where $l_i \in \{suggestion, non suggestion\}$.

The task of suggestion detection rests on the hypothesis that a large amount of opinionated text about a given entity or topic is likely to contain suggestions which could be useful to the stakeholders for that entity or topic. This hypothesis has been proven to be true when sentences from reviews and tweets about commercial entities were manually labeled (Table 1). Also, the survey presented by Asher et al. (2009) shows that although in a low proportion, opinionated texts do contain expressions of advice and recommendations.

The required datasets for suggestion based sentence classification task are a set of sentences which are labelled as *suggestion* and *non-suggestion*, where the labeled suggestions should be explicitly expressed.

Existing Datasets: Some datasets on suggestions for product improvement are unavailable due to their industrial ownership. To the best of our knowledge, only the below mentioned datasets are publicly available from the previous studies:

1) Tweet dataset about Microsoft phones: comprises of labeled tweets which give suggestions about product improvement (Dong et al., 2013). Due to the short nature of tweets, suggestions are labeled at the tweet level, rather than the sentence level.

2) Travel advice dataset: comprises of sentences from discussion threads labeled as *advice* (Wicaksono and Myaeng, 2013). We observe that the statements of facts (implicit suggestions/advice) are also tagged as advice in this dataset, for example, *The temperature may reach upto 40 degrees in summer.* Therefore, we re-labeled the dataset with the annotation guidelines for explicit suggestions, which reduced the number of positive instances from 2192 to 1314.

Table 2 lists the statistics of these datasets.

Introduced Datasets: In our previous work (Negi and Buitelaar, 2015b), we prepared two datasets from hotel and electronics reviews (Table 2) where suggestions targeted to the fellow customers are labeled. Similar to the existing Microsoft tweets dataset, the number of suggestions are very low in these datasets. As stated previously, we also formulate annotation guidelines for the explicit expression of suggestions, which led to a kappa score of upto 0.86 as the inter-annotator agreement. In another work (Negi et al., 2016), we further identify possible domains and collection methods, which are likely to provide suggestion rich datasets for training statistical classifiers.

1) Customer posts from a publicly accessible suggestion forums for the products *Feedly mobile app*[2], and *Windows App studio*[3]. We crawled

---

[2]https://feedly.uservoice.com/forums/192636-suggestions

[3]https://wpdev.uservoice.com/forums/110705-universal-windows-platform

Source, Entity/Topic	Sentence	Intended Receiver	Sentiment	Linguistic Properties
Reviews, Electronics	I would recommend doing the upgrade to be sure you have the best chance at trouble free operation.	Customer	Neutral	Subjunctive, Imperative, lexical clue: *recommend*
Reviews, Electronics	My one recommendation to creative is to get some marketing people to work on the names of these things	Brand owner	Negative	Imperative, lexical clue: *recommendation*
Reviews, Hotels	Be sure to specify a room at the back of the hotel.	Customer	Neutral	Imperative
Tweets, Windows Phone	Dear Microsoft, release a new zune with your wp7 launch on the 11th. It would be smart	Brand owner	Neutral	Imperative, subjunctive
Discussion thread, Travel	If you do book your own airfare, be sure you don't have problems if Insight has to cancel the tour or reschedule it	Thread participants	Neutral	Conditional, imperative

Table 1: Examples of similar linguistic properties in suggestions from different domains, about different entities and topics, and intended for different receivers

the suggestion for improvement posts for these products, and labeled only a subset of them due to the annotation costs. Although all the posts are about suggestions, they also comprise of explanatory and informative sentences around the suggestion sentences. With the availability of more annotation resources, this dataset can be easily extended.

2) We also prepared a new tweet dataset, where the tweets are first collected using the hashtags *suggestion, advice, recommendation, warning*, which appeared as top unigram features in our SVM based classification experiments. This sampling method increased the likelihood of the presence of suggestion tweets as compared to the Microsoft tweets dataset.

Table 2 details all the currently available datasets including the old and the new ones.

Sentence Classification: Conventional text classification approaches, including, rule based classifiers, and SVM based classifiers have been previously used for this task. We employ these two approaches on all the available datasets as baselines. In addition to the in-domain training and evaluation of statistical classifiers, we also perform a cross-domain training and evaluation. The reason for performing a cross domain training experiment is that the suggestions possess similar linguistic properties irrespective of the domain (Table 1). Since, it is expensive to prepare dedicated training dataset for each domain or use case, we aim for domain independent classification models.

We performed a first of its kind study of the employability of neural network architectures like Long Short Term Memory (LSTM), and Convolutional Neural Nets (CNN) for suggestion detection. The F-scores for positive class are shown in Table 2. A neural network based approach seems to be promising compared to the baseline

approaches, specifically in the case of domain independent training. Our intuition is that the ability of word embeddings to capture semantic and syntactic knowledge, as well as the ability of LSTM to capture word dependencies are the contributing factors to this.

There is a lot of scope for improvement in the current results. One challenge is that the sentences are often longer, whereas the suggestion is present only as a phrase or clause. Therefore, a future direction is to explore sequential classification approaches in this regard, where we can tag sentences at the word level, and train the classifiers to predict binary labels corresponding to whether a word is a part of suggestion or not. For example, My_1 $recommendation\_1$ is_1 to_1 $wait\_1$ on_1 $buying\_1$ one_1 $from\_1$ $this\_1$ $company\_1$ as_0 $they\_0$ $will\_0$ $surely\_0$ get_0 $sent\_0$ a_0 $message\_0$ of_0 $many\_0$ $returned\_0$ dvd_0 $players\_0$ $after\_0$ $christmas\_0$. LSTM NNs have also been proven to be a good choice for sequence labelling tasks (Huang et al., 2015).

3.3 Suggestion Representation and Summarisation

In order to apply suggestion mining to real life applications, a more structured representation of suggestions might be required. After the extraction of suggestion sentences from large datasets, there should be a way to cluster suggestions, link them to relevant topics and entities, and summarise them. One way of achieving this is to further extract information from these sentences, as shown in Table 3.

We start with the task of extracting the central phrase from a suggestion, which either corresponds to a recommended entity or a suggested action. As a first step in this direction, we experimented with keyphrase extraction. Keyphrase extraction has been mainly used for the detection of topical information, and is therefore noun-based

Dataset	Intended receiver	No. of suggestions	F1 score			
			Rules	SVM	LSTM	CNN
In-domain Evaluation						
Hotel Reviews	Customers	448 / 7534	0.285	0.543	**0.639**	0.578
Electronics reviews	Customers	324 / 3782	0.340	0.640	**0.672**	0.612
Travel advice	Thread participants	1314 / 5183	0.342	0.566	**0.617**	0.586
Tweets (Microsoft)	Brand owner	238 / 3000	0.325	**0.616**	0.550	0.441
New Tweets	Public	1126 / 4099	0.266	0.632	0.645	**0.661**
Suggestion Forum	Brand owners	1428 / 5724	0.605	0.712	**0.727**	0.713
Cross-domain Evaluation						
Training Dataset	Test Dataset	No. of suggestions (training)	F1 score			
			Rules	SVM	LSTM	CNN
Sugg-Forum	Hotel	1428 / 5724	0.285	0.211	**0.452**	0.363
Sugg-Forum	Electronics	1428 / 5724	0.340	0.180	**0.516**	0.393
Sugg-Forum	Travel advice	1428 / 5724	0.342	0.273	0.323	**0.453**
Sugg-Forum + Travel advice	Hotel	2742 / 10907	0.285	0.306	0.345	**0.393**
Sugg-Forum + Travel advice	Electronics	2742 / 10907	0.340	0.259	**0.503**	0.456
New Tweets	Microsoft Tweets	1126 / 4099	**0.325**	0.117	0.161	0.122

Table 2: Results of suggestion detection across datasets, using different methods

Full suggestion text	Entity	Beneficiary	Keyphrase
If you do end up here, be sure to specify a room at the back of the hotel	Room	Customer	Specify a room at the back of the hotel
If you are here, I recommend a Trabi safari	Trabi Safari	Customer	Trabi Safari
Chair upholstry seriously needs to be cleaned	Chair/Chair upholstry	Brand owner	chair upholstry need to be cleaned

Table 3: Aimed information extraction from suggestions

(Hasan and Ng, 2014). As Table 3 shows, we also need to detect verb based keyphrases in the case of advice or action based suggestions, however a noun based keyphrase would work in the case of suggestions which recommend an entity.

In the Table 4, we show the examples of keyphrases extracted using *TextRank* (Mihalcea and Tarau, 2004) algorithm on 3 different review datasets, i.e. ebook reader, camera, and hotel. TextRank and almost all of the keyphrase extraction algorithms rely on the occurrence and co-occurrence of candidate keyphrases (noun phrases) in a given corpus. We ran TextRank on the reviews and obtained a set of keyphrase. Table 4 shows whether the central phrases contained in a suggestion from the dataset were detected as a keyphrase by the algorithm or not. In the case of suggestion for improvement i.e. sentence 1, TextRank is able to capture relevant noun keyphrases. This can be attributed to a large number of sentences in the corpus which mention *price*, which is an important aspect of the reviewed entity. However, in the case of suggestions which are addressed to the other customers, reviewers often speak about aspects which do not appear frequently in reviews. This can be observed in sentence 2 and 3, where the keyphrase were not detected.

We plan to include keyphrase annotations to the sequence labels mentioned in section 3.2, in order to identify the suggestions as well as the keyphrases within those suggestions at the same time.

After the representation of suggestions in the proposed format, we plan to use the methods for text similarity and relatedness in order to cluster similar suggestions.

Suggestions	Extracted keyphrase	Desired keyphrase
Look around and compare price...the price of the Nook varies widely between stores.	Price	compare price
I suggest that you purchase additional memory	*none*	purchase additional memory
Would recommend the Kohi Noor indian around the corner, book in advance as it is small and well used by locals.	*none*	Kohi Noor Indian, book in advance

Table 4: Sample results from keyphrase extraction using the textRank algorithm

4 Related Work

To the best of our knowledge, all of the related work so far focussed on research question 2, i.e. detection of suggestions in a given text. In recent years, only a limited number of experiments have been performed in this regard, all of which frame the task as a sentence classification task.

Suggestion Detection: Ramanand et al. (2010) and Brun et al. (2013) employed manually crafted linguistic rules to identify suggestions for product improvement. Dong et al. (2013) performed classification of given tweets about Microsoft Windows' phone as suggestions for improvement or not. Wicaksono et al. (Wicaksono and Myaeng, 2013) detected advice containing sentences from travel related discussion threads. They employed sequential classifiers, based on Hidden Markov Model, and Conditional Random Fields. Most of the datasets are not available, and annotations for the available datasets are ambiguous with no detailed definition of what is considered as a *suggestion* or *advice*.

Text Classification using deep learning: Recent advances in the application of Neural Networks (NNs) to NLP tasks demonstrate their effectiveness in some of the text classification problems, like sentiment classification, pos tagging, and semantic categorisation. Long Short Term Memory NNs (Graves, 2012), and Convolutional NNs (Kim, 2014) are the two most popular neural network architectures in this regard. An end to end combination of CNN and LSTM (Zhou et al., 2015) has also shown improved results for sentiment analysis.

5 Conclusion

In this work we presented a research plan on suggestion mining. The problem in itself introduces a novel information mining task. Several useful datasets have already been released, with more to come. The related work in this direction is very limited, and has so far focussed on only one aspect of the problem. Our proposal proposes research contributions in three research aspects/questions, and presents initial results and analysis.

Since suggestions tend to exhibit similar linguistic structure, irrespective of topics and intended receiver of the suggestions, there is a scope of learning domain independent models for suggestion detection. Therefore, we test the discussed approaches both in a domain-independent setting as well, in order to test the domain-independence of models learnt in these approaches. Neural networks in general outperformed the results on existing test datasets, in both domain dependent and independent training. In light of these findings,

building neural network based classification architectures for intra-domain feature learning can be an interesting future direction for us.

The results also point towards the challenges and complexity of the task of suggestion mining. Building word level suggestion tagged datasets seems to be a promising direction in this regard, which can simultaneously address the tasks of suggestion detection and as keyphrase extraction for suggestion mining.

Our research findings and datasets can also be employed to similar problems, like classification of speech acts, summarisation, verb based keyphrase extraction, and cross domain classification model learning.

Acknowledgements

This work has been funded by the European Unions Horizon 2020 programme under grant agreement No 644632 MixedEmotions, and the Science Foundation Ireland under Grant Number SFI/12/RC/2289 (Insight Center).

References

[Asher et al.2009] Nicholas Asher, Farah Benamara, and Yannick Mathieu. 2009. Appraisal of Opinion Expressions in Discourse. *Lingvistic Investigationes*, 31.2:279–292.

[Brun and Hagege2013] C. Brun and C. Hagege. 2013. Suggestion mining: Detecting suggestions for improvements in users comments. In *Proceedings of 14th International Conference on Intelligent Text Processing and Computational Linguistics*.

[Dong et al.2013] Li Dong, Furu Wei, Yajuan Duan, Xiaohua Liu, Ming Zhou, and Ke Xu. 2013. The automated acquisition of suggestions from tweets. In Marie desJardins and Michael L. Littman, editors, *AAAI*. AAAI Press.

[Graves2012] Alex Graves. 2012. Supervised sequence labelling. In *Supervised Sequence Labelling with Recurrent Neural Networks*, pages 5–13. Springer Berlin Heidelberg.

[Hasan and Ng2014] Kazi Saidul Hasan and Vincent Ng. 2014. Automatic keyphrase extraction: A survey of the state of the art. In *Proceedings of the 52nd Annual Meeting of the Association for Computational Linguistics (Volume 1: Long Papers)*, pages 1262–1273, Baltimore, Maryland, June. Association for Computational Linguistics.

[Huang et al.2015] Zhiheng Huang, Wei Xu, and Kai Yu. 2015. Bidirectional LSTM-CRF models for sequence tagging. *CoRR*, abs/1508.01991.

[Kim2014] Yoon Kim. 2014. Convolutional neural networks for sentence classification. *arXiv preprint arXiv:1408.5882*.

[Mihalcea and Tarau2004] R. Mihalcea and P. Tarau. 2004. TextRank: Bringing order into texts. In *Proceedings of EMNLP-04and the 2004 Conference on Empirical Methods in Natural Language Processing*, July.

[Negi and Buitelaar2015a] Sapna Negi and Paul Buitelaar. 2015a. Curse or boon? presence of subjunctive mood in opinionated text. In *Proceedings of the 11th International Conference on Computational Semantics*, pages 101–106, London, UK, April. Association for Computational Linguistics.

[Negi and Buitelaar2015b] Sapna Negi and Paul Buitelaar. 2015b. Towards the extraction of customer-to-customer suggestions from reviews. In *Proceedings of the 2015 Conference on Empirical Methods in Natural Language Processing*, pages 2159–2167, Lisbon, Portugal, September. Association for Computational Linguistics.

[Negi et al.2016] Sapna Negi, Kartik Asooja, Shubham Mehrotra, and Paul Buitelaar. 2016. A distant supervision approach to semantic role labeling. In *Proceedings of the Fifth Joint Conference on Lexical and Computational Semantics*, Berlin, Germany, August. Association for Computational Linguistics.

[Ramanand et al.2010] J Ramanand, Krishna Bhavsar, and Niranjan Pedanekar. 2010. Wishful thinking - finding suggestions and 'buy' wishes from product reviews. In *Proceedings of the NAACL HLT 2010 Workshop on Computational Approaches to Analysis and Generation of Emotion in Text*, pages 54–61, Los Angeles, CA, June. Association for Computational Linguistics.

[Searle1969] John R. Searle. 1969. *Speech Acts: An Essay in the Philosophy of Language*. Cambridge University Press, Cambridge, London.

[Wicaksono and Myaeng2013] Alfan Farizki Wicaksono and Sung-Hyon Myaeng. 2013. Automatic extraction of advice-revealing sentences foradvice mining from online forums. In *K-CAP*, pages 97–104. ACM.

[Zhang et al.2011] Renxian Zhang, Dehong Gao, and Wenjie Li. 2011. What are tweeters doing: Recognizing speech acts in twitter. In *Analyzing Microtext*, volume WS-11-05 of *AAAI Workshops*. AAAI.

[Zhou et al.2015] Chunting Zhou, Chonglin Sun, Zhiyuan Liu, and Francis C. M. Lau. 2015. A C-LSTM neural network for text classification. *CoRR*, abs/1511.08630.

An Efficient Cross-lingual Model for Sentence Classification Using Convolutional Neural Network

Yandi Xia[1], Zhongyu Wei[12], Yang Liu[1]
[1]Computer Science Department, The University of Texas at Dallas
Richardson, Texas 75080, USA
[2]School of Data Science, Fudan University, Shanghai, P.R.China
{yandixia,zywei,yangl}@hlt.utdallas.edu

Abstract

In this paper, we propose a cross-lingual convolutional neural network (CNN) model that is based on word and phrase embeddings learned from unlabeled data in two languages and dependency grammar. Compared to traditional machine translation (MT) based methods for cross lingual sentence modeling, our model is much simpler and does not need parallel corpora or language specific features. We only use a bilingual dictionary and dependency parser. This makes our model particularly appealing for resource poor languages. We evaluate our model using English and Chinese data on several sentence classification tasks. We show that our model achieves a comparable and even better performance than the traditional MT-based method.

1 Introduction

With the rapid growth of global Internet, huge amounts of information are created in different languages. It is important to develop cross-lingual NLP systems in order to leverage information from other languages, especially languages with rich annotations. Traditionally, cross-lingual systems rely highly on machine translation (MT) systems (Wan et al., 2011; Wan, 2011; Rigutini et al., 2005; Ling et al., 2008; Amini et al., 2009; Guo and Xiao, 2012; Chen and Ji, 2009; Duh et al., 2011). They translate data in one language into the other, and then apply monolingual models. One problem of such cross-lingual systems is that there is hardly any decent MT system for resource-poor languages. Another problem is the lack of high quality parallel corpora for resource-poor languages, which is required by MT systems.

Other work tried to address these problems by developping language independent representation learning and structural correspondence learning (SCL) (Prettenhofer and Stein, 2010; Xiao and Guo, 2013). They showed some promising results on document level classification tasks. However, their methods require carefully designed language specific features and find the "pivot features" across languages, which can be very expensive and inefficient.

To solve these problems, we develop an efficient and feasible cross-lingual sentence model that is based on convolutional neural network (CNN). Sentence modeling using CNN has shown its great potential in recent years (Kalchbrenner et al., 2014; Kim, 2014; Ma et al., 2015). One of the advantages is that CNN requires much less expertise knowledge than traditional feature based models. The only input of the model, word embeddings, can be learned automatically from large unlabeled text data.

There are roughly two main differences between different languages, lexicon and grammar. Lexicon can be seen as a set of symbols with each symbol representing certain meanings. A bilingual dictionary easily enables us to map from one symbol set to another. As for grammar, it decides the organization of lexical symbols, i.e., word order. Different languages organize their words in different manners (see Figure 1a for an example). To reduce grammar difference, we propose to use dependency grammar as an intermediate grammar. As shown in Figure 1b, dependency grammar can yield a similar dependency tree between two sentences in different languages.

To bridge two different languages from aspects of both lexicon and grammar, our CNN-based cross-lingual model consists of two components, bilingual word embedding learning and CNN incorporating dependency information. We propose

Proceedings of the 54th Annual Meeting of the Association for Computational Linguistics – Student Research Workshop, pages 126–131,
Berlin, Germany, August 7-12, 2016. ©2016 Association for Computational Linguistics

a method to learn bilingual word embeddings as the input of CNN, using only a bilingual dictionary and unlabeled corpus. We then adopt a dependency-based CNN (DCNN) (Ma et al., 2015) to incorporate dependency tree information. We also design lexical features and phrase-based bilingual embeddings to improve our cross-lingual sentence model.

We evaluate our model on English and Chinese data. We train a cross-lingual model on English data and then test it on Chinese data. Our experiments show that compared to the MT based cross-lingual model, our model achieves a comparable and even better performance on several sentence classification tasks including question classification, opinion analysis and sentence level event detection.

2   Methods

Our method is based on the CNN sentence classification model. It consists of two key components. First, we propose a method to learn bilingual word embeddings with only a bilingual dictionary and unlabeled corpus. This includes both word and phrase based embeddings. Second, for the CNN model, we use dependency grammar as the intermediate grammar, i.e., dependency-based CNN (DCNN) (Ma et al., 2015) where we also propose some useful modifications to make the model more suitable for the cross-lingual tasks.

2.1   Bilingual word and phrase embeddings

In order to train the bilingual word embeddings, we first construct an artificial bilingual corpus containing mix-language texts. We assume that the embeddings for a word and its translation in another language should be similar. We thus aim to create a synthetic similar context for a bilingual word pair. For example, assume we have an English unlabeled corpus and we want to learn word embeddings of Chinese word "夏威夷" and its English counter-part "Hawaii", we can substitute half of "Hawaii" in the English corpus into "夏威夷". Based on the modified corpus, we can obtain similar embeddings for the bilingual word pair "Hawaii" and "夏威夷". Similarly, we can also substitute Chinese words in the Chinese unlabeled data with their English counter-parts.

We use a bilingual dictionary to find bilingual word pairs. Each word w in the corpus has $1/2$ chance to be replaced by its counter-part word in the other language. If there are multiple translations for w in the bilingual dictionary, we randomly choose its replacement with probability $1/k$, where k is the number of translations for w in the bilingual dictionary.

In the bilingual dictionary, many translations are phrase based, for example, "how many" and "多少". Intuitively phrases should be treated as a whole and translated to words or phrases in the other languages. Otherwise, "how many" will be translated word by word as "如何很多", which makes no sense in Chinese. Therefore, we propose a simple method to learn phrase based bilingual word embeddings. When creating the artificial mixed language corpus, if we need to substitute a word with its translated phrase, we connect all the words in the phrase with underscores so that they can be treated as one unit during word embedding learning. We also preprocess the data by identifying all the phrases and concatenating all the words in the phrases that appear in the bilingual dictionary. We thus can learn phrase based bilingual embeddings.

The original English and Chinese corpora are still useful for encoding pure monolingual information. Therefore, we mix them together with the artificial mixed language corpus to form the final corpus for word embedding learning. In the data, phrases are also identified and connected using the same strategy. We use the CBOW model (Mikolov et al., 2013) for the bilingual word embedding learning. CBOW follows the assumption that similar words are more likely to appear in similar context. It casts word embedding learning into a word prediction problem given the context of the word. Because the CBOW model ignores word order within the window of contextual words, it may fail to capture the grammar or word order difference between two languages. We set a relatively larger CBOW window size (20) so that the window can cover an average sentence length. This is expected to ignore the grammar difference within a sentence and allow the CBOW model to learn bilingual word embeddings based on sentence level word co-occurrence.

2.2   Dependency grammar based CNN

Using the learned bilingual word embeddings as input, we adopt CNN for sentence modeling. When doing convolution and max pooling, each window is treated as a unit, therefore, only local words' relations are captured. Due to different

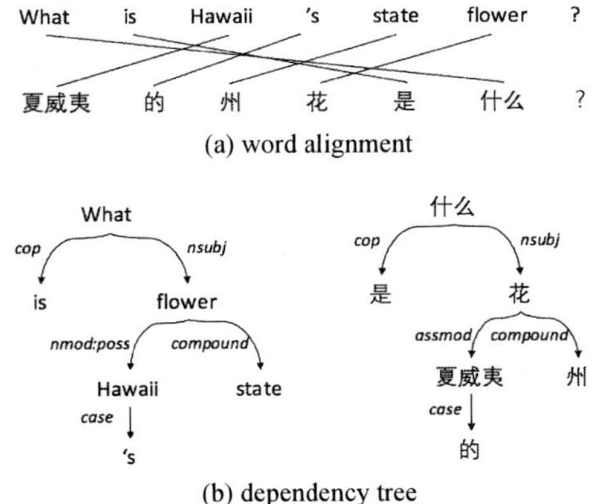

(a) word alignment

(b) dependency tree

Figure 1: An example to show dependency grammar can yield unified grammar between languages (Chinese and English).

grammars, local words' relation may vary across different languages. For example in Figure 1a, the basic CNN model will create six windows with size of 3 for each sentence: {Padding, Padding, What}, {Padding, What, is}, {What, is, Hawaii}, {is, Hawaii, 's}, {Hawaii, 's, state}, {'s, state, flower} for English, and {Padding, Padding, 夏威夷}, {Padding, 夏威夷, 的}, {夏威夷, 的, 州}, {的, 州, 花}, {州, 花, 是}, {花, 是, 什么} for Chinese. We can see that four windows in each sentence (out of six windows in that sentence) have different word ordering from the corresponding window in the other language.

To make relations captured in a window more meaningful for CNN, we adopt dependency based grammar as an intermediate grammar. As shown in Figure 1b, a dependency based CNN creates windows {What, ROOT, ROOT}, {is, What, ROOT}, {Hawaii, flower, What}, {'s, Hawaii, flower}, {state, flower, What}, {flower, What, ROOT} for English, and {夏威夷, 花, 什么}, {的, 夏威夷, 花}, {州, 花, 什么}, {花, 什么, ROOT}, {是, 什么, ROOT}, {什么, ROOT, ROOT} for Chinese. These dependency based windows capture similar word order and co-occurrence across languages. The order of the windows is not important as the max pooling layer ignores the global window order.

We therefore propose to incorporate dependency information into CNN. We evaluate the following three different setups.

(a) Dependency based CNN (DCNN): We adopt the dependency based CNN proposed by Ma et al. (2015), where instead of the natural word orders within a window, dependency based orders are used. For example, let x be the word embedding of current word w, then a dependency based window with size of 3 is $x \oplus Parent^1(x) \oplus Parent^2(x)$, where $Parent^1(x)$ and $Parent^2(x)$ are the embeddings of the parent and the grandparent of x respectively; $\oplus$ is concatenation operation. The dependency based windows will be passed through the convolution layer and max pooling layer and finally a softmax layer for classification. We use a window size of 3 (a short dependency path) here in order to make the model more robust across different languages.

(b) DCNN incorporating lexical features: Although dependency grammar is a good intermediate grammar, dependencies across languages are still not exactly the same. Second, dependency parsing is not perfect, especially for resource-poor languages. Therefore, it is possible that some word co-occurrence patterns cannot be captured. We thus add lexical features by adding an additional channel with window size equal to one, that is, each window has only one word. This lexicon input (a single word embedding) also passes through an independent convolution and pooling layer and the resulting feature is concatenated with the other abstract features.

(c) DCNN with phrase based grammar: In order to utilize phrase based bilingual embeddings, we make a modification in the dependency based CNN. If the input sentence contains a phrase in the bilingual dictionary, we combine the word nodes from the same phrase into a phrase node in the dependency tree. The combined phrase node will inherit all the parents and children from its contained word nodes. Then the phrase node will be treated as a single unit in the model.

3 Tasks and datasets

To evaluate our model, we select four sentence classification tasks including question classification, sentiment classification on movie review, sentiment classification on product review and sentence level event detection. For each task, we either use existing data or collect our own. It is difficult to find cross-lingual data with identical annotation schema for all the tasks. We thus collect English and Chinese corpora from tasks with similar annotation schema and take the overlapping part. For all the tasks, we train our model on English data, and test on Chinese data. To tune our model, we split Chinese dataset into validation and test sets.

Question classification (QC) aims to determine the category of a given question sentence. For English, we use the TREC[1] dataset. For Chinese, we use a QA corpus from HIT-IRLab[2]. We kept the six overlapped question types for both English and Chinese corpora. The final corpus includes 4,313 English questions and 4,031 Chinese questions (859 for testing, 859 for validation and 2,313 for training[3]).

Sentiment classification on movie review (SC-M) aims to classify a piece of given movie review into positive or negative. For English, we use IMDB polarity movie reviews from (Pang and Lee, 2004) (5,331 positive and 5,331 negative). For Chinese, we use the short Chinese movie reviews from Douban[4]. Like IMDB, users from Douban leave their comments along with a score for the movie. We collected 250 one star reviews (lowest score), and 250 five star reviews (highest score). We randomly split the 500 reviews into 200 for validation and 300 for testing.

Sentiment classification on product review (SC-P) aims to classify a piece of given product review into positive or negative. We use corpora from (Wan, 2011). Their Chinese dataset contains mostly short reviews. However, their English Amazon product reviews are generally longer, containing several sentences. Although our model is designed to take a single sentence as input, CNN can actually handle any input length. We remove reviews that are longer than 100 words and treat the remaining review as a single sentence. For dependency parsing, we combine the root of each sentence and make it a global dependency tree. In the end, we got 3,134 English product reviews (1,707 positive, 1,427 negative); 1000 (549 positive, 451 negative) and 314 (163 positive, 151 negative) Chinese ones for validation and testing respectively.

Sentence level event detection (ED) aims to determine if a sentence contains an event. ACE 2005 corpus[5] is ideal for cross-lingual tasks, be-

cause it contains annotated data for different languages with the same definition of events. Sentence is the smallest unit that contains a set of complete event information, i.e., triggers and corresponding arguments. To build the sentence level corpus, we first split document into sentences. For each sentence, if an event occurs (event triggers and arguments exist), we label the sentence as positive. Otherwise, we label it as negative. In the end we have 11,090 English sentences (3,688 positive, 7,402 negative). From the Chinese data we randomly selected 500 Chinese sentences (157 positive, 343 negative) for test, and 500 (138 positive, 362 negative) for validation. The remaining 5,039 ones (1767 positive, 3772 negative) are kept as training set. Because this is a detection task, we report F-score for it.

4 Experiment

We compare our bilingual word embedding based strategy to MT-based approach on the above four cross-lingual sentence classification tasks. Besides, we also evaluate the effectiveness of incorporating dependency information into CNN for sentence modeling.

4.1 Experiment setup

For the traditional MT-based cross-lingual method, we use the state-of-the-art statistical MT system Moses[6]. Language model is trained on Chinese gigawords corpus[7] with SRILM[8]. The parallel corpora used are from LDC[9]. We first translate English data into Chinese, and then apply the model trained on the translated dataset to the Chinese test data. For sentence classification, we use both basic CNN and DCNN (Ma et al., 2015).

We use monolingual word embeddings learned on the Chinese gigaword corpus for CNN and DCNN in MT-based method. For bilingual word embedding learning, we use "One Billion Word Language Modeling Benchmark"[10] and Chinese gigaword as unlabeled corpora for English and Chinese respectively. The bilingual dictionary is obtained from CC-CREDIT[11].

For CNN model training, we use the stochastic

---

[1]http://cogcomp.cs.illinois.edu/Data/QA/QC/

[2]http://ir.hit.edu.cn

[3]For QC and ED, we kept some samples as training set for an in-domain supervised model (refer to Section 4.2).

[4]http://www.douban.com

[5]http://projects.ldc.upenn.edu/ace/

[6]http://www.statmt.org/moses/

[7]https://catalog.ldc.upenn.edu/LDC2003T09

[8]http://www.speech.sri.com/projects/srilm/

[9]LDC: 2005T10, 2007T23, 2008T06, 2008T08, 2008T18, 2009T02, 2009T06, 2010T03

[10]http://www.statmt.org/lm-benchmark

[11]http://www.mandarintools.com/cedict.html

	QC	SC-M	SC-P	ED
	Accuracy			F-1
MT-based Method				
CNN	**83.00**	76.62	83.40	84.82
DCNN	82.89	75.97	81.50	84.40
Our Method With Bilingual Embedding				
CNN	68.10	64.29	64.80	82.06
DCNN	72.53	73.38	65.10	82.53
+Lex	79.28	75.00	78.60	83.17
+Lex+Phrase	82.19	**79.22**	**83.60**	**85.01**

Table 1: Results of different systems. +Lex: lexical features are used; +Phrase: phrase-based bilingual word embeddings and grammar are used.

gradient descent (SGD) learning method. We apply random dropout (Hinton et al., 2012) on the last fully connected layer for regularization. We use ADADELTA (Zeiler, 2012) algorithm to automatically control the learning rate and progress. The batch size for SGD and feature maps are tuned on the validation set for each task and fixed across different configurations. We preprocess all our corpora with Stanford CoreNLP (Manning et al., 2014), including word segmentation, sentence segmentation and dependency parsing.

4.2 Results

Table 1 shows the results of different systems. When using the MT based methods, the basic *CNN* achieves better results than *DCNN*. One possible reason is that the translation system produces errors, which may affect the performance of dependency parsing. For our method using bilingual word embeddings, basic *CNN* encodes only lexicon mapping information, and is not good at capturing grammar patterns. Therefore, it is natural this system has the lowest result. *DCNN* performs better than *CNN*, because it is able to capture additional grammar patterns across two languages by incorporating dependency information. Adding lexical features (*DCNN+Lex*) further improves performance. Given the fact that dependency parser is not perfect and dependency grammar between languages is not exactly the same, the grammar patterns that *DCNN* learned are not always reliable. The lexical feature here acts as an additional evidence to make the model more robust. *DCNN+Lex+Phrase* yields the best performance. The bilingual lexicon dictionary we use contains 54,168 Chinese words, and 29,355

of them have phrase-based translations (54.19%). Therefore, phrase-based bilingual word embeddings can represent sentences more accurately, and thus yield better results.

Compared to the MT-based approach, our cross-lingual model achieves comparable and even better performance. The advantage of our method is that we only use s dependency parser and bilingual dictionary, instead of a much more complicated machine translation system, which requires expertise knowledge about different languages, human designed features and expensive parallel corpus. Our method can be easily applied to any language pairs whose dependency parsers exist.

We further compare our cross-lingual model with a monolingual model for question classification and event detection. We have labeled Chinese training data for both tasks. We train a DCNN model on Chinese training data and then test on Chinese test set. For question classification, the monolingual model has an accuracy of 93.02%, and for event detection, its F-score is 87.28%. The event detection corpus has a consistent definition across two languages. Therefore, our cross-lingual system achieves close performance as the monolingual one. However, for question classification, the English and Chinese labeled data are constructed by two different teams and their annotation schemes are not identical. Therefore, the monolingual model performs much better than our cross-lingual model. Domain adaptation between two data sets may improve the performance for the bilingual model, but it is not the focus of this paper.

5 Conclusion

In this paper, we propose an efficient way to model cross-lingual sentences with only a bilingual dictionary and dependency parser. We evaluated our method on Chinese and English data and showed comparable and even better results than the traditional MT-based method on several sentence classification tasks. In addition, our method does not rely on expertise knowledge, human designed features and annotated resources. Therefore, it is easy to apply it to any language pair as long as there exist dependency parsers and a bilingual dictionary.

Acknowledgments

The work is partially supported by DARPA Contract No. FA8750-13-2-0041 and AFOSR award No. FA9550-15-1-0346.

References

Massih Amini, Nicolas Usunier, and Cyril Goutte. 2009. Learning from multiple partially observed views-an application to multilingual text categorization. In *Advances in neural information processing systems*, pages 28–36.

Zheng Chen and Heng Ji. 2009. Can one language bootstrap the other: a case study on event extraction. In *Proceedings of the NAACL HLT 2009 Workshop on Semi-Supervised Learning for Natural Language Processing*, pages 66–74. Association for Computational Linguistics.

Kevin Duh, Akinori Fujino, and Masaaki Nagata. 2011. Is machine translation ripe for cross-lingual sentiment classification? In *Proceedings of the 49th Annual Meeting of the Association for Computational Linguistics: Human Language Technologies: short papers-Volume 2*, pages 429–433. Association for Computational Linguistics.

Yuhong Guo and Min Xiao. 2012. Cross language text classification via subspace co-regularized multiview learning. *arXiv preprint arXiv:1206.6481*.

Geoffrey E Hinton, Nitish Srivastava, Alex Krizhevsky, Ilya Sutskever, and Ruslan R Salakhutdinov. 2012. Improving neural networks by preventing co-adaptation of feature detectors. *arXiv preprint arXiv:1207.0580*.

Nal Kalchbrenner, Edward Grefenstette, and Phil Blunsom. 2014. A convolutional neural network for modelling sentences. *arXiv preprint arXiv:1404.2188*.

Yoon Kim. 2014. Convolutional neural networks for sentence classification. *arXiv preprint arXiv:1408.5882*.

Xiao Ling, Gui-Rong Xue, Wenyuan Dai, Yun Jiang, Qiang Yang, and Yong Yu. 2008. Can chinese web pages be classified with english data source? In *Proceedings of the 17th international conference on World Wide Web*, pages 969–978. ACM.

Mingbo Ma, Liang Huang, Bowen Zhou, and Bing Xiang. 2015. Dependency-based convolutional neural networks for sentence embedding. In *Proceedings of the 53rd Annual Meeting of the Association for Computational Linguistics and the 7th International Joint Conference on Natural Language Processing (Volume 2: Short Papers)*, pages 174–179. Association for Computational Linguistics.

Christopher D. Manning, Mihai Surdeanu, John Bauer, Jenny Finkel, Steven J. Bethard, and David McClosky. 2014. The Stanford CoreNLP natural language processing toolkit. In *Association for Computational Linguistics (ACL) System Demonstrations*, pages 55–60.

Tomas Mikolov, Kai Chen, Greg Corrado, and Jeffrey Dean. 2013. Efficient estimation of word representations in vector space. *arXiv preprint arXiv:1301.3781*.

Bo Pang and Lillian Lee. 2004. A sentimental education: Sentiment analysis using subjectivity summarization based on minimum cuts. In *Proceedings of the 42nd Annual Meeting of the Association for Computational Linguistics*.

Peter Prettenhofer and Benno Stein. 2010. Cross-language text classification using structural correspondence learning. In *Proceedings of the 48th Annual Meeting of the Association for Computational Linguistics*, pages 1118–1127. Association for Computational Linguistics.

Leonardo Rigutini, Marco Maggini, and Bing Liu. 2005. An EM based training algorithm for cross-language text categorization. In *Web Intelligence, 2005. Proceedings. The 2005 IEEE/WIC/ACM International Conference on*, pages 529–535. IEEE.

Chang Wan, Rong Pan, and Jiefei Li. 2011. Bi-weighting domain adaptation for cross-language text classification. In *Proceedings of International Joint Conference on Artificial Intelligence*, volume 22, pages 1535–1540.

Xiaojun Wan. 2011. Bilingual co-training for sentiment classification of chinese product reviews. *Computational Linguistics*, 37(3):587–616.

Min Xiao and Yuhong Guo. 2013. Semi-supervised representation learning for cross-lingual text classification. In *Proceedings of the 2013 Conference on Empirical Methods in Natural Language Processing*, pages 1465–1475. Association for Computational Linguistics.

Matthew D Zeiler. 2012. Adadelta: An adaptive learning rate method. *arXiv preprint arXiv:1212.5701*.

QA-It: Classifying Non-Referential *It* for Question Answer Pairs

Timothy Lee
Math & Computer Science
Emory University
Atlanta, GA 30322, USA
`tlee54@emory.edu`

Alex Lutz
Math & Computer Science
Emory University
Atlanta, GA 30322, USA
`ajlutz@emory.edu`

Jinho D. Choi
Math & Computer Science
Emory University
Atlanta, GA 30322, USA
`jinho.choi@emory.edu`

Abstract

This paper introduces a new corpus, QA-It, for the classification of non-referential *it*. Our dataset is unique in a sense that it is annotated on question answer pairs collected from multiple genres, useful for developing advanced QA systems. Our annotation scheme makes clear distinctions between 4 types of *it*, providing guidelines for many erroneous cases. Several statistical models are built for the classification of *it*, showing encouraging results. To the best of our knowledge, this is the first time that such a corpus is created for question answering.

1 Introduction

One important factor in processing document-level text is to resolve coreference resolution; one of the least developed tasks left in natural language processing. Coreference resolution can be processed in two steps, mention detection and antecedent resolution. For mention detection, the classification of the pronoun *it* as either referential or non-referential is of critical importance because the identification of non-referential instances of *it* is essential to remove from the total list of possible mentions (Branco et al., 2005; Wiseman et al., 2015).

Although previous work has demonstrated a lot of promise for classifying all instances of *it* (Boyd et al., 2005; Müller, 2006; Bergsma et al., 2008; Li et al., 2009), it is still a difficult task, especially when performed on social networks data containing grammatical errors, ambiguity, and colloquial language. In specific, we found that the incorrect classification of non-referential *it* was one of the major reasons for the failure of a question answering system handling social networks data. In this paper, we first introduce our new corpus, QA-It, sampled from the Yahoo! Answers corpus and manually an-

notated with 4 categories of *it*, referential-nominal, referential-others, non-referential, and errors. We also present statistical models for the classification of these four categories, each showing incremental improvements from one another.

The manual annotation of this corpus is challenging because the rhetoric used in this dataset is often ambiguous; consequently, the automatic classification becomes undoubtedly more challenging. Our best model shows an accuracy of $\approx78\%$, which is lower than some of the results achieved by previous work, but expected because our dataset is much harder to comprehend even for humans, showing an inter-annotation agreement of $\approx65\%$. However, we believe that this corpus provides an initiative to development a better coreference resolution system for the setting of question answering.

2 Related Work

The identification of non-referential *it*, also known as pleonastic *it*, has been studied for many years, starting with Hobbs (1978). Although most of these earlier approaches are not used any more, the rules they discovered have helped for finding useful features for later machine learning approaches. Evans (2001) used 35 features and memory-based learning to classify 7 categories of *it* using data sampled from the SUSANNE and BNC corpora. Boyd et al. (2005) took this approach and added 25 more features to identify 5 categories of *it*.

Müller (2006) classified 6 categories of *it* using spoken dialogues from the ICSI Meeting corpus. Bergsma et al. (2008) used n-gram models to identify *it* as either referential or non-referential. Li et al. (2009) used search queries to help classify 7 categories of *it*. Figure 2 shows how the annotation scheme for non-referential *it* has changed over time. Our approach differs from the recent work because we not only identify instances of *it* as either refer-

Proceedings of the 54th Annual Meeting of the Association for Computational Linguistics – Student Research Workshop, pages 132–137,
Berlin, Germany, August 7-12, 2016. ©2016 Association for Computational Linguistics

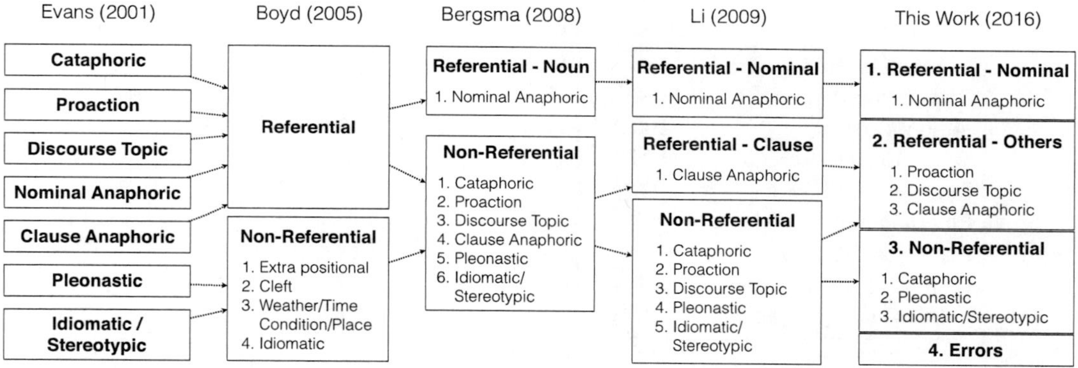

Figure 1: The chronicles of non-referential *it* annotation schemes.

ential or not, but also categorize whether referential *it* refers to a nominal or others, providing coreference resolution systems more valuable information. Furthermore, our corpus includes more colloquial language, which makes it harder to disambiguate different categories of *it*.

3 Data Collection

We inspected several corpora (e.g., Amazon product reviews, Wikipedia, New York Times, Yahoo! Answers), and estimated the maximum likelihood of non-referential *it* in each corpus. After thorough inspection, the Yahoo! Answers and the Amazon product reviews were found to contain the highest numbers of *it*; however, an overwhelming percentage of *it* in the Amazon product reviews was referential. On the other hand, the Yahoo! Answers showed great promise with over 35% instances of non-referential and referential-others *it*. Thus, question answer pairs were uniformly sampled from 9 genres in the Yahoo! Answers corpus:

[1]Computers and Internet, [2]Science and Mathematics, [3]Yahoo! Products, [4]Education and Reference, [5]Business and Finance, [6]Entertainment and Music, [7]Society and Culture, [8]Health, [9]Politics and Government

These genres contained the highest numbers of *it*. Each question answer pair was then ranked by the number of tokens it contained, ranging from 0 to 20, 20 to 40, all the way from 200 to 220, to see the impact of the document size on the classification of *it*. It is worth mentioning that our annotation was done on the document-level whereas annotations from most of the previous work were done on the sentence-level. While training our annotators, we confirmed that the contextual information was vital in classifying different categories of *it*.

4 Annotation Scheme

Instances of *it* are grouped into 4 categories in our annotation scheme; referential-nominal, referential-others, non-referential, and errors (Figure 2). Some of these categories are adapted from Evans (2001) who classified *it* into 7 categories; their categories captured almost every form of *it*, thus linguistically valuable, but a simpler scheme could enhance the annotation quality, potentially leading to more robust coreference resolution.

Boyd et al. (2005) focused on the detection of non-referential *it*, and although their scheme was effective, they did not distinguish referents that were nominals from the others (e.g., proaction, clause, discourse topic), which was not as suited for coreference resolution. Bergsma et al. (2008) attempted to solve this issue by defining that only instances of *it* referent to nominals were referential. Li et al. (2009) further elaborated above rules by adding referential-clause; their annotation scheme is similar to ours such that we both make the distinction between whether *it* refers to a nominal or a clause; however, we include proaction and discourse topic to referential-others as well as cataphoric instances to non-referential.

Our aim is to generate a dataset that is useful for a coreference system to handle both nominal and non-nominal referents. With our proposed scheme, it is up to a coreference resolution system whether or not to handle the referential-others category, including clause, proaction, and discourse topic, during the process of mention detection. Furthermore, the errors category is added to handle non-pronoun cases of *it*. Note that we only consider referential as those that do have antecedents. If the pronoun is cataphoric, it is categorized as non-referential.

Genre	Doc	Sen	Tok	C_1	C_2	C_3	C_4	C_*
1. Computers and Internet	100	918	11,586	222	31	24	3	280
2. Science and Mathematics	100	801	11,589	164	35	18	3	220
3. Yahoo! Products	100	1,027	11,803	176	36	25	3	240
4. Education and Reference	100	831	11,520	148	55	36	2	241
5. Business and Finance	100	817	11,267	139	57	37	0	233
6. Entertainment and Music	100	946	11,656	138	68	30	5	241
7. Society and Culture	100	864	11,589	120	57	47	2	226
8. Health	100	906	11,305	142	97	32	0	271
9. Politics and Government	100	876	11,482	99	81	51	0	231
Total	900	7,986	103,797	1,348	517	300	18	2,183

Table 1: Distributions of our corpus. Doc/Sen/Tok: number of documents/sentences/tokens. $C_{1..4}$: number of *it*-instances in categories described in Sections 4.1, 4.2, 4.3, and 4.4.

4.1 Referential - Nominal

This category is for anaphoric instances of *it* that clearly refer to nouns, noun phrases, or gerunds. This is the standard use of *it* that is already being referenced by coreference resolution models today.

4.2 Referential - Others

This category is for any anaphoric instances of *it* that do not refer to nominals. Some anaphora referents could be in the form of proaction, clause anaphoras, or discourse topic (Evans, 2001). Most coreference resolution models do not handle these cases, but as they still have anaphora referents, it would be valuable to indicate such category for the future advance of a coreference resolution system.

4.3 Non-Referential

This category is for any extraposition, clefts, and pronouns that do not have referent. This also includes cataphora (Evans, 2001). Our distinction of non-referential *it* is similar to the one made by Boyd et al. (2005), except that we do not include weather, condition, time, or place in this category because it would often be helpful to have those instances of *it* be referential:

What time is it now in Delaware US?
It would be approximately 9:00 am.

Many could argue that the second instance of *it* is non-referential for the above example. But when context is provided, it would be more informative to have *it* refer to "the time now in Delaware US" for coreference resolution. If *it* is simply marked as non-referential, we would essentially be losing the context that the time in Delaware is 9:00 am. Although this does not appear many times in our corpus, it is important to make this distinction based on the context because without the context, this instance of *it* would be simply marked as non-referential.

4.4 Errors

This category includes any uses of a non-pronoun form of *it* including IT (Information Technology), disfluencies, and ambiguous *it* in book/song titles.

When you leave a glass of water sitting around for a couple hours or so , do bubbles form *it it*

In the example above, the two instances of *it* serves no purpose and cannot be identified as a potential misspelling of another word. This category is not present in any of the previous work, but due to the nature of our corpus as mentioned in difficulties, it is included in our annotation scheme.

5 Corpus Analytics

5.1 Annotation Difficulties

The Yahoo! Answers contains numerous grammatical errors, ambiguous references, disfluency, fragments, and unintelligible question and answer pairs, all of which contributes to difficulties in annotation. Ambiguous referencing had been problematic throughout the annotation and sometimes an agreement was hard to reach between annotators:

After selling mobile phones, I got post dated cheques ($170,000). But he closed office and bank account. help me?... That's a lot of money to just let go. If it were $1,700.00 then I might just whoop his a** and let *it* go but for $170,000... are you kidding?...

Here, *it* can be either idiomatic, or refer to the "post dated cheque" or the "process of receiving the post dated cheque" such that disambiguating its category is difficult even with the context. There were more of such cases where we were not certain if the referent was referential-nominal, referential-others, or idiomatic; in which case, the annotators were instructed to use their best intuition to categorize.

5.2 Inter-Annotation Agreement

All instances of *it* were double annotated by students trained in both linguistics and computer science. Adjudication was performed by the authors of this paper. For the inter-annotator agreement, our annotation gave the Cohans Kappa score of 65.25% and the observed proportionate agreement score of 81.81%.

5.3 Analysis By Genre

The genre has a noticeable influence on the relative number of either referential or non-referential instances of *it*. The genres with the lowest percentage of referential-nominal are "Society and Culture" and "Politics and Government". These genres also contain the most abstract ideas and thoughts within the question and answer pairs. The genres which contain the most number of referential-nominal are "Computers and Internet", "Science and Mathematics", and "Yahoo! Products". This makes sense because in each of these categories, the questions and answers deal with specific, tangible objects such as "pressing a button on the computer to uninstall software". Overall, the more abstract the questions and answers get, the more likely it is to use non-referential *it* or referential-others.

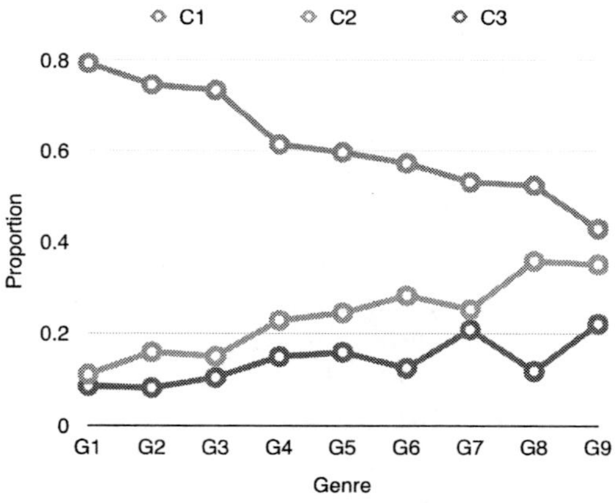

Figure 2: The proportion of referential-nominal for each genre. C1..3: the first 3 categories in Section 4, G1..9: the 9 genres in Table 1.

5.4 Analysis By Document Size

The document size shows a small influence on the categorization of *it*. The document group with the most instances of non-referential *it* is the smallest in size with a total number of tokens between 0 and 20. The rest of the document groups contains fewer instances of non-referential *it* although the differences are not as large as expected.

Document Size	C_1	C_2	C_3	C_4	C_*
0–20	21	60	20	0	101
20–40	14	84	33	0	131
40–60	27	100	33	1	161
60–80	24	129	42	2	197
100–120	29	132	56	2	219
120–140	28	148	53	3	232
140–160	32	163	68	2	265
160–180	28	158	74	6	266
180–200	43	190	70	0	303
200–220	54	184	68	2	308

Table 2: Distributions of our data for each document size.

5.5 Importance of Contextual Information

In certain cases, context is mandatory in determining the category of *it*:

> Q: Regarding **IT**, what are the fastest ways of getting superich?
> A: Find something everyone will need and then patent it. It could be anything that would do with or about computers. Look at RIM and the struggle it is now facing. With good maketing ANY enhancement or a new design could be worth millions. However, the biggest path to being rich is with maintenece or service of systems or with old programming languages.

For the first instance of *it*, if the annotators are only given the question, they possibly categorize it as referential-nominal or referential-others. However, we can confirm from further reading the context that *it* refers to the IT, "Information Technology".

6 Experiments

6.1 Corpus

Table 4 shows the distributions of our corpus, split into training (70%), development (10%), and evaluation (20%) sets. A total of 1,500, 209, and 474 instances of *it* is found in each set, respectively.

Model	Development Set					Evaluation Set				
	ACC	C_1	C_2	C_3	C_4	ACC	C_1	C_2	C_3	C_4
M_0	72.73	82.43	35.48	57.14	0.00	74.05	82.65	49.20	71.07	0.00
M_1	**73.21**	82.56	50.00	62.50	0.00	74.68	82.93	53.14	73.33	0.00
M_2	73.08	82.56	49.41	60.00	-	**75.21**	83.39	51.23	73.95	-
M_3	76.44	82.31	64.75		-	77.14	82.26	67.87		-
M_4	**76.92**	83.45	61.90		-	**78.21**	83.39	68.32		-

Table 3: Accuracies achieved by each model (in %). ACC: overall accuracy, $C_{1..4}$: F1 scores for 4 categories in Section 4. The highest accuracies are highlighted in bold.

All data are tokenized, sentence segmented, part-of-speech tagged, lemmatized, and dependency parsed by the open-source NLP toolkit, NLP4J (Choi and Palmer, 2012; Choi and McCallum, 2013).[1]

Set	Doc	Sen	Tok	C_1	C_2	C_3	C_4
TRN	630	5,650	72,824	927	353	209	11
DEV	90	787	10,348	139	42	27	1
TST	180	1,549	20,625	282	122	64	6

Table 4: Distributions of our data splits.

6.2 Feature Template

For each token w_i whose lemma is either *it* or *its*, features are extracted from the template in Table 5. w_{i-k} and w_{i+k} are the k'th preceding and succeeding tokens of w_i, respectively. $h(w_i)$ is the dependency head of w_i. The joint features in line 2 are motivated by the rules in Boyd et al. (2005). For instance, with a sufficient amount of training data, features extracted from $[w_{i+1}.\text{p} + w_{i+2}.\text{m}]$ should cover all rules such as $[it + verb + to/that/what/etc]$. Three additional features are used, the relative position of w_i within the sentence S_k (rpw; $w_i \in S_k$), the relative distance of w_i from the nearest preceding noun w_j (rdw; $w_j \in S_k$), and the relative position of S_k within the document D (rps; $S_k \in D$):

$$
\begin{aligned}
rpw &= i/t & &, t = \text{\# of tokens in } S_k. \\
rdw &= |i-j|/t & &, t = \text{\# of tokens in } S_k. \\
rps &= k/d & &, d = \text{\# of sentences in } D.
\end{aligned}
$$

$w_i.\text{p}, w_{i\pm1}.\text{p}, w_{i\pm2}.\text{p}, h(w_i).\text{p}, w_{i\pm1}.\text{m}, h(w_i).\text{m}$

$w_{i+1}.\text{p} + w_{i+2}.\text{m}, w_{i+1}.\text{p} + w_{i+2}.\text{p} + w_{i+3}.\text{m}$

$w_i.\text{d} , h(w_i).\text{dm}$

Table 5: Feature template used for our experiments. p: part-of-speech tag, m: lemma, d: dependency label, dm: set of dependents' lemmas.

It is worth mentioning that we experimented with features extracted from brown clusters (Brown et al., 1992) and word embeddings (Mikolov et al., 2013) trained on the Wikipedia articles, which did not lead to a more accurate result. It may be due to the different nature of our source data, Yahoo! Answers. We will explore the possibility of improving our model by facilitating distributional semantics trained on the social networks data.

6.3 Machine Learning

A stochastic adaptive gradient algorithm is used for statistical learning, which adapts per-coordinate learning rates to exploit rarely seen features while remaining scalable (Duchi et al., 2011). Regularized dual averaging is applied for ℓ_1 regularization, shown to work well with ADAGRAD (Xiao, 2010). In addition, mini-batch is applied, where each batch consists of instances from k-number of documents. The following hyperparameters are found during the development and used for all our experiments: the learning rate $\eta = 0.1$, the mini-batch boundary $k = 5$, the regularization parameter $\lambda = 0.001$.

6.4 Evaluation

Table 3 shows the accuracies achieved by our models. M_0 is the baseline model using only the features extracted from Table. M_1 uses the additional features of rpw, rdw, and rps in Section 6.2. The additional features show robust improvements on both the development and the evaluation sets. Notice that the F1 score for C_4 (errors) is consistently 0; this is not surprising given the tiny amount of training instances C_4 has. M_2 is experimented on datasets where annotations for C_4 are discarded. A small improvement is shown for M_2 on the evaluation set but not on the development set, where only 1 instance of C_4 is found.

M_3 and M_4 aim to classify instances of *it* into 2 classes by merging C_2 and C_3 during either training (M_3) or evaluation (M_4). Training with 3 categories and merging the predicted output into 2 categories during evaluation (M_4) gives higher accuracies than merging the gold labels and training with 2 categories (M_3) in our experiments.

7 Conclusion

This paper introduces a new corpus called, QA-It, sampled from nine different genres in the Yahoo! Answers corpus and manually annotated with four categories of *it*.[2] Unlike many previous work, our annotation is done on the document-level, which is useful for both human annotators and machine learning algorithms to disambiguate different types of *it*. Our dataset is challenging because it includes many grammatical errors, ambiguous references, disfluency, and fragments. Thorough corpus analysts are provided for a better understanding of our corpus. Our corpus is experimented with several statistical models. Our best model shows an accuracy of 78%; considering the challenging nature of our corpus, this is quite encouraging. Our work can be useful for those who need to perform coreference resolution for question answering systems.

In the future, we will double the size of our annotation so we can train a better model and have a more meaningful evaluation. We are also planning on developing a recurrent neural network model for the classification of *it*.

References

Shane Bergsma, Dekang Lin, and Randy Goebel. 2008. Distributional Identification of Non-Referential Pronouns. In *Proceedings of the Annual Conference of the Association for Computational Linguistics*, ACL'08, pages 10–18.

Adriane Boyd, Whitney Gegg-Harrison, and Donna Byron. 2005. Identifying Non-Referential it: A Machine Learning Approach Incorporating Linguistically Motivated Patterns. In *Proceedings of the ACL Workshop on Feature Engineering for Machine Learning in Natural Language Processing*, pages 40–47.

António Branco, Tony McEnery, and Ruslan Mitkov, editors. 2005. *Anaphora Processing: Linguistic, Cognitive and Computational Modelling*. John Benjamins Publishing Company.

Peter F. Brown, Peter V. deSouza, Robert L. Mercer, Vincent J. Della Pietra, and Jenifer C. Lai. 1992. Class-based n-gram Models of Natural Language. *Computational Linguistics*, 18(4):467–480.

Jinho D. Choi and Andrew McCallum. 2013. Transition-based Dependency Parsing with Selectional Branching. In *Proceedings of the 51st Annual Meeting of the Association for Computational Linguistics*, ACL'13, pages 1052–1062.

Jinho D. Choi and Martha Palmer. 2012. Fast and Robust Part-of-Speech Tagging Using Dynamic Model Selection. In *Proceedings of the 50th Annual Meeting of the Association for Computational Linguistics*, ACL'12, pages 363–367.

John Duchi, Elad Hazan, and Yoram Singer. 2011. Adaptive Subgradient Methods for Online Learning and Stochastic Optimization. *The Journal of Machine Learning Research*, 12(39):2121–2159.

Richard Evans. 2001. Applying Machine Learning Toward an Automatic Classification of It. *Literary and Linguistic Computing*, 16(1):45–57.

Jerry R. Hobbs. 1978. Resolving Pronoun References. *Lingua*, 44:331–338.

Yifan Li, Petr Musílek, Marek Reformat, and Loren Wyard-Scott. 2009. Identification of Pleonastic It Using the Web. *Journal Of Artificial Intelligence Research*, 34:339–389.

Tomas Mikolov, Ilya Sutskever, Kai Chen, Greg S Corrado, and Jeff Dean. 2013. Distributed Representations of Words and Phrases and their Compositionality. In *Proceedings of Advances in Neural Information Processing Systems 26*, NIPS'13, pages 3111–3119.

Christoph Müller. 2006. Automatic detection of non-referential it in spoken multi-party dialog. In *11th Conference of the European Chapter of the Association for Computational Linguistics*, EACL'06, pages 49–56.

Sam Wiseman, Alexander M. Rush, Stuart Shieber, and Jason Weston. 2015. Learning Anaphoricity and Antecedent Ranking Features for Coreference Resolution. In *Proceedings of the 53rd Annual Meeting of the Association for Computational Linguistics and the 7th International Joint Conference on Natural Language Processing (Volume 1: Long Papers)*, ACL'15, pages 1416–1426.

Lin Xiao. 2010. Dual Averaging Methods for Regularized Stochastic Learning and Online Optimization. *Journal of Machine Learning Research*, 11:2543–2596.

---

[2]`https://github.com/emorynlp/qa-it`

Building a Corpus for Japanese Wikification
with Fine-Grained Entity Classes

Davaajav Jargalsaikhan   Naoaki Okazaki   Koji Matsuda   Kentaro Inui
Tohoku University, Japan
{davaajav, okazaki, matsuda, inui}@ecei.toholu.ac.jp

Abstract

In this research, we build a Wikification corpus for advancing Japanese Entity Linking. This corpus consists of 340 Japanese newspaper articles with 25,675 entity mentions. All entity mentions are labeled by a fine-grained semantic classes (200 classes), and 19,121 mentions were successfully linked to Japanese Wikipedia articles. Even with the fine-grained semantic classes, we found it hard to define the target of entity linking annotations and to utilize the fine-grained semantic classes to improve the accuracy of entity linking.

1   Introduction

Entity linking (EL) recognizes mentions in a text and associates them to their corresponding entries in a knowledge base (KB), for example, Wikipedia[1], Freebase (Bollacker et al., 2008), and DBPedia (Lehmann et al., 2015). In particular, when linked to Wikipedia articles, the task is called Wikifiation (Mihalcea and Csomai, 2007). Let us consider the following sentence.

> On the 2nd of June, the team of Japan will play World Cup (W Cup) qualification match against Honduras in the second round of Kirin Cup at Kobe Wing Stadium, the venue for the World Cup.

Wikification is expected to link "Soccer" to the Wikipedia article titled *Soccer*, "World Cup" and "W Cup"[2] to *FIFA World Cup 2002*, "team of Japan" to *Japan Football Team*, "Kobe City" to *Kobe*, "Kobe Wing Stadium" to *Misaki Park Stadium*. Since there is no entry for "Second Round of Kirin Cup", the mention is labeled as NIL.

---

[1] https://www.wikipedia.org/
[2] "W Cup" is a Japanese-style abbreviation of "World Cup".

EL is useful for various NLP tasks, e.g., Question-Answering (Khalid et al., 2008), Information Retrieval (Blanco et al., 2015), Knowledge Base Population (Dredze et al., 2010), Co-Reference Resolution (Hajishirzi et al., 2013). There are about a dozen of datasets targeting EL in English, including UIUC datasets (ACE, MSNBC) (Ratinov et al., 2011), AIDA datasets (Hoffart et al., 2011), and TAC-KBP datasets (2009–2012 datasets) (McNamee and Dang, 2009).

Ling et al. (2015) discussed various challenges in EL. They argued that the existing datasets are inconsistent with each other. For instance, TAC-KBP targets only mentions belonging to PERSON, LOCATION, ORGANIZATION classes. Although these entity classes may be dominant in articles, other tasks may require information on natural phenomena, product names, and institution names. In contrast, the MSNBC corpus does not limit entity classes, linking mentions to any Wikipedia article. However, the MSNBC corpus does not have a NIL label even if a mention belongs to an important class such as PERSON or LOCATION, unlike the TAC-KBP corpus.

There are few studies addressing on Japanese EL. Furukawa et al. (2014) conducted a study on recognizing technical terms appearing in academic articles and linking them to English Wikipedia articles. Hayashi et al. (2014) proposed an EL method that simultaneously performs both English and Japanese Wikification, given parallel texts in both languages. Nakamura et al. (2015) links keywords in social media into English Wikipedia, aiming at a cross-language system that recognizes topics of social media written in any language. Osada et al. (2015) proposed a method to link mentions in news articles for organizing local news of different prefectures in Japan.

However, these studies do not necessarily ad-

Proceedings of the 54th Annual Meeting of the Association for Computational Linguistics – Student Research Workshop, pages 138–144,
Berlin, Germany, August 7-12, 2016. ©2016 Association for Computational Linguistics

vance EL on a Japanese KB. As of January 2016, Japanese Wikipedia and English Wikipedia include about 1 million and 5 million, respectively, articles. However, there are only around 0.56 million inter-language links between Japanese and English. Since most of the existing KBs (e.g., Freebase and DBPedia) originate from Wikipedia, we cannot expect that English KBs cover entities that are specific to Japanese culture, locals, and economics. Moreover, a Japanese EL system is useful for populating English knowledge base as well, harvesting source documents written in Japanese.

To make matters worse, we do not have a corpus for Japanese EL, i.e., Japanese mentions associated with Japanese KB. Although (Murawaki and Mori, 2016) concern with Japanese EL, the corpus they have built is not necessarily a corpus for Japanese EL. The motivation behind their work comes from the difficulty of word segmentation for unsegmented languages, like Chinese or Japanese. (Murawaki and Mori, 2016) approach the word segmentation problem from point of view of Wikification. Their focus is on the word segmentation rather than on the linking.

In this research, we build a Japanese Wikification corpus in which mentions in Japanese documents are associated with Japanese Wikipedia articles. The corpus consists of 340 newspaper articles from Balanced Corpus of Contemporary Written Japanese (BCCWJ) [3] annotated with fine-grained named entity labels defined by Sekine's Extended Named Entity Hierarchy (Sekine et al., 2002) [4].

2 Dataset Construction

To give a better understanding of our dataset we briefly compare it with existing English datasets. The most comparable ones are UIUC (Ratinov et al., 2011) and TAC-KBP 2009–2012 datasets (McNamee and Dang, 2009). Although, AIDA datasets are widely used for Disambiguation of Entities, AIDA uses YAGO, an unique Knowledge Base derived from Wikipedia, GeoNames and Wordnet, which makes it difficult to compare. UIUC is similar to our dataset in a sense that it links to any Wikipedia article without any semantic class restrictions, unlike TAC-KBP which

is limited to mentions that belong to PERSON, LOCATION or ORGANIZATION classes only. When an article is not present in Wikipedia, UIUC does not record this information in any way. On the contrary, TAC-KBP [5] and our datasets have NIL tag used to mark a mention when it does not have an entry in KB.

2.1 Design Policy

Ling et al. (2015) argued that the task definition of EL itself is challenging: whether to target only named entities (NEs) or to include general nouns; whether to limit semantic classes of target NEs; how to define NE boundaries; how specific the links should be; and how to handle metonymy.

The original (Hashimoto et al., 2008) corpus is also faced with similar challenges: mention abbreviations that result in the string representation that is an exact match to the string representation of another mention, abbreviated or not (for example, "Tokyo (City)" and "TV Tokyo"), metonymy and synecdoche.

As for the mention "World Cup" in the example in Section 1, we have three possible candidates entities, *World Cup*, *FIFA World Cup*, and *2002 FIFA World Cup*. Although all of them look reasonable, *2002 FIFA World Cup* is the most suitable, being more specific than others. At the same time, we cannot expect that Wikipedia includes the most specific entities. For example, let us suppose that we have a text discussing a possible venue for 2034 FIFA World Cup. As of January 2016, Wikipedia does not include an article about 2034 FIFA World Cup[6]. Thus, it may be a difficult decision whether to link it to *FIFA World Cup* or make it NIL.

Moreover, the mention "Kobe Wing Stadium" includes nested NE mentions, "Kobe (City)" and "Kobe Wing Stadium". Furthermore, although the article titled "Kobe Wing Stadium" does exist in Japanese Wikipedia, the article does not explain the stadium itself but explains the company running the stadium. Japanese Wikipedia includes a separate article *Misaki Park Stadium* describing the stadium. In addition, the mention "Honduras" does not refer to Honduras as a country, but as the national soccer team of Honduras.

In order to separate these issues raised by NEs

---

[3]http://pj.ninjal.ac.jp/corpus_center/bccwj/en/

[4]https://sites.google.com/site/extendednamedentityhierarchy/

[5]TAC-KBP 2012 requires NIL to be clustered in accordance to the semantic classes.

[6]Surprisingly, Wikipedia includes articles for the future World Cups up to 2030.

from the EL task, we decided to build a Wikification corpus on top of a portion of BCCWJ corpora with Extended Named Entity labels annotated (Hashimoto et al., 2008). This corpus consists of 340 newspaper articles where NE boundaries and semantic classes are annotated. This design strategy has some advantages. First, we can omit the discussion on semantic classes and boundaries of NEs. Second, we can analyze the impact of semantic classes of NEs to the task of EL.

2.2 Annotation Procedure

We have used *brat rapid annotation tool* (Stenetorp et al., 2012) to effectively link mentions to Wikipedia articles. Brat has a functionality of importing external KBs (e.g., Freebase or Wikipedia) for EL. We have prepared a KB for Brat using a snapshot of Japanese Wikipedia accessed on November 2015. We associate a mention to a Wikipedia ID so that we can uniquely locate an article even when the title of the article is changed. We configure Brat so that it can present a title and a lead sentence (short description) of each article during annotation.

Because this is the first attempt to build a Japanese Wikification dataset on a fine-grained NE corpus, we did not limit the semantic classes of target NEs in order to analyze the importance of different semantic classes. However, based on preliminary investigation results, we decided to exclude the following semantic classes from targets of the annotation: `Timex` (Temporal Expression, 12 classes), `Numex` (Numerical Expression, 34 classes), `Address` (e.g., postal address and urls, 1 class), `Title_Other` (e.g., *Mr.*, *Mrs.*, 1 class), `Facility_Part` (e.g, *9th floor, second basement*, 1 class). Mentions belonging to other classes were linked to their corresponding Wikipedia pages.

We asked three Japanese native speakers to link mentions into Wikipedia articles using Brat. We gave the following instructions to obtain consistent annotations:

1. Choose the entity that is the most specific in possible candidates.

2. Do not link a mention into a disambiguation page, category page, nor WikiMedia page.

3. Link a mention into a section of an article only when no suitable article exists for the

Attribute	Value
# articles	340
# mentions	25,675
# links	19,121
# NILs	6,554
# distinct mentions	7,118
# distinct entities	6,008

Table 1: Statistics of the corpus built by this work.

Annotator pair	Agreement
Annotators 1 and 2	0.910
Annotators 2 and 3	0.924

Table 2: Inter-annotator agreement.

mention.

2.3 Annotation Results

Table 1 reports the statistics of the corpus built by this work. Out of 25,675 mentions satisfying the conditions explained in Section 2.2, 19,121 mentions were linked to Japanese Wikipedia articles. In total, 7,118 distinct mentions were linked to 6,008 distinct entities. Table 2 shows the high inter- annotator agreement (the Cohen-Kappa's coefficient) of the corpus[7].

In order to find important/unimportant semantic classes of NEs for EL, we computed the link rate for each semantic class. Link rate of a semantic class is the ratio of the number of linkable (non-NIL) mentions belonging that class to the total number of mentions of that class occurring throughout the corpus. Table 3 presents semantic classes with the highest and lowest link rates[8]. Popular NE classes such as `Province` and `Pro_Sports_Organization` had high link rates. Semantic classes such as Book and `Occasion_Other` had low link rates because these entities are rare and uncommon. However, we also found it difficult to limit the target of entity linking based only on semantic classes because the importance of the semantic classes with

---

[7]We cannot compute the inter-annotator agreement between Annotators 1 and 3, who have no overlap articles for annotation.

[8]In this analysis, we removed semantic classes appearing less than 100 times in the corpus. We concluded that those minor semantic classes do little help in revealing the nature of the dataset we have built. Most of them had perfect or near to zperfect link rates with mentions being rare and uniquely identifiable.

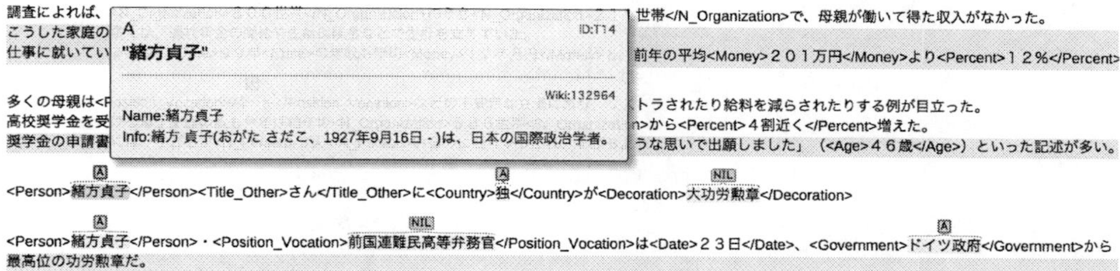

Figure 1: A screenshot of the annotation senvironment with Brat.

low link rates depends on the application; for example, Occasion_Other, which has the lowest link rate, may be crucial for event extraction from text.

In the research on word sense disambiguation (WSD), it is common to assume that the identical expressions have the same sense throughout the text. This assumption is called *one-sense-per-discourse*. In our corpus, 322 out of 340 (94.7%) articles satisfy the assumption. A few instances include: expressions "Bush" referred to both *George H. W. Bush* and *George W. Bush* (the former is often referred as Bush Senior and the latter as Bush Junior); and expressions "Tokyo" referred to both *Tokyo Television* and *Tokyo city*.

2.4 Difficult Annotation Cases

We report cases where annotators found difficult to choose an entity from multiple potential candidates. Mention boundaries from the original corpus are indicated by underline.

Nested entities

It was assumed that the role initially served as a temporary peacemaker to persuade Ali al-Sistani, the spiritual leader of Shia Muslims: Position_Vocation.

Since the mention in the sentence refers to the highest ranking position of a specific religion, it is inappropriate to link the mention to the article *Spiritual Leader* nor *Shia Muslim*. Therefore, we decided to mark this mention as NIL.

Entity changes over time

In his greeting speech, the representative Ito expressed his opinion on the upcoming gubernatorial election: Event_Other and Sapporo city mayoral election.

This article was about the Hokkaido Prefecture gubernatorial election held in 2003. Since the BCCWJ corpus does not provide timestamps of articles, it is difficult to identify the exact event. However, this article has a clue in another place, "the progress of the developmental project from 2001". For this reason, the annotators could resolve the mention to *2003 Hokkaido Prefecture gubernatorial election*. Generally, it is difficult to identify events that are held periodically. The similar issue occurs in mentions regarding position/profession (e.g., "former president") and sport events (e.g., "World Cup").

Japanese EL is similar to English El: the same challenges of mention ambiguity (nested entities, metonymy) still persist. With the Japanese Wikification, a variation of the task that takes advantage of the cross-lingual nature of Wikipedia is worth exploring.

3 Wikification Experiment

In this section, we conduct an experiment of Wikification on the corpus built by this work. Wikification is decomposed into two steps: recognizing a mention m in the text, and predicting the corresponding entity e for the mention m. Because the corpus was built on the corpus with NE mentions recognized, we omit the step of entity mention recognition.

3.1 Wikification without fine-grained semantic classes

Our experiment is based on the disambiguation method that uses the probability distribution of anchor texts (Spitkovsky and Chang, 2012). Given a mention m, the method predicts an entity $\hat{e}$ that yields the highest probability $p(e|m)$,

$$\hat{e} = \operatorname*{argmax}_{e \in E} p(e|m). \tag{1}$$

Category	Example	Link Rate	# of Links	# of Occurrences
Province	Fukuoka Prefecture	0.983	678	690
Country	United States of America	0.976	1924	1964
GPE_Other	Ginza	0.974	115	118
Political_Party	Liberal Democratic Party	0.967	236	244
Pro_Sports_Organization	Yomiuri Giants	0.997	290	300
City	Sendai City	0.947	1354	1430
Company_Group	JR	0.928	103	111
Mammal	Kangaroo	0.906	164	181
International_Organization	NATO	0.891	188	211
Company	NTT	0.883	647	733
...				
Game	Summer Olympics	0.576	167	290
Conference	34th G8 summit	0.548	74	135
Public_Institution	Takatsuki City Office	0.451	105	233
Book	Sazae-san	0.412	49	119
Political_Organization_Other	Takeshita faction	0.407	68	167
Organization_Other	General Coordination Division	0.393	55	140
GOE_Other	White House	0.363	99	274
Plan	Income Doubling Plan	0.273	32	117
Character	Mickey Mouse	0.145	29	200
Occasion_Other	Tsukuba EXPO	0.113	28	226

Table 3: 10 classes with the highest and the lowest link rates among the classes that occurred more than 100 times

Here, E is the set of all articles in Japanese Wikipedia. The conditional probability $p(e|m)$ is estimated by the anchor texts in Japanese Wikipedia,

$$p(e|m) = \frac{\text{\# occurrences of } m \text{ as anchors to } e}{\text{\#occurrences of } m \text{ as anchors}}. \tag{2}$$

If $\forall e : p(e|m) = 0$ for the mention m, we mark the mention as NIL. Ignoring contexts of mentions, this method relies on the popularity of entities in the anchor texts of the mention m. The accuracy of this method was 53.31% (13,493 mentions out of 25,309).

3.2 Wikification with fine-grained semantic classes

Furthermore, we explore the usefulness of the fine-grained semantic classes for Wikification. This method estimates probability distributions conditioned on a mention m and its semantic class c. Ideally, we would like to predict an entity $\hat{e}$ with,

$$\hat{e} = \operatorname*{argmax}_{e \in E, c \in C} p(e|m, c) \tag{3}$$

However, it is hard to estimate the probability distribution $p(e|m, c)$ directly from the Wikipedia articles. Instead, we decompose $p(e|m, c)$ into $p(e|m)p(e|c)$ to obtain,

$$\hat{e} = \operatorname*{argmax}_{e \in E, c \in C} p(e|m)p(e|c). \tag{4}$$

Here, C is the set of all semantic classes included in Sekine's Extended Named Entity Hierarchy. In addition, we apply Bayes' rule to $p(e|c)$,

$$\hat{e} = \operatorname*{argmax}_{e \in E, c \in C} p(e|m)p(c|e)p(e) \tag{5}$$

The probability distribution $p(c|e)$ bridges Wikipedia articles and semantic classes defined in Sekine's Extended Named Entity Hierarchy. We adapt a method to predict a semantic class of a Wikipedia article (Suzuki et al., 2016) for estimating $p(c|e)$. The accuracy of this method was 53.26% (13,480 mentions out of 25,309), which is slightly lower than that of the previous method. The new method improved 627 instances mainly with LOCATION Category (e.g., country names and city names). For example,

> The venue is Aichi Welfare Pension Hall in Ikeshita, Nagoya
>
> Semantic Class: City   Correct: *Nagoya City*
>
> Old Method: *Nagoya Station*
>
> New Method: *Nagoya City*

Because *Nagoya Station* is more popular in anchor texts in Japanese Wikipedia, the old method predicts *Nagoya Station* as the entity for the mention *Nagoya*. In contrast, the new method could leverage the semantic class, City to avoid the mistake. We could observe similar improvements for distinguishing Country – Language, Person – Location, Location – Sports Team.

However, the new method degraded 664 instances mainly because the fine-grained entity classes tried to map them into too specific entities. More than half of such instances belonged to POSITION_VOCATION semantic class. For example, mention "Prime Minister" was mistakingly mapped to *Prime Minister of Japan* instead of *Prime Minister*.

4 Future Work

In our future work, we will incorporate the context information of the text in the Wikification process and further investigate the definition of the target of entity linking annotations. Although incorporating semantic classes of entities has a potential to improve Wikification quality, some problems still remain even with the semantic classes. Here, we explain some interesting cases.

Name variations

> During the summer, a JASRAC Correct:
> *Japanese Society for Rights of Authors, Composers and Publishers*
> Predicted: NIL staff came to the shop to explain it.

This type of mistakes are caused by the lack of aliases and redirects in Wikipedia. In this example, the mention 'JASRAC' was predicted as NIL because Wikipedia did not include JASRAC as an alias for Japanese Society for Rights of Authors, Composers and Publishers.

Link bias in Wikipedia

> Thousands have participated in the funeral held at World Trade Center
> Correct: *World Trade Center (1973-2001)*
> Predicted: *World Trade Center (Tokyo)*, which is known as "Ground Zero".

In this example, the mention "World Trade Center" refers to *World Trade Center (1973–2001)* with strong clues in the surrounding context "Ground Zero". Both of the presented methods predict it as *World Trade Center (Tokyo)* because there is a building with the identical name in Japan. Using Japanese Wikipedia articles for estimating the probability distribution, Japanese entities are more likely to be predicted.

5 Conclusion

In this research, we have build a Wikification corpus for advancing Japanese Entity Linking. We

have conducted Wikification experiment using using fine grained semantic classes. Although we expect an effect of the fine-grained semantic classes, we could no observe an improvement in terms of the accuracy on the corpus. The definition of the target of entity linking annotations requires further investigation. We are distributing the corpus on the Web site `http://www.cl.ecei.tohoku.ac.jp/jawikify`.

Acknowledgments

This work was partially supported by *Research and Development on Real World Big Data Integration and Analysis*, MEXT and JSPS KAKENHI Grant number 15H05318.

References

Roi Blanco, Giuseppe Ottaviano, and Edgar Meij. 2015. Fast and space-efficient entity linking for queries. In *Proc. of WSDM*, pages 179–188.

Kurt Bollacker, Colin Evans, Praveen Paritosh, Tim Sturge, and Jamie Taylor. 2008. Freebase: A collaboratively created graph database for structuring human knowledge. In *Proceedings of the 2008 ACM SIGMOD International Conference on Management of Data*, pages 1247–1250.

Mark Dredze, Paul McNamee, Delip Rao, Adam Gerber, and Tim Finin. 2010. Entity disambiguation for knowledge base population. In *Proc. of COLING*, pages 277–285.

Tatsuya Furukawa, Takeshi Sagara, and Akiko Aizawa. 2014. Semantic disambiguation for cross-lingual entity linking (in Japanese). *Journal of Japan Society of Information and Knowledge*, 24(2):172–177.

Hannaneh Hajishirzi, Leila Zilles, Daniel S. Weld, and Luke Zettlemoyer. 2013. Joint coreference resolution and named-entity linking with multi-pass sieves. In *Proc. of EMNLP*, pages 289–299.

Taichi Hashimoto, Takashi Inui, and Koji Murakami. 2008. Constructing extended named entity annotated corpora (in Japanese). In *IPSJ Natural Lnaguage Processing (2008-NL-188)*, pages 113–120.

Yoshihiko Hayashi, Kenji Hayashi, Masaaki Nagata, and Takaaki Tanaka. 2014. Improving Wikification of bitexts by completing cross-lingual information. In *The 28th Annual Conference of the Japanese Society for Artificial Intelligence*, pages 1A2–2.

Johannes Hoffart, Mohamed Amir Yosef, Ilaria Bordino, Hagen Fürstenau, Manfred Pinkal, Marc Spaniol, Bilyana Taneva, Stefan Thater, and Gerhard Weikum. 2011. Robust disambiguation of named entities in text. In *Proc. of EMNLP*, pages 782–792.

Mahboob Alam Khalid, Valentin Jijkoun, and Maarten De Rijke. 2008. The impact of named entity normalization on information retrieval for question answering. In *Proc. of ECIR*, pages 705–710.

Jens Lehmann, Robert Isele, Max Jakob, Anja Jentzsch, Dimitris Kontokostas, Pablo N. Mendes, Sebastian Hellmann, Mohamed Morsey, Patrick van Kleef, Sören Auer, and Christian Bizer. 2015. DBpedia — a large-scale, multilingual knowledge base extracted from Wikipedia. *Semantic Web*, 6(2):167–195.

Xiao Ling, Sameer Singh, and Daniel Weld. 2015. Design challenges for entity linking. *TACL*, 3:315–328.

Paul McNamee and Hoa Trang Dang. 2009. Overview of the TAC 2009 knowledge base population track. In *Text Analysis Conference (TAC)*, pages 111–113.

Rada Mihalcea and Andras Csomai. 2007. Wikify!: Linking documents to encyclopedic knowledge. In *Proc. of CIKM*, pages 233–242.

Yugo Murawaki and Shinsuke Mori. 2016. Wicification for scriptio continua. In *Proc. of LREC*, pages 1346–1351.

Tatsuya Nakamura, Masumi Shirakawa, Takahiro Hara, and Shojiro Nishio. 2015. An entity linking method for closs-lingual topic extraction from social media (in Japanese). In *DEIM Forum 2015*, pages A3–1.

Seiya Osada, Keigo Suenaga, Yoshizumi Shogo, Kazumasa Shoji, Tsuneharu Yoshida, and Yasuaki Hashimoto. 2015. Assigning geographical point information for document via entity linking (in Japanese). In *Proceedings of the Twenty-first Annual Meeting of the Association for Natural Language Processing*, pages A4–4.

Lev Ratinov, Dan Roth, Doug Downey, and Mike Anderson. 2011. Local and global algorithms for disambiguation to Wikipedia. In *Proc. of ACL-HLT*, pages 1375–1384.

Satoshi Sekine, Kiyoshi Sudo, and Chikashi Nobata. 2002. Extended named entity hierarchy. In *Proceedings of LREC 2002*.

Valentin I. Spitkovsky and Angel X. Chang. 2012. A cross-lingual dictionary for english Wikipedia concepts. In *Proc. of LREC*, pages 3168–3175.

Pontus Stenetorp, Sampo Pyysalo, Goran Topic, Tomoko Ohta, Sophia Ananiadou, and Jun'ichi Tsujii. 2012. brat: a web-based tool for nlp-assisted text annotation. In *Proceedings of the Demonstrations Session at EACL*.

Masatoshi Suzuki, Koji Matsuda, Satoshi Sekine, Naoaki Okazaki, and Kentaro Inui. 2016. Multi-label classification of wikipedia articles into fine-grained named entity types (in japanese). Proceedings of the Twenty-second Annual Meeting of the Association for Natural Language Processing.

A Personalized Markov Clustering and Deep Learning Approach for Arabic Text Categorization

Vasu Jindal
University of Texas at Dallas
Richardson, TX 75080
vasu.jindal@utdallas.edu

Abstract

Text categorization has become a key research field in the NLP community. However, most works in this area are focused on Western languages ignoring other Semitic languages like Arabic. These languages are of immense political and social importance necessitating robust categorization techniques. In this paper, we present a novel three-stage technique to efficiently classify Arabic documents into different categories based on the words they contain. We leverage the significance of root-words in Arabic and incorporate a combination of Markov clustering and Deep Belief Networks to classify Arabic words into separate groups (clusters). Our approach is tested on two public datasets giving a F-Measure of 91.02%.

1 Introduction

In the emerging era of big data technology, there has been a widespread increase in information obtained from text documents. Furthermore, with the rapid availability of machine-readable documents, text classification techniques have gained tremendous interest during the recent years. Consequently, automatic categorization of numerous new documents to different categories has become critical for political, social and for news research purposes.

Text categorization techniques have been widely investigated by researchers around the world. However, most of the recent developments in this field are focused on popular Western languages, ignoring Semitic and Middle-Eastern languages like Arabic, Hebrew, Urdu and Persian. As discussed further in related works in Section 2.1, most classification algorithms utilized English and Chinese to validate their methods while works on Arabic are extremely rare. This is primarily due to significant dialect differences between these languages and their complex morphology. Additionally, the presence of various inflections in Arabic as opposed to English makes it difficult for the NLP community to validate techniques on the popular Middle Eastern languages. According to the US Department of Cultural Affairs, Arabic and Urdu are categorized as critical languages and United Nations heavily emphasizes on the social and political importance of these languages. Arabic is listed as one of the six official languages of the United Nations.

In this paper, we present a novel three stage approach to classify Arabic text documents into different categories combining Markov Clustering, Fuzzy-C-means and Deep Learning. To the best of our knowledge, this is the first work that leverages the heavy influence of root-words in Arabic to extract features for both clustering and deep learning to perform classification of Arabic documents. First, we segment each document and extract root-word information. Then we perform clustering with root-word based features using Fuzzy-C-Means and Markov clustering. This allows us to separate documents into unsupervised groups (clusters). We then train a deep belief network (DBN) for each cluster using Restricted Boltzmann Machines. This personalization which is essentially training DBN for each cluster improves the classification accuracy and features extraction. Finally, we generate network graphs of these clusters which can be used for similarity relatedness or summarization in future works. This is the first work to use a modified combination of Markov clustering and personalized deep learning to classify documents into different categories.

The rest of the paper is organized as follows: Section 2 discusses the literature review and Ara-

145

Proceedings of the 54th Annual Meeting of the Association for Computational Linguistics – Student Research Workshop, pages 145–151,
Berlin, Germany, August 7-12, 2016. ©2016 Association for Computational Linguistics

bic morphology. Section 3 focuses on methodology for Markov clustering and deep learning. Section 4 discusses our experimental results and finally, Section 5 summarizes the paper and presents conclusions and future work.

2 Background

2.1 Related Works

As mentioned previously, even though numerous works in text categorization have been proposed for Western languages, works on categorizing Semitic languages like Arabic are very rare in the NLP community.

Most previous works on Arabic text categorization treats documents as a bag-of-words where the text is represented as a vector of weighted frequencies for each of the distinct words or tokens. (Diederich et al. 2003; Sebastiani et al. 2002). We use a similar approach to extract features from documents based on root-word frequency. Early efforts to categorize Arabic documents were performed using Naive Bayes algorithm (El-Kourdi et al., 2004), maximum entropy (Sawaf et al., 2001) and support vector machines (Gharib et al., 2009).

N-gram frequency statistics technique was used with Manhattan distance to categorize documents by Khreisat (Khreisat, 2006) El-Halees described a method based on association rules to classify Arabic documents (El-Halees, 2007). Hmeidi I. uses two machine learning methods for Arabic text categorization: K-Nearest Neighbor (KNN) and support vector machines (SVM) (Hmeidi et al., 2008). An approach for feature selection in Arabic text categorization was proposed using information gain and Chi-square (Yang and Pedersen, 1997). Abu-Errub A. proposed a new Arabic text classification algorithm using Tf-Idf and Chi square measurements (Abu-Errub, 2014). However, all these methods were not very efficient for large datasets giving an accuracy of less than 70% and were unable to classify documents with different diacritics. Diacritics are signs or accents whose pronunciation or presence in a word can result in a different meaning.

Recently, a new technique using a combination of kNN and Rocchio classifier for text categorization was introduced (Mohammad et al., 2016). This approach specifically solves the Word Sense Disambiguation (WSD) problem in a supervised approach using lexical samples of five Arabic words. Although, this method achieved

higher accuracy than previous works, usage of only five Arabic words limits usage for larger datasets. Our proposed approach generates multiple roots of each Arabic words addressing the issue of different diacritics in Arabic.

2.2 Arabic Morphology

Arabic belongs to the family of Semitic languages and has significant morphological, syntactical and semantical differences from other languages. It consists of 28 letters and can be extended to 90 by added shapes, marks, and vowels. Furthermore, Arabic is written from right to left and letters have different styles based on the position of its appearance in the word. The base words of Arabic inflect to express eight main features. Verbs inflect for aspect, mood, person and voice. Nouns and adjectives inflect for case and state. Verbs, nouns and adjectives inflect for both gender and number. Arabic morphology consists from a bare root verb form that is trilateral, quadrilateral, or pentaliteral. The derivational morphology can be lexeme = Root + Pattern or inflection morphology (word = Lexeme + Features) where features are noun specific, verb specific or single letter conjunctions. In contrast, in most European languages words are formed by concatenating morphemes. For example in German, 'Zeitgeit'(the spirit of the times) is simply 'Zeit'(time) + 'geist'(spirit) i.e the root and pattern are essentially interleaved.

Stem pattern are often difficult to parse in Arabic as they interlock with root consonants (Abdelali, 2004). Arabic is also influenced by infixes which may be consonants and vowels and can be misinterpreted as root-words. One of the major problem is usage of a consonant, hamza. Hamza is not always pronounced and can be a vowel. This creates a severe orthographic problem as words may have differently positioned hamzas making them different strings yet having similar meaning.

Furthermore, diacritics are critical in categorizing Arabic documents. For example, consider the two words "zhb" mean "to go" and "gold" differing by just one diacritic. The two words can only be distinguished using diacritics. The word "go" may appear in a variety of text documents while "gold" may likely appear in documents containing other finance related words. This is where our personalized deep learning approach is extremely efficient for Arabic as discussed in future sections. For the purpose of clarity, we use the term "root-words" throughout this paper to represent the roots of an Arabic word.

3 Methodology

Figure 1 presents an overview of our algorithm. In summary, our approach consists of a pre-processing stage, two stages of clustering and finally a learning stage. In the pre-processing stage documents are tokenized and segmented into different words and the Tf-Idf weighted root-word counts are extracted. Subsequently, we cluster the documents by a combination of Markov Clustering and Fuzzy C-means in Step 2. Finally, in step 3, we use deep learning models on each obtained cluster to personalize learning for each root word cluster. Personalization essentially means to train a separate deep belief network for each cluster. Each of these stages is discussed in subsequent sections.

3.1 Pre-Processing

In the pre-processing stage we first remove the punctuation marks, auxiliary verbs, pronouns, conjunctions etc. As we stated in section 2.2, it is very important for processing Arabic to properly use the semantic information provided by root-words (Kanaan et al., 2009). Therefore, representing words presented in a document in the root pattern increases efficiency of classification. Root extraction or stemming for the Arabic dataset is performed using a letter weight and order scheme. For example, the root meaning "write" has the form k-t-b. More words can be formed using vowels and additional consonants in the root word. Some of the words that can be formed using k-t-b are kitab meaning "book", kutub meaning "books", katib meaning "writer", kuttab representing "writers", kataba meaning "he wrote", yaktubu meaning "he writes", etc.

In our method we assign weights to letters of Arabic and subsequently rank them based on their frequency in the document. Root-words of the Arabic word are selected by recurring patterns with the maximum weight. Furthermore, we calculate the standard Tf-Idf frequency of each root word to use as features in clustering and deep learning. Tf-Idf (term frequency-inverse document frequency) is one of the widely used feature selection techniques in information retrieval (Baeza-Yates et al., 1999). Tf measures the importance of a term in a given document while Idf signifies the relative importance of a term in a collection of documents. In the next section, we will discuss the clustering step of our approach.

3.2 Estimation of Initial Number of Clusters

The words frequencies (Tf-Idf) and root-word frequencies are used from the pre-processing stage and grouped into clusters. Once the words are clustered, we consider each document and find which cluster of words it may belong. This is done by rank-matching based approach discussed later. The clustering step is described below.

Consider each document to be P

$$P = \begin{bmatrix} p_{0,0} & p_{0,1} & \cdots & p_{0,W-1} \\ \vdots & \vdots & \cdots & \vdots \\ p_{H-1,0} & p_{H-1,2} & \cdots & p_{H-1,W-1} \end{bmatrix} \quad (1)$$

where $p_{i,0}$ indicate extracted words tokenized from the documents. $p_{i,j}$ are the similar root-words of $p_{i,0}$.

We first estimate the initial number of categories that may be present in a corpus of text documents. The estimation of initial number of clusters is critical for text categorization as many Arabic documents may contain synonyms, different morphologies of Arabic and yet may have a close meaning. We perform estimation by computing the total number of modes found in all eigenvectors of the data. Modes in each eigenvector of the data are detected using kernel density estimation. Then, significance test of the gradient and second derivative of a kernel density estimation is computed. A similar approach was used for bioinformatics data (Pouyan et al., 2015). Briefly, if $E = \{e_1, e_2, ..., e_M\}$ denotes eigenvectors of dataset X, a kernel Gaussian is considered as follows:

$$\kappa(l) = \frac{1}{\sqrt{2\pi}} exp(\frac{-l^2}{2}) \quad (2)$$

where $\kappa(.)$ is the Gaussian kernel and h is the bandwidth. The estimator gradient is written as follows:

$$\Delta \hat{f}(l) = \frac{2}{N \cdot h^2} \cdot \sum_{i=1}^{N} \kappa(\frac{l - e_i}{h}) \cdot (l - e_i) \quad (3)$$

The number of modes is approximated using the number of times, the gradient changes from positive to negative for each projection of data on the eigenvectors. K represents initial number of clusters approximated by summation of all the modes in eigenvectors.

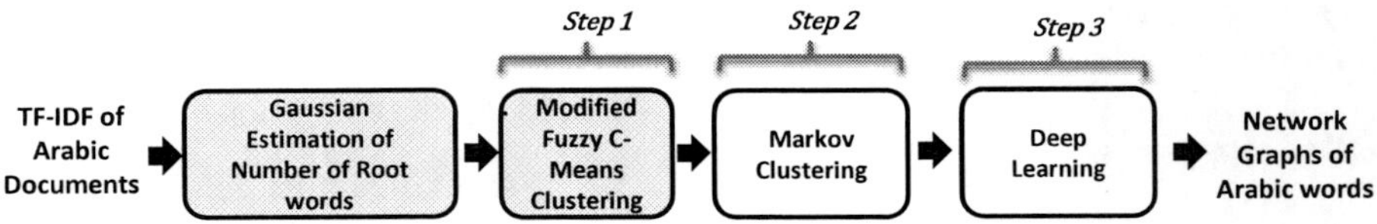

Figure 1: The general view of our proposed method

3.3 Initial Clustering Using Fuzzy-C-Mean

We leverage the heavy influence of root-words in Arabic for clustering words (tf-idf) from the pre-processing stage. As described in section 2.1, new words in Arabic can be formed by filling vowels or consonants. For example, k-t-b is a triliteral root word as it contains a sequence of three consonants. Accordingly, an improved version of Fuzzy-C-Means clustering is developed to calculate the membership probability of each words to its root word. The clusters we obtain are intended to correspond to the different root-words in document. Concisely, $\chi = \{\mu_1, ..., \mu_j, ..., \mu_K\}$ will be centers of K root-words $C = \{c_1, ..., c_j, ..., c_K\}$ which represents potential similarities of N-letter words $X = [x_1, x_2, ..., x_n]^\top$. Words are assigned to different root word clusters by minimizing the following optimization model:

$$\begin{cases} Minimize \ \{J_m = \sum_{i=1}^{N} \sum_{j=1}^{K} u_{ij}^m D_m(x_i, \mu_j)\} \\ \\ \text{subject to: } \sum_{j=1}^{K} u_{ij} = 1 \qquad \forall i = 1, 2, ..., N \end{cases}$$

$$(4)$$

where word x_i belongs to root word c_j with the membership probability of u_{ij}. The fuzzification coefficient is selected as $m = 2$ in this work. $D_m(x_i, \mu_j)$ implies the *Mahalanobis Distance* between word x_i and root word c_j. Since membership probability depends on the dispersion of cluster c_j, we use Mahalanobis Distance instead of Euclidean Distance as a distance metric between x_i and population c_j.

A Lagrangian multiplier is used to minimize the optimization problem of Fuzzy-C-Means given in Equation 4. The initial cluster set C will be available after applying the revised Fuzzy-C-Means and used in future steps.

3.4 Merging Clusters Using Markov Clustering

The number of initial clusters may have been overestimated by kernel density estimation in the first stage. We address this issue using Markov clustering, a fast, divisive and scalable clustering algorithm based on stochastic modelling of flow of networks (Van Dongen, 2001). We apply Markov clustering on the initial cluster centers $\mu_1, ..., \mu_K$ to extract the main skeleton of the data cloud. Markov clustering (MCL) has recently emerged as a popular clustering technique for determining cluster networks. The algorithm computes the probability of random walks through a graph by applying two main methods: expansion and inflation. When MCL is applied on centers of initial clusters, the centers corresponding to initial populations will be clustered in the same segments. We extract the final categories of the text documents by merging these clusters. MCL is required as the previous step may have estimated duplicate clusters based on similar diacritics or morphologies. Therefore, these redundant clusters are merged in this stage.

Once the words are clustered, we consider each document and find which most similar cluster of words it may belong to. This is done by rank-matching based approach. We find the maximum match between the 40% most frequent words in the document and every cluster. Cluster of words consisting of the highest number of words from top 40% frequent words in the document is assigned to the document.

3.5 Deep Learning

We further use the state-of-the-art deep learning for extracting features from the clusters and use them for future clustering. We create separate deep belief network classifier for each cluster, which allows us to capture differences in between dialects, topics etc. To reiterate, our novel contribution is a personalized deep learning model for

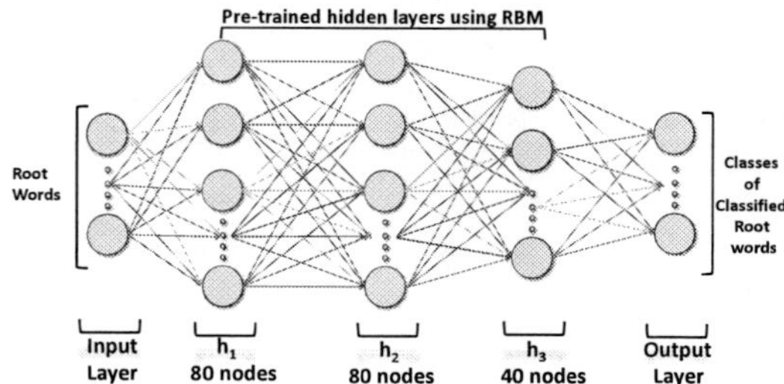

Figure 2: Deep Neural Network for C_1

each root word cluster. Personalized means training of each model for each specific root word, dialects and diacritics. The classifiers get more fine-grained by training one classifier for every cluster.

This personalization poses several advantages: the features learned using deep learning are personalized for each root word. Consequently, the technique is robust against different dialects, scripts and way of writing. Secondly, personalized deep learning models extract features from diacritics. As previously described in section 2.2, diacritics makes Arabic word classification very challenging. By extracting features from diacritics in the context of appeared root-words, our personalized deep learning approach efficiently solves this problem.

We separately train deep belief networks (DBN) on each cluster obtained from Stage 2. For example the deep network contains one input layer, three hidden layers and one output layer for Cluster 1 with hidden layers consisting of 80, 80 and 40 nodes respectively. The input of these classification models are words in each clusters. The activation function of hidden units is the sigmoid function which is traditionally used in nonlinear neural networks. Furthermore, higher number of parameters in neural networks generally makes parameter estimation much more difficult. Therefore, it is inefficient to start training of deep neural networks from random initial weight and bias values. We incorporate Restricted Boltzmann Machines (RBM) to pre-train the network and find good initial weights for training deep belief networks (Le Roux and Bengio, 2008).

Let D_i be a DBN model for cluster C_i. The hidden layers of each D_i are first trained as RBMs using unlabeled inputs. We use Contrastive Divergence-1 (CD-1) algorithm to obtain samples after 1-step Gibbs sampling (Hinton, 2002). CD-

1 allows accurate estimation of gradient's direction and minimize reconstruction error. Due to this pre-training, D_i learns an identity function with same desired output as the original input. Furthermore, it enhances the robustness of D_i by learning feature representations of the Arabic words before the final supervised learning stage.

Subsequently, the pre-trained DBN network is fine-tuned by vanilla back-propagation with labeled segments as the input layer. Figure 2 gives the abstract structure of final resulting D_1 after tuning and is also used for identification for cluster C_1. If a new document is added for text categorization then we find it's nearest neighbor cluster and use the deep learning model specific to that cluster. Finally, we plot the network graphs of the extracted cluster words for visualization of the association of these words.

4 Experimental Results

We evaluate our three-stage technique using two popular datasets previously used in Arabic text categorization: 10,000 documents from Al-Jazeera news website (http://www.aljazeera.net) and 6,000 Saudi Press Agency (Al-Harbi et al., 2008) documents. The results are reported using 10-fold cross validation. Our proposed method achieves a precision of 91.2% and recall of 90.9% giving F-measure of 91.02%.

Clustering is performed on a set consisting of the total 12,000 documents, randomly sampled from separately from Al-Jazeera and Saudi Press Agency. We further ran deep learning on each of these clusters and extracted network graphs. Two example networks are presented in Figure 3 and 4. We compare our results with existing approaches in Table 1. We can see that our technique improves substantially on the previous published works. Furthermore, it is capable to categorize different diacritics by using clusters based on root-words. Most misclassified cases in our algorithm due to random outliers and/or mix categories in a document. An example of a random outlier are some recent words which are not influenced by root-words. This can be further improved by using a larger dataset in future works and using new discriminative features for clustering and deep learning.

5 Conclusion and Future Work

This paper presents a novel three-stage technique for Arabic text categorization using a combina-

Table 1: Performance of our algorithm on Al-Jazeera Dataset

Technique	Precision	Recall	Root-words based?	Robust to Diacritcs?
Naive Bayes (El-Kourdi et al., 2004)	62.6%	57.4%	No	No
SVM (Hmeidi et al.,2008)	71.2%	66.7%	No	No
kNN (Mohammad AH et al., 2016)	83.0%	80.2%	No	No
Ours	**91.2%**	**90.9%**	**Yes**	**Yes**

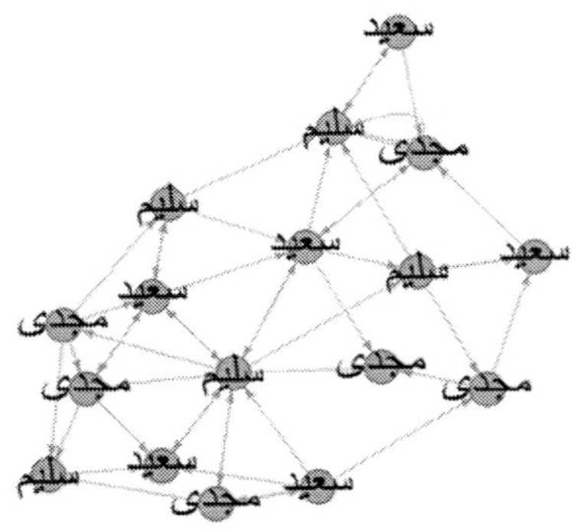

Figure 3: Network of a document's words from Cluster 1

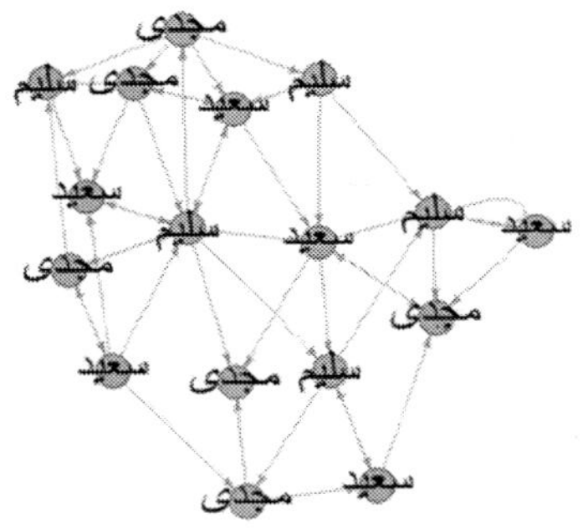

Figure 4: Network of a document's words from Cluster 2

tion of clustering and deep learning. We leverage the influence of root-words in Arabic to extract the features. Our technique is robust against different diacritics and complex morphology of Semitic languages. Furthermore, this procedure can be extended to Persian and Semitic languages like Hebrew which heavily depend on root-words. Future work includes extracting more discriminative features of root-words using deep learning and improving training of our models using larger datasets. We also plan to explore other Arabic morphologies like lemmas used in Arabic dependency parsing (Marton et al., 2003).

6   References

Ahmed Abdelali. 2004. Localization in modern standard Arabic. Journal of the American Society for Information Science and technology, 55(1):23-28.

Aymen Abu-Errub. 2014. Arabic text classification algorithm using tf-idf and chi square measurements. International Journal of Computer Applications, 93(6).

S Al-Harbi, A Almuhareb, A Al-Thubaity, MS Khorsheed, and A Al-Rajeh. 2008. Automatic Arabic text classification. Journes internationals, France, pp. 77–83.

Ricardo Baeza-Yates, Berthier Ribeiro-Neto, et al. 1999. Modern information retrieval, volume 463. ACM press New York.

Joachim Diederich, Jorg Kindermann, Edda Leopold,and Gerhard Paass. 2003. Authorship attribution with support vector machines. Applied intelligence, 19(1-2):109-123.

Alaa El-Halees. 2007. Arabic text classification using maximum entropy. The Islamic University Journal(Series of Natural Studies and Engineering), 15(1):157-167.

Mohamed El Kourdi, Amine Bensaid, and Tajje-eddine Rachidi. 2004. Automatic arabic document categorization based on the Naive bayes algorithm. In Proceedings of the Workshop on Computational Approaches to Arabic Script-based Languages, pages 51-58. Association for Computational Linguistics.

Tarek F Gharib, Mena B Habib, and Zaki T Fayed. 2009. Arabic text classification using support vector machines. International Journal of Computer Applications, 16(4):192-199.

Geoffrey E Hinton. 2002. Training products of experts by minimizing Contrastive Divergence. Neural computation, 14(8):1771-1800.

Ismail Hmeidi, Bilal Hawashin, and Eyas El-Qawasmeh. 2008. Performance of kNN and SVM classifiers on full word arabic articles. Advanced Engineering Informatics, 22(1):106–111.

Ghassan Kanaan, Riyad Al-Shalabi, Sameh Ghwanmeh, and Hamda Al-Maadeed. 2009. A comparison of text-classification techniques applied to arabic text. Journal of the American society for Information Science and Technology, 60(9):1836-1844.

Laila Khreisat. 2006. Arabic text classification using N-gram frequency statistics a comparative study. DMIN, 2006:78-82.

Nicolas Le Roux and Yoshua Bengio. 2008. Representational power of restricted boltzmann machines and deep belief networks. Neural computation, 20(6):1631-1649.

Yuval Marton, Nizar Habash, and Owen Rambow. 2013. Dependency parsing of modern standard arabic with lexical and inflectional features. Computational Linguistics, 39(1):161-194.

Adel Hamdan Mohammad, Omar Al-Momani, and Tariq Alwadan. 2016. Arabic text categorization using k-nearest neighbour, decision trees (c4.5) and rocchio classifier: A comparative study.

M Baran Pouyan, V Jindal, J Birjandtalab, and M Nourani. 2015. A two-stage clustering technique for automatic biaxial gating of flow cytometry data. In Proceedings of 2015 IEEE International Conference on Bioinformatics and Biomedicine (BIBM), pages 511-516.

Hassan Sawaf, Jorg Zaplo, and Hermann Ney. 2001. Statistical classification methods for arabic news articles. Natural Language Processing in ACL'2001, Toulouse, France.

Fabrizio Sebastiani. 2002. Machine learning in automated text categorization. ACM computing surveys (CSUR), 34(1):1-47.

Stijn Marinus Van Dongen. 2001. Graph clustering by flow simulation.

Yiming Yang and Jan O Pedersen. 1997. A comparative study on feature selection in text categorization. In ICML, volume 97, pages 412-420.

Author Index

Abercrombie, Gavin, 107
Asoh, Hideki, 22

Benzschawel, Eric, 15

Choi, Jinho D., 132
Chu, Chenhui, 8
Clark, Aidan, 114

Daks, Alon, 114

Fares, Murhaf, 72

Grover, Claire, 43

Haagsma, Hessel, 65
Hladka, Barbora, 86
Hovy, Dirk, 107

Inui, Kentaro, 138

Jargalsaikhan, Davaajav, 138
Jindal, Vasu, 145

Kajiwara, Tomoyuki, 1
Kobayashi, Ichiro, 22
Kodaira, Tomonori, 1
Komachi, Mamoru, 1
Kříž, Vincent, 86
Kurohashi, Sadao, 8

Lam, Alron Jan, 30
Lee, Timothy, 132
Liu, Yang, 126
Llewellyn, Clare, 43
Lutz, Alex, 132

Matsuda, Koji, 138
Matsuo, Eri, 22
Mehta, Parth, 100
Milajevs, Dmitrijs, 58
Moradiannasab, Omid, 80
Muszyńska, Ewa, 93

Nakazawa, Toshiaki, 8
Negi, Sapna, 119
Nishida, Satoshi, 22

Nishimoto, Shinji, 22

Oberlander, Jon, 43
Okazaki, Naoaki, 138
Otsuki, Hitoshi, 8

Purver, Matthew, 58

Sadrzadeh, Mehrnoosh, 58
Sharma, Dipti Misra, 37

Tobaili, Taha, 51

V V, Devadath, 37

Wei, Zhongyu, 126

Xia, Yandi, 126